AMERICA PERCEIVED:

A View from Abroad in the 17th Century

AMERICA PERCEIVED

- America Perceived: A View From Abroad in the 17th Century

- America Perceived: A View From Abroad in the 18th Century

- America Perceived: A View From Abroad in the 19th Century

- America Perceived: A View From Abroad in the 20th Century

AMERICA PERCEIVED:

A View from Abroad
in the 17th Century

Edited by
James Axtell

Pendulum Press, Inc.

West Haven, Connecticut   El Monte, California

Clothbound Edition   *ISBN 0-88301-144-1*   *Complete Set*
                              0-88301-145-X   *This Volume*

Paperback Edition   *ISBN 0-88301-123-9*   *Complete Set*
                              0-88301-124-7   *This Volume*

Library of Congress Catalog Card Number   73-94107

Published by
Pendulum Press, Inc.
An Academic Industries, Inc. Company
The Academic Building
Saw Mill Road
West Haven, Connecticut 06516

Printed in the United States of America

CONTENTS

ABOUT THE EDITOR

James Axtell, after receiving his B.A. from Yale University, went on to study at Oxford International Summer School, and later received his Ph.D. from Cambridge University. Mr. Axtell has taught at Yale University and currently is Associate Professor of history at Sarah Lawrence College. He has published many articles, reviews, and essays and has served as general editor of several educational publications. He is the author of the forthcoming book, *The School upon a Hill: Education and Society in Colonial New England.*

FOREWORD

> Oh wad some power the giftie gie us
> To see ourselves as others see us!
> It wad frae monie a blunder free us,
>   An' foolish notion.
>   Robert Burns, "To a Louse" (1786)

AMERICA PERCEIVED was created as a companion to THE AMERICAN PEOPLE series and as an independent collection of primary sources for the study of American history. Like its companion, it is founded on the belief that the study of history in the schools and junior levels of college generally begins at the wrong end. That study usually begins with abstract and pre-digested *conclusions*—the conclusions of other historians as filtered through the pen of a textbook writer—and not with the primary sources of the past and unanswered *questions* —the starting place of the historian himself.

Since we all need, use, and think about the past in our daily lives, we are all historians. The question is whether we can be skillful, accurate, and useful historians. The only way to become such is to exercise our historical skills and interests until we gain competence. But we have to exercise them in the same ways the best historians do or we will be kidding ourselves that we are *doing* history when in fact we are only absorbing sponge-like the results of someone else's historical competence.

Historical competence must begin with one crucial skill—the ability to distinguish between past and present. Without a sharp sense of the past as a different time from our own, we will be unable to accord the people of the past the respect that we would like to receive from

7

the people of the future. And without according them that respect, we will be unable to recognize their integrity as individuals or to understand them as human beings like ourselves.

A good sense of the past depends primarily on a good sense of the present, on experience, and on the imaginative empathy to relate ourselves to human situations not our own. Since most students have had a relatively brief experience of life and have not yet given full expression to their imaginative sympathies, THE AMERICAN PEOPLE was designed to draw upon the one essential prerequisite for the study of history that all students possess—the lives they have lived from birth to young adulthood. It asked us to look at the American experience from the *inside*, through the eyes of the participants who lived through the American life cycles, with the understanding gained from living through our own. AMERICA PERCEIVED seeks to draw more upon our imaginative sympathy by asking us to look at America from the *outside*, through the eyes of visitors, travellers, and critics whose lives and values were very different from those of the Americans they saw.

One view (inside or outside) is not necessarily better—that is, more accurate, sensitive, objective, complete—than the other. Both views are necessary to take the full measure of the country in all its complexity. The value of the view ultimately depends upon the observer. The quality of a foreigner's observations depends less upon his initial attitude toward America than upon his personal qualities—his objectivity, breadth of vision, accuracy of perception, sensitivity to human character, and tolerance of cultural difference. For example, although a perceptive visitor may come to America expecting the worst, his observations may be of great value because he can accurately see some of the country's dark spots and contradictions that perhaps remain hidden to Americans or to other visitors who come expecting only the best. On the other hand, the observations of an insensitive visitor who comes expecting the best may be of small value because he is too accepting of what well-meaning Americans tell him or because he is unable to see the country's faults and contradictions as well as its more obvious strengths and consistencies.

Foreign observers possess one quality that gives special value to their views of America: their foreignness. They are the products of different cultures which do not share all the assumptions, values, and standards of Americans. They see the world differently than Americans because they have been taught by their culture to see the world differently. In any culture there are aspects of life—they may be good or bad—which for some reason its own members are either unable to see or take so much for granted that they are never mentioned. But few cultures develop exactly the same blind spots about the same aspects of life. Consequently, the visiting members of one culture may be able to see those unrecognized or unmentioned aspects of another culture simply because they are used to seeing them—or not seeing them as the case may be—in their own culture. It is this angle of vision that gives the perceptions of foreigners their primary historical value.

But foreigners' observations usually have one built-in limitation: they are static snapshots of America frozen in time. Because of their relatively short stay, travellers seldom capture a full view of the historical development of the country that made it what it is when they see it. They record only the end product of a long process. Of course curiosity, historical research, and a good interviewing technique can overcome some of this limitation, but they can seldom erase it completely. Consequently, to gain an idea of historical change—as well as stability—we must place these snapshots in chronological order and compare them. This is sometimes difficult because travellers may not focus upon comparable subjects in successive periods, but in general the same range of subjects will capture visitors' interest, especially in a period of moderate or slow change. Visitors are adept at avoiding fads.

Since the experience of each student is the only prerequisite for the study of primary sources at the first level, annotations and introductory material have been reduced to a minimum, simply enough to identify the sources, their authors, and the circumstances in which they were written.

But the remains of the past are mute by themselves. Many sources have survived that can tell us what happened in the past and why, but they have to be questioned properly to reveal their secrets. So by way of illustration, a number of questions have been asked in each chapter, but these should be supplemented by the students whose experiences and knowledge and interests are, after all, the flywheel of the educational process. Although the questions and sources are divided into chapters, they should be used freely in the other chapters;

the collection should be treated as a whole. And although most of the illustrative questions are confined to the sources at hand, questions that extend to the present should be asked to anchor the acquired knowledge of the past in the immediate experience of the present. Only then will learning be real and lasting and history brought to life.

INTRODUCTION

Founding a new society in a new world was a tricky business. First, the European colonists had to confront and cope with an environment—woods, land, air, and water—that was often markedly different from their own. In this task there were few guides: a handful of explorer's journals and descriptions, sometimes fabulous, usually exaggerated in one direction or another. Experience alone was the best guide, with all its potential for costly error.

But in this "vast and howling wilderness" (as one settler called it) lived another source of guidance: the *first* Americans, the Indians as they were mistakenly called by Columbus. The Indians had lived close to the land for centuries, knew every bird, fish, animal, plant, and tree by name—the names they had given them, and had travelled nearly every square mile of the continent at one time in their search for food, war, or adventure. Moreover, they were initially friendly and receptive to the strange bearded men who came from the sea in giant canoes and spoke a garbled tongue.

When the first colonists needed land, food, directions, or instruction in the flora and fauna of America, the Indians were prompt to give them, asking in return only courtesy and justice. But when the colonists' hunger for land outstripped their sense of justice, the Indians were compelled to defend their lands and to revenge their loss of life and honor. Thus the image of the warlike Indian warrior was born, leaving forever after a deep impression on American culture and upon the foreigners who visited the New World in the 17th century.

Another difficulty encountered by the colonists were the overlapping claims to many parts of America by the major European states. Armed with charters and grants that often allotted them lands "from sea to sea," many colonists found themselves confronted with foreign set-tlers already in possession of the land or proposing to settle there by authority of an equally official grant from *their* government. And on more than one occasion, two groups of settlers from the *same* country arrived with grants to the same piece of land. Consequently, the inherent problems of founding new societies in a new environment were compounded by the chaotic legal foundations upon which they ultimately rested.

All of these problems and more were observed and described by the European visitors who appear in the pages of this volume. In one sense, everyone who came to America—settlers as well as explorers and travellers—can be considered visitors, at least initially, simply because the Indians were the original inhabitants of the country. It all depends on your perspective and sense of time. Nevertheless, we have tried to choose observers who were truly visitors in the sense that they eventually returned to Europe for some period or perma-nently. It is their view from abroad that allows us a unique opportunity to perceive the emerging character and meaning of America in the 17th century.

I. THE VAST AND HOWLING WILDERNESS

Before the first colonists had even set sail, the American wilderness had been drawn by their imaginations as a land of milk and honey, an Eden where the evils of a dying Europe could be avoided and the promise of God's Word brought to fruition. Upon arrival, however, their picture of America had to be revised to accord with the sometimes harsh realities they found. What evidence exists that their initial picture was *not* thoroughly revised in the first few years of settlement? In what ways did it change? Was the American wilderness a dense forest? Were there any exceptions? Were the exceptions more valuable to the settlers than the forests? Why was wood so noteworthy to the visitors? In what ways was America considered to be superior to Europe? In what ways inferior? In what ways did the Indians aid the European settlement of America? Did they teach the settlers anything about the "New" World? Was there any difference between the Indian and European philosophies of Nature and conservation? What American "beasts" were new to the settlers? How accurately did they describe them in their earliest accounts? Why was the beaver so noteworthy? What were America's chief "incommodities" or defects? Were they serious enough to impede further colonization?

One of the first descriptions of New-Englands Plantation *was written by the Rev. Francis Higginson, the first minister of Salem, Massachusetts, or as the Indians called it, Neihum-kek. Born in Leicestershire in 1588, he had graduated Master of Arts from Jesus College, Cambridge, in 1613. Two years later he accepted the religious care*

of his home parish of Claybrooke, where he ministered until his non-
conformity with the official practices of the Church of England com-
pelled him to leave for America in 1629. His "Short and True De-
scription of the Commodities and Discommodities of that Countrey"
was published in London in 1630. The following version is taken from
Peter Force's collection of Tracts and Other Papers, Relating Principally to the Origin, Settlement, and Progress of the Colonies in North
America, from the Discovery of the Country to the Year 1776
(Washington, 1836), volume 1.

Letting passe our Voyage by Sea, we will now begin our discourse
on the shore of *New-England*. And because the life and wel-fare of
everie Creature here below, and the commodiousnesse of the Countrey
whereas such Creatures live, doth by the most wise ordering of Gods
providence, depend next unto himselfe, upon the temperature and disposition of the foure Elements, Earth, Water, Aire and Fire (For as
of the mixture of all these, all sublunarie things are composed; so
by the more or lesse injoyment of the wholesome temper and convenient use of these, consisteth the onely well-being both of Man and
Beast in a more or lesse comfortable measure in all Countreys under
the Heavens) Therefore I will endeavour to shew you what *New-
England* is by the consideration of each of these apart, and truly
endeavour by Gods helpe to report nothing but the naked truth, and
that both to tell you of the discommodities as well as of the commodities, though as the idle Proverbe is, *Travellers may lye by
authoritie*, and so may take too much sinfull libertie that way. Yet
I may say of my selfe as once *Nehemiah* did in another case: *Shall
such a Man as I lye?* No verily; It becommeth not a Preacher of Truth
to be a Writer of Falshood in any degree: and therefore I have beene
carefull to report nothing of *New-England* but what I have partly seene
with mine owne Eyes, and partly heard and enquired from the
Mouthes of verie honest and religious persons, who by living in the
Countrey a good space of time have had experience and knowledge
of the state thereof, and whose testimonies I doe beleeve as my selfe.
First therefore of the Earth of *New-England* and all the appurte-
nances thereof; It is a Land of divers and sundry sorts all about
Masathulets Bay, and at *Charles* River is as fat blacke Earth as can
be seene any where: and in other places you have a clay soyle, in

other gravell, in other sandy, as it is all about our Plantation at *Salem*, for so our Towne is now named, *Psal.* 76.2.

The forme of the Earth here in the superficies of it is neither too flat in the plainnesse, nor too high in Hils, but partakes of both in a mediocritie, and fit for Pasture, or for Plow or Meddow ground, as Men please to employ it: though all the Countrey be as it were a thicke Wood for the generall, yet in divers places there is much ground cleared by the *Indians*, and especially about the Plantation: and I am told that about three miles from us a Man may stand on a little hilly place and see divers thousands of acres of ground as good as need to be, and not a Tree in the same. It is thought here is good Clay to make Bricke and Tyles and Earthen-Pots as needs to be. At this instant we are setting a Bricke-Kil on worke to make Brickes and Tyles for the building of our Houses. For Stone, here is plentie of Slates at the Ile of Slate in *Masathulets* Bay, and Lime-stone, Free-stone, and Smooth-stone, and Iron-stone, and Marble-stone also in such store, that we have great Rockes of it, and a Harbour hard by. Our Plantation is from thence called Marble-harbour.

Of Minerals there hath yet beene but little trial made, yet we are not without great hope of being furnished in that Soyle.

The fertilitie of the Soyle is to be admired at, as appeareth in the aboundance of Grasse that groweth everie where both verie thicke, verie long, and verie high in divers places: but it groweth very wildly with a great stalke and a broad and ranker blade, because it never had been eaten with Cattle, nor mowed with a Sythe, and seldome trampled on by foot. It is scarce to be beleeved how our Kine and Goats, Horses and Hogges doe thrive and prosper here and like well of this Countrey.

In our Plantation we have already a quart of Milke for a penny: but the aboundant encrease of Corne proves this Countrey to be a wonderment. Thirtie, fortie, fiftie, sixtie, are ordinarie here: yea *Josephs* encrease in *Egypt* is out-stript here with us. Our Planters hope to have more then a hundred fould this yeere: and all this while I am within compasse; what will you say of two hundred fould and upwards? It is almost incredible what great gaine some of our English Planters have had by our Indian Corne. Credible persons have assured me, and the partie himselfe avouched the truth of it to me, that of the setting of 13 Gallons of Corne he hath had encrease of it 52 Hogsheads, everie Hogshead holding seven Bushels of *London* measure, and everie Bushell was by him sold and trusted to the *Indians* for so much Beaver as was worth 18 shillings; and so of this 13 Gallons of Corne which was worth 6 shillings 8 pence, he made about 327 pounds of it the yeere following, as by reckoning will appeare: where you may see how God blesseth husbandry in this Land. There is not such great and beautifull eares of Corne I suppose any where else to be found but in this Countrey: being also of varietie of colours, as red, blew and yellow, &c. and of one Corne there springeth foure or five hundred. I have sent you many Eares of divers colours that you might see the truth of it.

Little Children here by setting of Corne may earne much more then their owne maintenance.

They have tryed our *English* Corne at new *Plimouth* Plantation, so that all our severall Graines will grow here verie well, and have a fitting Soyle for their nature.

Our Governour hath store of greene Pease growing in his Garden as good as ever I eat in *England*.

This Countrey aboundeth naturally with store of Roots of great varietie and good to eat. Our Turnips, Parsnips and Carrots are here both bigger and sweeter then is ordinarily to be found in *England*. Here are also store of Pumpions, Cowcumbers, and other things of that nature which I know not. Also, divers excellent Pot-herbs grow abundantly among the Grasse, as Strawberrie leaves in all places of the Countrey, and the plentie of Strawberries in their time, and Penyroyall, Wintersaverie, Sorrell, Brookelime, Liverwort, Carvell and Watercresses, also Leekes and Onions are ordinarie, and divers Physicall [medical] Herbes. Here are also aboundance of other sweet Herbes delightful to the smell, whose names we know not, &c. and plentie of single Damaske Roses verie sweet; and two kinds of Herbes that beare two kind of Flowers very sweet, which they say, are as good to make Cordage or Cloath as any Hempe or Flaxe we have.

Excellent Vines are here up and downe in the Woods. Our Governour hath already planted a Vineyard with great hope of encrease.

Also, Mulberies, Plums, Raspberies, Corrance, Chesnuts, Filberds, Walnuts, Smalnuts, Hurtleberies and Hawes of Whitethrone neere as good as our Cherries in *England*, they grow in plentie here.

For Wood there is no better in the World I thinke, here being foure sorts of Oke differing both in the Leafe, Timber, and Colour, all excellent good. There is also good Ash, Eleme, Willow, Birch,

Beech, Saxafras, Juniper Cipres, Cedar, Spruce, Pines and Firre that will yeeld abundance of Terpentine, Pitch, Tarre, Masts and other materials for building both of Ships and Houses. Also here are store of Sumacke Trees, they are good for dying and tanning of Leather, likewise such Trees yeeld a precious Gum called White Benjamen, that they say is excellent for perfumes. Also here be divers Roots and Berries wherewith the *Indians* dye excellent holyday colours that no raine nor washing can alter. Also, wee have materials to make Sope-Ashes and Salt-Peter in aboundance.

For Beasts there are some Beares, and they say some Lyons [cougars] also; for they have been seen at Cape *Anne*. Also here are severall sorts of Deere, some whereof bring three or foure young ones at once, which is not ordinarie in *England*. Also Wolves, Foxes, Beavers, Otters, Martins, great wild Cats, and a great Beast called a Molke [moose] as bigge as an Oxe. I have seen the Skins of all these Beasts since I came to this Plantation excepting Lyons. Also here are great store of Squerrels, some greater, and some smaller and lesser: there are some of the lesser sort, they tell me, that by a certaine Skin will fly from Tree to Tree though they stand farre distant.

Of the Waters of New-England *with the things belonging to the same.*

New-England hath Water enough both salt and fresh, the greatest Sea in the World, the *Atlanticke* Sea runs all along the Coast thereof. There are aboundance of Ilands along the Shore, some full of Wood and Mast to feed Swine; and others cleere of Wood, and fruitfull to beare Corne. Also we have store of excellent harbours for Ships, as at Cape *Anne*, and at *Masathulets* Bay, and at *Salem*, and at many other places: and they are the better because for Strangers there is a verie difficult and dangerous passage into them, but unto such as are well acquainted with them, they are easie and safe enough. The aboundance of Sea-Fish are almost beyond beleeving, and sure I should scarce have beleeved it except I had seene it with mine owne Eyes. I saw great store of Whales, and Crampusse, and such aboundance of Makerils that it would astonish one to behold, likewise Cod-Fish aboundance on the Coast, and in their season are plentifully taken. There is a Fish called a Basse, a most sweet and wholesome Fish as ever I did eat, it is altogether as good as our fresh Sammon, and the season of their comming was begun when we came first to

New-England in *June*, and so continued about three months space.
Of this Fish our Fishers take many hundreds together, which I have
seene lying on the shore to my admiration; yea, their Nets ordinarily
take more then they are able to hale to Land, and for want of Boats
and Men they are constrained to let a many goe after they have taken
them, and yet sometimes they fill two Boats at a time with them.
And besides Basse we take plentie of Scate and Thornbacke, and
abundance of Lobsters, that the least Boy in the Plantation may both
catch and eat what he will of them. For my owne part I was soone
cloyed with them, they were so great, and fat, and lussious. I have
seene some my selfe that have weighed 16 pound, but others have
had divers time so great Lobsters as have weighed 25 pound, as they
assured me. Also here is aboundance of Herring, Turbut, Sturgion,
Cuskes, Hadocks, Mullets, Eeles, Crabs, Muskles and Oysters. Beside
there is probabilitie that the Countrey is of an excellent temper for
the making of Salt: for since our comming our Fishermen have brought
home verie good Salt which they found candied by the standing of
the sea water and the heat of the Sunne, upon a Rock by the Sea
shore: and in divers Salt Marishes that some have gone through, they
have found some Salt in some places crushing under their Feet and
cleaving to their Shoes.

And as for fresh Water the Countrey is full of daintie Springs, and
some great Rivers, and some lesser Brookes; and at *Masathulets* Bay
they digged Wels and found Water at three Foot deepe in most places:
and neere *Salem* they have as fine cleare Water as we can desire,
and we may digge Wels and find Water where we list.

Thus we see both Land and Sea abound with store of blessings
for the comfortable sustenance of Mans life in *New-England*.

Of the Aire of New-England *with the Temper and Creatures in it*.

The Temper of the Aire of *New-England* is one speciall thing that
commends this place. Experience doth manifest that there is hardly
a more healthfull place to be found in the World that agreeth better
with our English Bodyes. Many that have beene weake and sickly
in old *England*, by comming hither have beene thoroughly healed and
growne healthful and strong. For here is an extraordinarie cleere and
dry Aire that is of a most healing nature to all such as are of a Cold,
Melancholy, Flegmatick, Reumaticke temper of Body. None can more

truly speake hereof by their owne experience then my selfe. My Friends that knew me can well tell how verie sickly I have been and continually in Physick [medicine], being much troubled with a tormenting paine through an extraordinarie weaknesse of my Stomache, and aboundance of Melancholicke humours; but since I came hither on this Voyage, I thanke God I have had perfect health, and freed from paine and vomitings, having a Stomacke to digest the hardest and coursest fare who before could not eat finest meat, and whereas my Stomacke could onely digest and did require such drinke as was both strong and stale, now I can and doe oftentimes drink *New-England* water verie well, and I that have not gone without a Cap for many yeeres together, neither durst leave off the same, have now cast away my Cap, and doe weare none at all in the day time: and whereas beforetime I cloathed my selfe with double cloathes and thicke Wastcoats to keepe me warme, even in the Summer time, I doe now goe as thin clad as any, onely wearing a light Stuffe Cassocke upon my Shirt and Stuffe Breeches of one thickness without Linings. Besides I have one of my Children that was fo[r]merly most lamentably handled with sore breaking out of both his hands and feet of the Kings-Evill, but since he came hither he is verie well over hee was, and there is hope of perfect recoverie shortly, even by the verie wholesomnesse of the Aire, altering, digesting and drying up the cold and crude humours of the Body: and therefore I thinke it is a wise course for all cold complections to come to take Physicke in *New-England*: for a sup of *New-Englands* Aire is better then a whole draft of old *Englands* Ale.

In the Summer time in the midst of *July* and *August*, it is a good deale hotter then in old *England*: and in Winter, *January* and *February* are much colder as they say: but the Spring and Autume are of a middle temper.

Fowles of the Aire are plentifull here, and of all sorts as we have in *England* as farre as I can learne, and a great many of strange Fowles which we know not. Whilst I was writing these things, one of our Men brought home an Eagle which he had killed in the Wood: they say they are good meat. Also here are many kinds of excellent Hawkes, both Sea Hawkes and Land Hawkes: and my selfe walking in the Woods with another in company, sprung a Partridge so bigge that through the heavinesse of his Body could fly but a little way: they that have killed them, say they are as bigge as our Hens. Here are likewise aboundance of Turkies often killed in the Woods, farre greater then our English Turkies, and exceeding fat, sweet and fleshy, for here they have aboundance of feeding all the yeere long, as Strawberries, in Summer all places are full of them, and all manner of Berries and Fruits. In the Winter time I have seene Flockes of Pidgeons, and have eaten of them: they doe flye from Tree to Tree as other Birds doe, which our Pidgeons will not doe in *England*: they are of all colours as ours are, but their wings and tayles are farr longer, and therefore it is likely they fly swifter to escape the terrible Hawkes in this Countrey. In Winter time this Countrey doth abound with wild Geese, wild Duckes, and other Sea Fowle, that a great part of winter the Planters have eaten nothing but roastmeat of divers Fowles which they have killed.

Thus you have heard of the Earth, Water and Air of *New-England*, now it may be you expect something to be said of the Fire proportionable to the rest of the Elements.

Indeed I thinke *New-England* may boast of this Element more then of all the rest: for though it be here somthing cold in the winter, yet here we have plentie of Fire to warme us, and that a great deale cheaper then they sell Billets and Faggots in *London*: nay all *Europe* is not able to afford to make so great Fires as *New-England*. A poore Seruant here that is to possesse but 50 Acres of Land, may afford to give more wood for Timber and Fire as good as the world yeelds, then many Noble Men in *England* can afford to doe. Here is good living for those that love good Fires. And although *New-England* have no Tallow to make Candles of, yet by the aboundance of the Fish thereof, it can afford Oyle for Lamps. Yea our Pine-Trees that are the most plentifull of all wood, doth allow us plentie of Candles, which are verie usefull in a House: and they are such Candles as the *Indians* commonly use, having no other, and they are nothing else but the wood of the Pine Tree cloven in two little slices something thin, which are so full of the moysture of Turpentine and Pitch, that they burne as cleere as a Torch. I have sent you some of them that you may see the experience of them.

Thus of *New-Englands* commodities, now I will tell you of some discommodities that are here to be found.

First, In the Summer season for these three months *June, July* and *August*, we are troubled much with little Flyes called Musketoes, being the same they are troubled with in *Lincolnshiere* and the Fens: and they are nothing but Gnats, which except they be smoked out of their Howses are troublesome in the night season.

Secondly, In the Winter season for two months space the Earth is commonly covered with Snow, which is accompanied with sharp biting Frosts, something more sharpe then is in old *England*, and therefore are forced to make great Fires.

Thirdly, This Countrey being verie full of Woods and Wildernesses, doth also much abound with Snakes and Serpents of strange colours and huge greatnesse: yea there are some Serpents called Rattle Snakes, that have Rattles in their Tayles that will not flye from a Man as others will, but will flye upon him and sting him so mortally, that he will dye within a quarter of an houre after, except the partie stinged have about him some of the root of an Hearbe called Snake weed to bite on, and then he shall receive no harme: but yet seldome falles it out that any hurt is done by these. About three yeeres since an *Indian* was stung to death by one of them, but we heard of none since that time.

Fourthly and lastly, Here wants as yet the good company of honest Christains to bring with them Horses, Kine and Sheepe to make use of this fruitfull Land: great pittie it is to see so much good ground for Corne and for Grasse as any is under the Heavens, to lye altogether unoccupied, when so many honest Men and their Families in old *England* through the populousnesse thereof, do make very hard shift to live one by the other. . . .

The *Indians* are not able to make use of the one fourth part of the Land, neither have they any settled places, as Townes to dwell in, nor any ground as they challenge for their owne possession, but change their habitation from place to place. . . .

[Many Indians] about twelve yeeres since were swept away by a great and grievous Plague that was amongst them, so that there are verie few left to inhabite the Countrey. . . .

They doe generally professe to like well of our comming and planting here; partly because there is abundance of ground that they cannot possesse nor make use of, and partly because our being here will be a meanes both of reliefe to them when they want, and also a defence from their Enemies, wherewith (I say) before this Plantation begun, they were often indangered.

New Englands Prospect *(London, 1634) was based upon "some few years travels and experience" of William Wood, who said he had lived in New England "these foure yeares, and intend God willing to returne shortly againe." Little is known of the author save the popularity of his book, which reached a third edition by 1639 and a fourth as late as 1764. The following description of the New England wilderness from the pen of an observant early visitor is taken from the Prince Society reprint of his book (Boston, 1865), pp. 15-29.*

Of the Hearbes, Fruites, Woods, Waters and Mineralls.

The ground affoards very good kitchin Gardens, for Turneps, Parsnips, Carrots, Radishes, and Pumpions, Muskmillions, Isquouterquashes, Coucumbers, Onyons, and whatsoever growes well in *England*, growes as well there, many things being better and larger: there is likewise growing all manner of Hearbes for meate, and medicine, and that not onely in planted Gardens, but in the Woods, without eyther the art or the helpe of man, as sweet Marjoran, Purselane, Sorrell, Peneriall, Yarrow, Mirtle, Saxifarilla, Bayes, &c. There is likewise Strawberries in abundance, very large ones, some being two inches about; one may gather halfe a bushell in a forenoone: In other seasons there bee Gooseberries, Bilberies, Resberies, Treackleberies, Hurtleberries, Currants; which being dryed in the Sunne are little inferiour to those that our Grocers sell in *England*: This land likewise affoards Hempe and Flax, some naturally, and some planted by the *English*, with Rapes if they bee well managed. For such commodities as lie underground, I cannot out of mine owne experience or knowledge say much, having taken no great notice of such things; but it is certainely reported that there is Iron, stone; and the *Indians* informe us that they can leade us to the mountaines of blacke Lead, and have showne us lead ore, if our small judgement in such things doe not deceive us: and though no body dare confidently conclude, yet dare they not utterly deny, but that the *Spaniards* bliss may lye hid in the barren Mountaines, such as have coasted the countrey affirme that they know where to fetch Seacole if wood were scant; there is plenty of stone both rough and smooth, usefull for many things, with quarries of Slate, out of which they get covering for houses, with good clay,

whereof they make Tiles and Brickes, and pavements for their necessary uses.

For the Countrey it is as well watered as any land under the Sunne,
every family, or every two families having a spring of sweet waters
betwixt them, which is farre different from the waters of *England*,
being not so sharpe, but of a fatter substance, and of a more jetty
colour; it is thought there can be no better water in the world, yet
dare I not preferre it before good Beere, as some have done, but any
man will choose it before bad Beere, Wheay, or Buttermilke. Those
that drinke it be as healthfull, fresh, and lustie, as they that drinke
beere; These springs be not onely within land, but likewise bordering
upon the Sea coasts, so that some times the tides overflow some of
them, which is accounted rare in the most parts of *England*. No man
hitherto hath beene constrained to digge deepe for his water, or to
fetch it farre, or to fetch of severall waters for severall uses; one kind
of water serving for washing, and brewing and other things. Now
besides these springs, there be divers spacious ponds in many places
of the Countrey, out of which runne many sweet streames, which are
constant in their course both winter and summer, whereat the Cattle
quench their thirst, and upon which may be built water mills, as the
plantation encreases.

The next commoditie the land affords, is good store of Woods, &
that not onely such as may be needful for fewell, but likewise for
the building of Ships, and houses, & Mils, and all manner of water-
worke about which Wood is needefull. The Timber of the Countrey
growes straight, and tall, some trees being twenty, some thirty foot
high, before they spread forth their branches; generally the Trees be
not very thicke, though there be many that will serve for Mill posts,
some beeing three foote and a halfe o're. And whereas it is generally
conceived, that the woods grow so thicke, that there is no more cleare
ground than is hewed out by labour of man; it is nothing so; in many
places, divers Acres being cleare, so that one may ride a hunting in
most places of the land, if he will venture himselfe for being lost:
there is no underwood saving in swamps, and low grounds that are
wet, in which the *English* get Osiers, and Hasles, and such small wood
as is for their use. Of these swamps, some be ten, some twenty, some
thirty miles long, being preserved by the wetnesse of the soile wherein
they grow; for it being the custome of the *Indians* to burne the wood

in *November*, when the grasse is withered, and leaves dryed, it consumes all the underwood, and rubbish, which otherwise would over grow the Country, making it unpassable, and spoile their much affected hunting: so that by this meanes in those places where the *Indians* inhabit, there is scarce a bush or bramble, or any combersome underwood to bee seene in the more champion ground. Small wood growing in these places where the fire could not come, is preserved. In some places where the *Indians* dyed of the Plague some foureteene yeares agoe, is much underwood, as in the mid way betwixt *Wessaguscus* and *Plimouth*, because it hath not beene burned; certaine Rivers stopping the fire from comming to cleare that place of the countrey, hath made it unusefull and troublesome to travell thorow, in so much that it is called ragged plaine, because it teares and rents the cloathes of them that passe. Now because it may be necessary for mechanicall artificers to know what Timber, and wood of use is in the Countrey, I will recite the most usefull as followeth.

Trees both in hills and plaines, in plenty be,
The long liv'd Oake, and mournefull Cypris tree,
Skie towring pines, and Chesnuts coated rough,
The lasting Cedar, with the Walnut tough:
The rozin dropping Firre for masts in use,
The boatmen seeke for Oares light, neate growne sprewse,
The brittle Ash, the ever trembling Aspes,
The broad-spread Elme, whose concave harbours waspes,
The water spungie Alder good for nought,
Small Elderne by th' Indian Fletchers sought,
The knottie Maple, pallid Birtch, Hawthornes,
The Horne bound tree that to be cloven scornes;
Which from the tender Vine oft takes his spouse,
Who twinds imbracing armes about his boughes.
Within this Indian Orchard fruites be some,
The ruddie Cherrie, and the jettie Plumbe,
Snake murthering Hazell, with sweet Saxaphrage,
Whose spurnes in beere allayes hot fevers rage.
The Diars Shumach, with more trees there be,
That are both good to use, and rare to see.

Though many of these trees may seeme to have epithites contrary to the nature of them as they grow in *England*, yet are they agreeable with the Trees of that Countrie. The chiefe and common Timber for ordinary use is Oake, and Walnut: Of Oakes there be three kindes, the red Oake, white, and blacke; as these are different in kinde, so are they chosen for such uses as they are most fit for, one kind being more fit for clappboard, others for sawne board, some fitter for shipping, others for houses. These Trees affoard much Mast for Hogges, especially every third yeare, bearing a bigger Acorne than our *English* Oake. The Wallnut tree is something different from the *English* Wallnut, being a great deale more tough, and more serviceable, and altogether as heavie: and whereas our Gunnes that are stocked with *English* Wallnut, are soone broaken and cracked in frost, beeing a brittle Wood; we are driven to stocke them new with the Country Wallnut, which will indure all blowes, and weather; lasting time out of minde. These trees beare a very good Nut, something smaller, but nothing inferiour in sweetnesse and goodnesse to the *English* Nut, having no bitter pill. There is likewise a tree in some part of the Countrey, that beares a Nut as bigge as a small peare. The Cedar tree is a tree of no great growth, not bearing above a foot and a halfe square at the most, neither is it very high. I suppose they be much inferiour to the Cedars of *Lebanon* so much commended in holy writ. This wood is more desired for ornament than substance, being of colour red and white like Eugh, smelling as sweete as Juniper; it is commonly used for seeling of houses, and making of Chests, boxes, and staves. The Firre and Pine bee trees that grow in many places, shooting up exceeding high, especially the Pine: they doe afford good masts, good board, Rozin and Turpentine. Out of these Pines is gotten the candlewood that is so much spoken of, which may serve for a shift amongst poore folkes; but I cannot commend it for singular good, because it is something sluttish, dropping a pitchie kinde of substance where it stands. Here no doubt might be good done with saw mils; for I have seene of these stately highgrowne trees, ten miles together close by the Riverside, from whence by shipping they might be conveyed to any desired Port. Likewise it is not improbable that Pitch and Tarre may be forced from these trees, which beare no other kinde of fruite. For that countrey Ash, it is much different from the Ash of *England*, being brittle and good for little, so that Wallnut is used for it. The Horne-bound tree is a tough kind of Wood, that requires so much paines in riving as is almost incredible, being the best for to make bolles and dishes, not being subject to cracke or leake. This tree growing with broad spread Armes, the vines winde their curling branches about them; which vines affoard great store of grapes, which are very big both for the grape and Cluster, sweet and good: These be of two sorts, red and white, there is likewise a smaller kind of grape, which groweth in the Islands which is sooner ripe and more delectable; so that there is no knowne reason why as good wine may not be made in those parts, as well as in *Burdeaux* in *France*; being under the same degree. It is great pittie no man sets upon such a venture, whereby he might in small time inrich himselfe, and benefit the Countrie, I know nothing which doth hinder but want of skilfull men to manage such an imployment: For the countrey is hot enough, the ground good enough, and many convenient hills which lye toward the south Sunne, as if they were there placed for the purpose. The Cherrie trees yeeld great store of Cherries, which grow on clusters like grapes; they be much smaller than our *English* Cherrie, nothing neare so good if they be not very ripe: they so furre the mouth that the tongue will cleave to the roofe, and the throate wax horse with swallowing those red Bullies (as I may call them,) being little better in taste. *English* ordering may bring them to be an *English* Cherrie, but yet they are as wilde as the *Indians*. The Plummes of the Countrey be better for Plummes than the Cherries be for Cherries, they be blacke and yellow about the bignesse of a Damson, of a reasonable good taste. The white thorne affords hawes as bigge as an *English* Cherrie, which is esteemed above a Cherrie for his goodnesse and pleasantnesse to the taste.

Of the Beasts that live on the land.

Having related unto you the pleasant situation of the Countrey, the healthfulnesse of the climate, the nature of the soile, with his vegetatives, and other commodities; it will not be amisse to informe you of such irrationall creatures as are daily bred and continually nourished in this countrey, which doe much conduce to the well being of the Inhabitants, affording not onely meate for the belly, but cloathing for the backe. The beasts be as followeth.

The kingly Lyon, and the strong arm'd Beare
The large limbed Mooses, with the tripping Deare,

Quill darting Porcupines, and Rackcoones bee,
Castelld in the hollow of an aged tree;
The skipping Squerrell, Rabbet, purblinde Hare,
Immured in the selfesame Castle are,
Least red-eyed Ferrets, wily Foxes should
Them undermine, if rampird but with mould.
The grim fac't Ounce, and ravenous howling Woolfe,
Whose meagre paunch suckes like a swallowing gulfe.
Blacke glistering Otters, and rich coated Bever,
The Civet sented Musquash smelling ever.

Concerning Lyons [cougars], I will not say that I ever saw any
my selfe, but some affirme that they have seene a Lyon at *Cape Anne*
which is not above six leagues from *Boston*: some likewise being lost
in woods, have heard such terrible roarings, as have made them much
agast; which must eyther be Devills or Lyons; there being no other
creatures which use to roare saving Beares, which have not such a
terrible kind of roaring: besides, *Plimouth* men have traded for Lyons
skinnes in former times. But sure it is that there be Lyons on that
Continent, for the *Virginians* saw an old Lyon in their plantations,
who having lost his Jackall, which was wont to hunt his prey, was
brought so poore that he could goe no further. For Beares they be
common, being a great blacke kind of Beare, which be most fierce
in Strawberry time, at which time they have young ones; at this time
likewise they will goe upright like a man, and clime trees, and
swimme to the Islands; which if the *Indians* see, there will be more
sportfull Beare bayting than Paris Garden can affoard. For seeing the
Beares take water, an *Indian* will leape after him, where they goe
to water cuffes for bloody noses, and scratched fides; in the end the
man gets the victory, riding the Beare over the watery plaine till he
can beare him no longer. In the winter they take themselves to the
clifts of rockes, and thicke swamps, to shelter them from the cold;
and foode being scant in those cold and hard times, they live onely
by sleeping and sucking their pawes, which keepeth them as fat as
they are in Summer; there would be more of them if it were not for
the Woolves, which devoure them; a kennell of those ravening run-
nagadoes, setting on a poore single Beare, will teare him as a Dogge
will teare a Kid: it would be a good change if the countrey had for
every Woolfe a Beare, upon the condition all the woolves were

banished; so should the inhabitants be not onely rid of their greatest annoyance, but furnished with more store of provisions, Beares being accounted very good meate, esteemed of all men above Venison: againe they never prey upon the *English* cattle, or offer to assault the person of any man, unlesse being vexed with a shot, and a man run upon them before they be dead, in which case they will stand in their owne defence, as may appeare by this instance. Two men going a fowling, appointed at evening to meete at a certaine pond side, to share equally, and to returne home; one of these Gunners having killed a Seale or Sea calfe, brought it to the side of the pond where hee was to meete his comrade, afterwards returning to the Sea side for more gaine; and having loaded himselfe with more Geese and Duckes, he repaired to the pond, where hee saw a great Beare feeding on his Seale, which caused him to throw down his loade, and give the Beare a salute; which though it was but with Goose shot, yet tumbled him over and over, whereupon the man supposing him to be in a manner dead, ran and beate him with the hand of his Gunne; The Beare perceiving him to be such a coward to strike him when he was down, scrambled up, standing at defiance with him, scratching his legges, tearing his cloathes and face, who stood it out till his six foot Gunne was broken in the middle, then being deprived of his weapon, he ran up to the shoulders into the pond, where hee remained till the Beare was gone, and his mate come in, who accompanied him home.

The beast called a Moose, is not much unlike red Deare, this beast is as bigge as an Oxe; slow of foote, headed like a Bucke, with a broade beame, some being two yards wide in the head, their flesh is as good as Beefe, their hides good for cloathing; The *English* have some thoughts of keeping them tame, and to accustome them to the yoake, which will be a great commoditie: First because they are so fruitfull, bringing forth three at a time, being likewise very uberous. Secondly, because they will live in winter without any fodder. There be not many of these in the *Massachusets bay*, but forty miles to the Northeast there be great store of them; These pore beasts likewise are much devoured by the Woolves: The ordinary Deare be much bigger than the Deare of *England*, of a brighter colour, more inclining to red, with spotted bellies; the most store of these be in winter, when the more Northerne parts of the countrey bee cold for them; they desire to be neare the Sea, so that they may swimme to the Islands when they are chased by the Woolves: It is not to be thought into what great multitudes they would encrease, were it not for the common devourer the Woolfe; They have generally three at a time, which they hide a mile one from another, giving them sucke by turnes; thus they doe, that if the Woolfe should finde one, he might misse of the other. These Deare be fat in the deepe of winter; In Summer it is hard catching of them with the best Greyhounds that may be procured, because they bee swift of foote. Some credible persons have affirmed, that they have seene a Deare leape three score feet at little or no forcement; besides, there be so many old trees, rotten stumps, and *Indian* barnes, that a dog cannot well run without being shoulder-shot: yet would I not disswade any from carrying good dogges; for in the winter time they be very usefull; for when the snow is hard frozen, the Deare being heavie, sinkes into the snow, the doggs being light runne upon the top and overtake them, and pull them downe: some by this meanes have gotten twenty Buckes and Does in a winter, the hornes of these Deare grow in such a straight manner, (overhanging their heads) that they cannot feede upon such things as grow low, till they have cast their old hornes: of these Deare there be a great many, and more in the *Massachusets bay*, than in any other place, which is a great helpe and refreshment to these planters. The Porcupine is a small thing not much unlike a Hedgehog; something bigger, who stands upon his guard and proclaimes a *Noli me tangere* [*Touch me not*], to man and beast, that shall approach too neare him, darting his quills into their legges, and hides. The Rackoone is a deepe furred beast, not much unlike a Badger, having a tayle like a Fox, as good meate as a Lambe; there is one of them in the Tower [of London.] These beasts in the day time sleepe in hollow trees, in the moone shine night they goe to feede on clammes at a low tide, by the Sea side, where the *English* hunt them with their dogges. The Squerrells be of three sorts, first the great gray Squerrell, which is almost as bigge as an *English* Rabbet; of these there be the greatest plenty, one may kill a dozen of them in an afternoone, about three of the clocke they begin to walke. The second is a small Squerrell, not unlike the *English* Squerrell, which doth much trouble the planters of Corne, so that they are constrained to set divers Trappes, and to carry their Cats into the Corne fields, till their corne be three weekes old. The third kind is a flying Squerrell, which is not very bigge, slender of body, with a great deale of loose skinne which shee spreads square when shee flyes, which the winde gets, and so wafts her Bat-like body from place to place; it is a creature more for sight and won-derment, than eyther pleasure or profit. The Rabbets be much like ours in *England*. The Hares be some of them white, and a yard long; these two harmelesse creatures are glad to shelter themselves from the harmefull Foxes, in hollow trees, having a hole at the entrance no bigger than they can creepe in at: if they should make them holes in the ground, as our *English* Rabbets doe, the undermining Renoilds [Foxes] would rob them of their lives, and extirpate their generation. The beasts of offence be Squunckes, Ferrets, Foxes, whose impudence sometimes drives them to the good wives Hen roost, to fill their Paunch: some of these be blacke; their furre is of much esteeme.

The Ounce or the wilde Cat, is as big as a mungrell dog, this crea-ture is by nature feirce, and more dangerous to bee met withall than any other creature, not fearing eyther dogge or man; he useth to kill Deare, which hee thus effecteth: Knowing the Deares tracts, hee will lye lurking in long weedes, the Deare passing by he suddenly leapes upon his backe, from thence gets to his necke, and scratcheth out his throate; he hath likewise a devise to get Geese, for being much of the colour of a Goose he will place himselfe close by the water, holding up his bob taile, which is like a Goose necke; the Geese see-ing this counterfet Goose, approach nigh to visit him, who with a suddaine jerke apprehends his mistrustlesse prey. The *English* kill many of these, accounting them very good meate. Their skinnes be a very deepe kind of Furre, spotted white and black on the belly. The Woolves bee in some respect different from them of other coun-tries; it was never knowne yet that a Woolfe ever set upon a man or woman. Neyther do they trouble horses or cowes; but swine, goates and red calves which they take for Deare, be often destroyed by them, so that a red calfe is cheaper than a blacke one in that regard; in Autumne and the beginning of the Spring, these ravenous rangers doe most frequent our *English* habitations, following the Deare which come downe at that time to those parts. They be made much like a Mungrell, being big boned, lanke paunched, deepe breasted, having a thicke necke, and head, pricke eares, and long snoute, with danger-ous teeth, long staring haire, and a great bush taile; it is thought of many, that our *English* Mastiffes might be too hard for them; but it is no such matter, for they care no more for an ordinary Mastiffe, than an ordinary Mastiffe cares for a Curre; many good Dogges have

beene spoyled with them. Once a faire Grayhound hearing them at
their howlings run out to chide them, who was torne in peeces before
he could be rescued. One of them makes no more bones to runne
away with a Pigge, than a Dogge to runne away with a Marrow bone.
It is observed that they have no joynts from the head to the tayle,
which prevents them from leaping, or suddaine turning, as may
appeare by what I shall shew you. A certaine man having shot a
Woolfe, as he was feeding upon a Swine, breaking his legge onely,
hee knew not how to devise his death, on a suddaine, the Woolfe
being a blacke one, he was loath to spoyle his furre with a second
shot, his skinne being worth five or sixe pound Sterling; wherefore
hee resolved to get him by the tayle, and thrust him into a River
that was hard by; which effected, the Woolfe being not able to turne
his joyntlesse body to bite him, was taken. That they cannot leape,
may appeare by this Woolfe, whose mouth watering at a few poore
impaled Kiddes, would needes leape over a five-foote pale to be at
them; but his foote slipping in the rise, he fell a little short of his
desire, and being hung in the Carpenters stockes, howled so loud,
that he frighted away the Kids, and called the *English*, who killed
him. These be killed dayly in some place or other, either by the *English*, or *Indian*; who have a certaine rate for every head: Yet is there
little hope of their utter destruction, the Countrey being so spacious,
and they so numerous, travelling in the Swamps by Kennels: sometimes ten or twelve are of a company. Late at night, and early in
the morning, they set up their howlings, and call their companies
together at night to hunt, at morning to sleepe; in a word they be
the greatest inconveniency the Countrey hath, both for matter of dam-
mage to private men in particular, and the whole Countrey in generall.

Beasts living in the water.

For all creatures that liv'd both by Land and Water, they be first
Otters, which be most of them blacke, whose furre is much used for
Muffes, and are held almost as deare as Beaver. The flesh of them
is none of the best meate, but their Oyle is of rare use for many
things. Secondly, Martins, a good furre for their bignes: Thirdly,
Musquashes, which be much like a Beaver for shape, but nothing
neare so bigge; the Male hath two stones [testicles] which smell as
sweete as Muske, and being killed in Winter, never lose their sweete

smell: These skinnes are no bigger than a Coney-skinne, yet are sold for five shillings a peice, being sent for Tokens into *England*. One good skinne will perfume a whole house-full of cloathes, if it be right and good. Fourthly, the Beaver, concerning whom if I should at large discourse, according to knowledge or information, I might make a Volumne. The wisdome and understanding of this Beast, will almost conclude him a reasonable creature: His shape is thicke and short, having likewise short legs, feete like a Mole before, and behinde like a Goose, a broad tayle in forme like a shooe-soale, very tough and strong; his head is something like an Otters head, saving that his teeth before, be placed like the teeth of a Rabbet, two above, and two beneath; sharpe and broad, with which he cuts downe Trees as thicke as a mans thigh, afterwards dividing them into lengths, according to the use they are appointed for. If one Bever be too weake to carry the logge, then another helpes him; if they two be too weake, then *Multorum manibus grande levatur onus* [*Many hands will lift the burden*]; foure more adding their helpe, being placed three to three, which set their teeth in one anothers tough tayles, and laying the loade on the two hindermost, they draw the logge to the desired place. That this may not seeme altogether incredible, remember that the like almost may be seene in our Ants, which will joyne sometimes seaven or eight together in the carrying of a burthen. These Creatures build themselves houses of wood and clay, close by the Ponds sides, and knowing the Seasons, build them answerable houses, having them three stories high, so that as land-floods are raised by great Raines, as the waters arise, they mount higher in their houses; as they asswage, they descend lower againe. These houses are so strong, that no creature saving an industrious man with his penetrating tooles can prejudice them, their ingresse and egresse being under water. These make likewise very good Ponds, knowing whence a streame runnes from betweene two rising Hils, they will there pitch down piles of Wood, placing smaller rubbish before it with clay and sods, not leaving, till by their Art and Industry they have made a firme and curious damme-head, which may draw admiration from wise understanding men. These creatures keepe themselves to their owne families, never parting so long as they are able to keepe house together: And it is commonly sayd, if any Beaver accidentally light into a strange place, he is made a drudge so long as he lives there, to carry at the greater end of the logge, unlesse he creepe away by stealth. Their wisedome secures them from the *English*, who seldome, or never kills any of them, being not patient to lay a long siege, or to be so often deceived by their cunning evasions, so that all the Beaver which the *English* have, comes first from the *Indians*, whose time and experience fits them for that imployment.

Adriaen Van der Donck, a law graduate of the University of Leyden, came to the New Netherlands in 1641 as the resident legal officer for the large Van Rensselaer patroonship along the Hudson River. In 1649 he returned to Holland to protest Peter Stuyvesant's mismanagement of the colony. Five years of bureaucratic red tape enabled him to write his Description of the New Netherlands *(1665). The first English translation was made in 1841 by Jeremiah Johnson and published in the* Collections of the New York Historical Society, *2nd series, volume 1. The following excerpt is taken from Thomas F. O'Donnell's reprint of that translation (Syracuse, 1968), pp. 19-23, 43-49, 110-120.*

Of the Wood, the Natural Productions, and Fruits of the Land

The New Netherlands, with other matters, is very fruitful, and fortunate in its fine woods; so much so, that the whole country is covered with wood, and in our manner of speaking, there is all too much of it, and in our way. Still it comes to hand to build vessels and houses, and to enclose the farms &c. The oak trees are very large; from sixty to seventy feet high without knots, and from two to three fathoms thick, being of various sizes. There are several kinds of oak, such as white, smooth bark, rough bark, grey bark and black bark. It is all durable wood, being as good as the oak of the Rhine or the Weser when properly worked, according to the opinion of our woodcutters, who are judges of timber and are sawyers. The nut-wood grows as tall as the oak, but not so heavy. It is probable that this kind of wood will be useful for many purposes, it grows straight and is tough and hard. We now use it for cogs and rounds in our mills and for threshing-flails, swivel-trees, and other farming purposes. It also is excellent firewood, surpassing every other kind, and setting at naught

our old adage, "The man is yet to come, who can find better wood
to burn than oak." This wood is far better as well for heat as duration.
It possesses a peculiar sap, which causes it to burn freely, whether
green or dry. If we draw it up out of the fresh water where it has
lain a long time, still, on account of its hardness, it is even then
uncommonly durable on the fire. We all agree, that no turf, or other
common fuel is equal to nut-wood. When it is dry, it keeps fire and
sparkles like matches. Our women prefer nut-coals to turf for their
stoves, because they last longer, and are not buried in ashes. This
kind of wood is found all over the New Netherlands in such abundance, that it cannot become scarce in the first hundred years with
an increased population. There also is oak and ash enough to supply
its place for many purposes. The land also is so natural to produce
wood, that in a few years large trees will be grown, which I can
say with certainty from my own observation; and that unless there
be natural changes or great improvidence, there can be no scarcity
of wood in this country.

It has happened when I have been out with the natives (*Wilden*,
for so we name those who are not born of Christian parents), that
we have come to a piece of young woodland. When I have told them,
in conversation, that they would do well to clear off such land,
because it would bear good corn, that they said, "it is but twenty
years since we planted corn there, and now it is woods again." I
asked them severally if it were true, when they all answered in the
affirmative. This relation was also corroborated by others. To return
to the subject: this woodland was composed of oak, nut, and other
kinds of wood, but principally of oak and nut; and there were several
trees in the same which were a fathom in circumference. The wood
was so closely grown that it was difficult to pass through it on
horseback. As the wood appeared young and thrifty, I give credit to
the relation of the natives. I have also observed that the youngest
woodlands are always covered closest with wood, and where the
growth is small, the woods are so thick as to render walking through
the same difficult. But where the woods are old, the timber is large
and heavy, whereby the underwood is shaded, which causes it to die
and perish.

The Indians have a yearly custom (which some of our Christians
have also adopted) of burning the woods, plains and meadows in the
fall of the year, when the leaves have fallen, and when the grass and

vegetable substances are dry. Those places which are then passed over are fired in the spring in April. This practice is named by us and the Indians, "bush-burning." which is done for several reasons: First, to render hunting easier, as the bush and vegetable growth renders the walking difficult for the hunter, and the crackling of the dry substances betrays him and frightens away the game. Secondly, to thin out and clear the woods of all dead substances and grass, which grow better the ensuing spring. Thirdly, to circumscribe and enclose the game within the lines of the fire, when it is more easily taken, and also, because the game is more easily tracked over the burned parts of the woods.

The bush burning presents a grand and sublime appearance. On seeing it from without, we would imagine that not only the dry leaves, vegetables and limbs would be burnt, but that the whole woods would be consumed where the fire passes, for it frequently spreads and rages with such violence, that it is awful to behold; and when the fire approaches houses, gardens, and wooden enclosures, then great care and vigilance are necessary for their preservation, for I have seen several houses which have recently been destroyed, before the owners were apprized of their danger.

Notwithstanding the apparent danger of the entire destruction of the woodlands by the burning, still the green trees do not suffer. The outside bark is scorched three or four feet high, which does them no injury, for the trees are not killed. It however sometimes happens that in the thick pine woods, wherein the fallen trees lie across each other, and have become dry, that the blaze ascends and strikes the tops of the trees, setting the same on fire, which is immediately increased by the resinous knots and leaves, which promote the blaze, and is passed by the wind from tree to tree, by which the entire tops of the trees are sometimes burnt off, while the bodies remain standing. Frequently great injuries are done by such fires, but the burning down of entire woods never happens. I have seen many instances of wood-burning in the colony of Rensselaerwyck, where there is much pine wood. Those fires appear grand at night from the passing vessels in the river, when the woods are burning on both sides of the same. Then we can see a great distance by the light of the blazing trees, the flames being driven by the wind, and fed by the tops of the trees. But the dead and dying trees remain burning in their standing positions, which appear sublime and beautiful when seen at a distance.

Hence it will appear that there actually is such an abundance of wood in the New Netherlands, that, with ordinary care, it will never be scarce there. There always are, however, in every country, some people so improvident, that even they may come short here, and for this reason we judge that it should not be destroyed needlessly. There, however, is such an abundance of wood, that they who cultivate the land for planting and sowing can do nothing better than destroy it, and thus clear off the land for tillage, which is done by cutting down the trees and collecting the wood into great heaps and burning the same, to get it out of their way. Yellow and white pine timber, in all their varieties, is abundant here, and we have heard the Northerners say (who reside here) that the pine is as good here as the pine of Norway. But the pine does not grow as well near the salt water, except in some places. Inland, however, and high up the rivers, it grows in large forests, and it is abundant, and heavy enough for masts and spars for ships. There also are chestnuts here, like those of the Netherlands, which are spread over the woods. Chestnuts would be plentier if it were not for the Indians, who destroy the trees by stripping off the bark for covering for their houses. They, and the Netherlanders also, cut down the trees in the chestnut season, and cut off the limbs to gather the nuts, which also lessens the trees. We also find several kinds of beech trees, but those bear very little. Amongst the other trees, the water-beeches grow very large along the brooks, heavier and larger than most of the trees of the country. When those trees begin to bud, then the bark becomes a beautiful white, resembling the handsomest satin. This tree retains the leaves later than any other tree of the woods. Trees of this kind are considered more ornamental and handsomer than the linden trees for the purpose of planting near dwelling-houses. We can give no comparison with this species of trees, and can give the same no better name to make the wood known. There also is wild ash, some trees large; and maple trees, the wood resembling cedar; white-wood trees, which grow very large—the Indians frequently make their canoes of this wood, hence we name it *Canoe-wood*; we use it for flooring, because it is bright and free of knots. There are also two kinds of ash, with linden, birch, yew, poplar, sapine, alder, willow, thorn trees, sassafras, persimmon, mulberry, wild cherry, crab, and several other kinds of wood, the names of which are unknown to us, but the wood is suitable for a variety of purposes. Some of the trees bear fruit. The oak trees in alternate years bear many acorns of the chestnut species. The nuts grow about as large as our persimmons, but they are not as good as ours. The mulberries are better and sweeter than ours, and ripen earlier. Several kinds of plums, wild or small cherries, juniper, small kinds of apples, many hazelnuts, black currants, gooseberries, blue India figs, and strawberries in abundance all over the country, some of which ripen at half May, and we have them until July; blueberries, raspberries, black-caps, &c., with artichokes, ground-acorns, ground beans, wild onions, and leeks like ours, with several other kinds of roots and fruits, known to the Indians, who use the same which are disregarded by the Netherlanders, because they have introduced every kind of garden vegetables, which thrive and yield well. The country also produces an abundance of fruits like the Spanish capers, which could be preserved in like manner.

Of the Wild Animals

Although the New Netherlands lay in a fine climate, and although the country in winter seems rather cold, nevertheless lions [cougars] are found there, but not by the Christians, who have traversed the land wide and broad and have not seen one. It is only known to us by the skins of the females, which are sometimes brought in by the Indians for sale; who on inquiry say, that the lions are found far to the southwest, distant fifteen or twenty days' journey, in very high mountains, and that the males are too active and fierce to be taken.

Many bears are found in the country, but none like the grey and pale-haired bears of Muscovy and Greenland. The bears are of a shining pitch black colour; their skins are proper for muffs. Although there are many of these beasts, yet from the acute sharpness of their smelling, they are seldom seen by the Christians. Whenever they smell a person they run off. When the Indians go a-hunting, they dress themselves as Esau did, in clothes which have the flavour of the woods (except in their sleeping and hiding season, whereon we will treat hereafter) that they may not be discovered by their smell. The bears are sometimes seen by the Christians, when they are approached from the leeward side, or when they swim across water courses. The bears are harmless unless they are attacked or wounded, and then they defend themselves fiercely as long as they can. A person who intends to shoot a bear, should be careful to have a tree near him to retreat to for safety; for if his shot does not take good effect, and the bear is not killed instantly, which, on account of their toughness, seldom happens, then the hunter is in danger; for then the bear instantly makes a stopper of leaves or of any other substance, as instinct directs, wherewith the animal closes the wound, and directly proceeds towards the hunter, if in sight, or to the place whence the smoke ascends and the gun was fired. In the meantime the hunter should be up the tree, which should be thick and full of limbs, otherwise the bear would also climb the tree easily. In this position the hunter has the advantage, and should be prepared to despatch his adversary; otherwise he must remain in his sanctuary until the rage of the animal is abated, which has frequently lasted two hours, and he retires. Hunters have related these particulars, who have preserved themselves as related.

The bears of this country are not ravenous, and do not subsist on flesh and carrion, as the bears of Muscovy and Greenland do. They subsist on grass, herbs, nuts, acorns and chestnuts, which, we are told by the Indians, they will gather and eat on the trees. It is also affirmed by the Christians, that they have seen bears on trees gathering and eating the fruit. When they wish to come down, then they place their heads between their legs, and let themselves fall to the earth; and whether they fall high or low, they spring up and go their way. Bears are sometimes shot when on the trees.

The Indians and the Christians are firmly of opinion that the bears sleep and lay concealed twelve weeks in succession in a year. In the fall they always are fat. During the winter they eat nothing, but lie down on one side with a foot in the mouth, whereon they suck growling six weeks; they then turn on the other side and lay six weeks more, and continue to suck as before. For this purpose they usually retire to the mountains, and seek shelter under projecting rocks in a burrow, or in a thick brushy wood, wherein many large trees have fallen, where they also seek shelter from the wind, snow and rain. The Indians say that the greatest number of bears are taken during their sleeping season, when they are most easily killed. The heaviest bears which are taken (judging from their skins) are about the size of a common heifer. The animals also are very fat, as before stated, the pork frequently being six or seven fingers in thickness. The Indians esteem the fore quarters and the plucks [the heart and liver] as excellent food. I have never tasted the meat, but several Christians who have eaten the bear's flesh say it is as good as any swine's flesh or pork can be.

Buffaloes are also tolerably plenty. These animals mostly keep towards the southwest, where few people go. Their meat is excellent, and more desirable than the flesh of the deer, although it is much coarser. Their skins when dressed are heavy enough for collars and harness. These animals are not very wild, and some persons are of opinion that they may be domesticated and tamed. It is also supposed that a female buffalo, put to a Holland bull, would produce a cross breed which would give excellent milking cattle, and that the males would form fine hardy working animals when castrated. Persons who have got them when young say they become very tame as they grow older and forget the wild woods and that they fatten well. It is remarked that the half of those animals have disappeared and left the country, and that if a cross breed succeeded, it would become more natural to the climate.

The deer are incredibly numerous in the country. Although the Indians throughout the year and every year (but mostly in the fall) kill many thousands, and the wolves, after the fawns are cast, and while they are young, also destroy many, still the land abounds with them everywhere, and their numbers appear to remain undiminished. We seldom pass through the fields without seeing deer more or less, and we frequently see them in flocks. Their meat digests easily, and is good food. Venison is so easily obtained that a good buck cashes for five guilders, and often for much less.

There are also white bucks and does, and others of a black colour in the country. The Indians aver that the haunts of the white deer are much frequented by the common deer, and that those of the black species are not frequented by the common deer. These are the sayings of the Indians. The truth remains to be ascertained relating to the preference between the animals.

There is also another kind of animals in the country, which are represented to be large, and which are known to the people of Canada, who relate strange things concerning the same. I have heard from the mouth of a Jesuit, who had been taken prisoner by the Mohawk Indians and released by our people, and come to me, that there were many wild forest oxen in Canada and *Nova Francia* [New France], which in Latin they name *boves silvestres* (the moose or elk), which are as large as horses, having long hair on their necks like the mane of a horse, and cloven hoofs, but that, like the buffalo, the animals were not fierce. I have also been frequently told by the Mohawk Indians, that far in the interior parts of the country, there were animals which were seldom seen, of the size and form of horses, with cloven hoofs, having one horn in the forehead, from a foot and a half to two feet in length, and that because of their fleetness and strength they were seldom caught or ensnared. I have never seen any certain token or sign of such animals, but that such creatures exist in the country, is supported by the concurrent declarations of the Indian hunters. There are Christians who say that they have seen the skins of this species of animal, but without the horns.

Wolves are numerous in the country, but these are not so large and ravenous as the Netherlands wolves are. They will not readily attack anything, except small animals, such as deer (but most commonly when young), calves, sheep, goats, and hogs. But when a drove of hogs are together, they do not permit the wolves to do them any injury, as those animals defend and assist each other.

The wolves in winter know how to beset and take deer. When the snow is upon the earth, eight or ten wolves, hunter-like, prowl in the chase in company. Sometimes a single wolf will chase and follow a single deer, until the animal is wearied, and falls a prey; but if the deer in the pursuit crosses a stream of water, then the wolf is done, because he dare not follow, and remains on the margin of the stream to see his chase escape. Wolves frequently drive deer into the rivers and streams. Many are taken in the water by persons who reside in the neighbourhood of rivers and streams, by the means of boats, with which they pursue the animals. If the deer is so near the shore as to be likely to gain the land before the boat can be near enough to take the prize, the person or persons in the boat shout and holloa loudly, when the echo from the land and woods frightens the animal off from the place to which it was swimming, and fearing to land it is easily taken by these stratagems.

Some persons are of opinion that a driven deer will not betake itself to fresh water for safety, but we of the New Netherlands know to the contrary, and that there is no difference. When deer are chased upon an island near the sea, or on land near the sea, they will enter the open ocean, and frequently swim so far from shore that they never find their way to the land again.

Beavers are numerous in the New Netherlands. We will treat at large of these animals hereafter. There are also fine otters in the country, very fine fishes, and wildcats, which have skins nearly resembling the skin of the lioness; these animals also resemble them in form, but they have short tails, like the hares and conies. Foxes and racoons are plenty; the skins of the latter are streaked, resembling seals, and are excellent applications for bruises and lameness. When their meat is roasted, it is delicious food, but when stewed, it is too luscious, on account of its fatness. The racoons usually shelter in hollow trees, wherein they lay up food for the winter, which they seldom leave, except for drink. It is a pleasure to take racoons; the trees wherein they shelter are discovered by the scratching of the bark, which is done by the racoons in climbing and descending the trees. When their haunts are discovered, the trees are cut down. By the fall of a tree, the racoons are stunned, and on leaving their holes they stagger as if drunk, and fall an easy prey to the hunter. Minks, hares, and conies (rabbits) are plenty in the country. Tame rabbits run at large in New England. Muskrats are abundant; these creatures smell so strong of musk, that it can hardly be endured: when the skins are old and dry, the smell is retained, and all articles which are kept with the skins, are impregnated with the musky smell. *Maeters*, and black and gray squirrels, are also numerous. One kind of squirrels can fly several rods at a time; this species have a thin skin on both sides from the fore to the hind legs, which they extend and flap like wings, with which they fly swiftly to the desired place. Ground hogs, English skunks, drummers, and several other kinds of animals, for which we have no names, are known and found in the country. Their description is passed over.

Of the Land and Water Fowls; and first, of the Birds of Prey

Birds of prey are numerous in the New Netherlands; among which there are two species of eagles, so different in appearance that they hardly resemble each other. The one is the common kind, which is known in Holland. The other kind is somewhat larger, and the feathers are much browner, except the whole head, a part of the neck, the whole tail, and the striking feathers, which are as white as snow, and render the bird beautiful. This kind are called white-heads, and they are plenty. Falcons, sparrow-hawks, sailing-hawks, castrills, church-hawks, fish-hawks, and several other kinds, for which I have no name, are plenty; but every kind feed on flesh or fish, as they can best take the same. Those hawks might easily be trained to catch game, to which nature with art would perfect them. The small kind live on small birds; the larger kinds watch for woodpeckers, corn-birds, quails, &c.; each that kind which it can overcome. But the eagles look for higher game, and bring terror where they appear. They usually frequent places where the trees are old, and where the ground is free from underwood, near the bay sides, or near large rivers, where from the tops of the trees they can have their eyes over the fish, the swans, the geese and the ducks, with which they can supply themselves; but they do not commonly feed on fowl, because they prefer fish. They frequently strike a fish, and jerk it living from the waters. When a bird is crippled by a gunner, or is otherwise disabled, then the eagle's eye will see them, where the human eyes have looked in vain. The eagles soar very high in the air, beyond the vision of man, and on those flights they are always looking out for prey, or for a dead carcase, near which they are commonly seen. They seldom kill corn birds, or fowls which live on fruit. Eagles are fond of the flesh of deer, for which they watch the places where the wolves kill deer, and have left a carcass partly eaten, which they discover on the wing. Many persons who know the nature of the eagle, and observe their sailing, have followed in their direction and have found the deer for which the eagle went, partly destroyed and eaten by wolves. It also happens that the hunters wound deer which escape, and die from the loss of blood. Such are also sometimes found uninjured by the direction of the eagles. There is also another bird of prey in the country, which has a head like the head of a large cat. Its feathers are of a light ash colour. The people of the country have no name for the bird. The Director Kieft says, the bird is known in France, and is named *Grand Dux*, where it is held in high estimation by the nobility, who have them trained for sporting. They are difficult to break, but when well trained they are frequently sold for 100 French crowns per bird.

THE BEAVER

Under the title of the wild animals of the New Netherlands, we remain indebted for a description of the uncommon and natural habits of the beavers. . . . This animal has attracted many persons to the country. We will begin by stating the opinions of the ancient and later writers on the beaver, and by following the truth show how far they have wandered from it on this matter.

Pliny, the great naturalist, in his XXXII Book, Chap. 3, says that the limbs of the beaver, whereby he means the *testicles*, are very useful for many purposes in medicine. And that the animals when sought by the hunters for their testes, and when closely pursued, would castrate themselves with their teeth and leave the parts for the hunters, which the creatures knew to be the prize sought after. This most of the old naturalists and physicians believed to be true; although some denied the same, still they held that the beaver cods, which they named castorium, possessed many medicinal virtues.

They write that the beavers could bite very sharp; that they could fell trees as if cut with an axe. Olaus and Albertus remark on their carrying of wood for their houses. They also state that the beavers' tails are very long, and that that part is fish; that beavers will attack men and bite them severely, with many other things differing widely from the truth. Hence it may be inferred that neither of them have ever seen a beaver, but have related their uncertain propositions upon the credit of ignorant, unlettered persons. We may give credit to their declarations, when they relate that they used beaver flesh and cods for medicines. This was their art; the virtue of the specific lay in the faith of the patients, which they saw suited their designs.

We will now relate in connection the disorders for which they say the medicines prepared from beaver testicles were infallible remedies. The smelling of beaver cods will produce sneezing and cause sleep—connected with the oil of roses and hogs-lard, and rubbed on the head of a drowsy person, it will produce wakefulness. Taken in water, it serves to remove idiocy. The sleeping are awakened by rubbing with cod oil. Two quarts of the oil, mixed with polay-water, will restore the menses to women, and remove the second birth. Beaver oil is good for dizziness, for trembling, for the rheumatism, for lameness, for the pain in the stomach, and for apoplexy, when the stomach is greased with it. Again, when taken inwardly, it removes the falling sickness and stoppages in the body, pain in the bowels, and poison. It cures the tooth-ache; dropped in the ear, it cures the ear-ache. Tingling and rustling in the ears is cured by a few drops of *Macolim* sap. Beaver oil, mixed with the best honey and rubbed on the eyes, restores the sharpness of sight. Beaver water is an antidote for all poisons, but to preserve it good it must be kept in the bladder. Those who have the gout should wear slippers and shoes made of beaver skins.

After relating all those things we will proceed to an accurate description of the beaver, as we have found and known the animal. And that none may believe that I treat upon a subject which is unknown to me, the reader will please observe that in the New Netherlands, and in the adjacent country, about eighty thousand beavers have been killed annually, during my residence of nine years in the country. I have frequently eaten beaver flesh, and have raised and kept their young. I have also handled and exchanged many thousand skins.

A beaver is a four-footed animal that feeds on vegetables, and keeps in water and on land, coated with fur and hair, short-legged, quick, timid and subtle, and commonly as thick as it is long. The Greek name of this animal is *castor*, the Latin is *eyber* [fiber], the Dutch is *beever*. The other names by which it is known in Europe are mostly derived from the foregoing. It has feet like the otter or like other wild and tame creatures which keep on land.

The food of the beaver is not, as some suppose, fish and prey like the otter's; to which end the beaver has been described and delineated with a fish in its mouth, and to be part fish and part flesh. It feeds on the bark of several kinds of wood, on roots, rushes, and greens, which it finds in the woods, fields, and bushes, near the water sides. The kinds of bark whereon it feeds are of the water willow, birch, and maple trees, which grow plentifully near the water sides, and of all other trees which are not sour or bitter to the taste, which they dislike.

The beavers keep (as is said, which is true) in the water and on land; therefore they may be named land and water animals, but they are mostly on the dry land, and get most of their food on land, consisting of bark and herbage. The wood and grass used in the construction of their house are got on the land; they remain whole nights on land, and they cannot live and remain long under the water, particularly when they are chased and fatigued. In the water they obtain a scanty subsistence from the bark of roots of trees which extend into the water from the margin of the water courses, and the weeds and bushes which grow in some places, but mostly on the margin of the water. The true and certain reason why the beavers keep so much in the water arises from their natural timidity, which is supported by the testimony of the great beaver catchers. Being naturally timid, the creature can best preserve and secure itself much better and easier in the water than on land. To that end, as will be detailed hereafter, they construct their abodes over the water, having apertures in the lower stories that communicate with the water, from which they can readily retreat under water to places of safety, which they have always prepared near their houses; these consist of a hollow or hole entwining under water from the side of the stream whereon their houses are erected and ascending under the bank, into which they retreat on the approach of danger—wherein they seem to be so safe and secure that no person can molest them.

The beaver's skin is rough, but very thickly set with fine wool (fur) of an ash grey colour, inclining to blue. The outward points also incline to a russet or brown colour. From the beaver fur, or wool, the best hats are made that are worn, which are named beavers or castoreums, after the materials from which the same are made, being at present known over all Europe. Outside of the coat of fur many shining hairs appear, which are called wind hairs, that more properly are winter hairs, for those fall out in summer and appear again in the fall. This outer coat is of a chestnut brown colour—the browner the better—it sometimes will be somewhat reddish. When hats are made of the fur, the rough hairs are plucked out, being useless. The skins usually are first sent to Russia (Muscovy) where they are highly esteemed for the outside shining hair, and on that their greatest recommendation depends with the Russians. There the skins are used for mantle linings, and are also cut into stripes for borders, as we cut the rabbit skins. Therefore we name the same *peltries*. Whoever there has the most and costliest fur trimmings is esteemed the greatest, as with us, the finest stuffs and gold and silver embroidery are considered the appendages of the great. After the hairs have fallen out, or are worn, and the peltries become old and dirty, and apparently useless, we get the articles back and convert the fur into hats, before which it cannot be well used for this purpose, for unless the beaver has been worn and is greasy and dirty, it will not felt properly—therefore those old peltries are most valuable. The coats which the Indians make of beaver skins, and have worn a long time around their bodies, until the same have become foul with sweat and grease—those afterwards are used by the hatters and make the best hats. They also work it with the combed wool or fur (which is so called) because the beaver skins before the same are sent to Russia are combed, by which process much of the fur is taken out of the long hair (or wind hair) with a comb—this is also worked with the peltry fur, after its return from Russia.

The beavers have very short legs, appearing as if there were no middle bones, and when they run, their legs are scarcely observable, and appear as if their feet were joined to their bodies, with which they move. Their claws or paws are bare and blackish, with strong, brown nails, bound with a thick, strong skin, like swans' feet, which they resemble, but are not so broad, being shorter before than behind. The hinder part of the body is short, much like that of a goose or swan. The forefeet (as the creature has a short neck, or is almost without a neck, the head being near the shoulders) stand near the head. Therefore when they run, which they do with great activity, their whole body appears to touch the ground and appears to be too heavy for their small short legs; but far from it, they are well provided by nature with strong sinews and muscles and are very strong.

The beavers are so quick that they not only can run wonderfully over the earth, when we consider their formation, avoiding men and dogs; but in the water they seem as active as fishes. Therefore the Indians must take them in traps; or when they lay in their burrows in the earth, they know how to take and kill them with long rammers (which have lances affixed at the ends) inserted at the holes of their burrows. That the beavers according to the meaning of Olaus, Magnus, and Albertus, will be inclined to bite and wound persons dreadfully, is a mistake; for it is a timid creature, which seeks to preserve itself by flight if possible, and as it has a sharp scent and hearing, we seldom happen to see it on the land. Nor will it ever keep near man like the otters, which the latter sometimes do. The beavers keep in deep swamps, at the waters and morasses, where no settlements are. Still when they are beset and bitten by dogs, they can defend themselves very well, and do great injury to a common dog, when they take hold of the same with their foreteeth; but as to their attacking men with violence, it is erroneous. I have seen and conversed with hundreds of beaver hunters, but have never known more than one who had been bitten by a beaver in his shoulder and received a bad wound. This happened when the hunter's dog and a beaver were striving for the mastery, and the hunter stooped down to help his dog; when the beaver missing the dog probably, in terror and misery, bit the hunter in his shoulder.

That the beavers are subtle animals appears by the construction of their houses, and in rearing their young, which we will presently relate, with their continual watch, which they keep to prevent surprise and being taken; which, we are informed, they keep at every house, for the beavers commonly have six or seven in a family in every house, at which they in turn keep watch. It is certain that when it freezes hard, which it frequently does where the most and best beavers resort, there always sits one, not as Albertus and Magnus assert, with half of the body in the water (for this would be impossible in severe frost). The beaver can keep above water without pain, which they nevertheless on the contrary feel; but I assert that one of the family always sits near the running water, for they always build on running waters, that with the striking of their tails they keep it open; the noise of which resembles the continual striking of a person with his flat hand, by which means they prevent the freezing of the water and keep it open. This is not done because, as the doctors say, they cannot remain out of water without pain, but to keep the entrance of the houses open, so that they can seek food, and in case of danger, that they can readily with little difficulty retreat to their strongholds, which they always have near their houses under the banks of the water courses.

The form of a beaver resembles the shape of a cucumber which has a short stem, or a duck that has the neck and head cut off, or like a ball of yarn wound in long form and flattened a little, being often thicker than long, or like a swine which is flat on the back, with its belly hanging down. The dead beaver resembles a dead mole which is somewhat flattened with the foot.

When full grown, the skins are about an ell [27 inches] long and an ell broad; they are not round, but frequently nearly square. From this size up to five quarters, the skins are merchantable—they are seldom larger. From December to the first of June, the skins are good, and then they are killed. The fall skins have the winter hairs in part, with very little fur. The summer skins and those taken from ungrown beavers are of little value. Still the Indians kill all they find when they are hunting.

Their houses, as Sextius, Albertus, and Olaus say, they construct always over a running stream, with several stories, four, five, or more, above each other, of curious workmanship, and worthy of speculation. Every apartment and story in their houses is made perfectly tight with wood, grass and clay to the top, which keeps out the rain. They lodge in those houses in whole families, and parts of families, and break out like bees, with their increase when disturbed. The wood used in the construction of their houses is of the soft kind, such as maple, pine, white-wood, &c. which they find laying along the water courses. When this supply is insufficient, they have recourse to the nearest trees, which is done as follows. When a beaver intends to fell a tree, it selects one of a proper size, of about six inches diameter, the bark of which is not bad tasted. The beaver then begins cutting with its front teeth, of which it has two in the upper and two in the lower jaw; very strong and about half an inch long, more or less, according to its age. Those teeth are yellow on the outside. When this is scraped off and taken inwardly, it will cure the jaundice. With those teeth, which are common to the squirrels and other animals, they commence gnawing, making a cut of about a hand's breadth or more around the tree, which they work at until the tree falls, and then the ends resemble the turned whip-tops used by children. Whether they look up when the tree falls, to observe its direction, I have never heard. But I have seen many trees which had been cut down by the beavers, that had fallen fast against trees that stood near by, that were left by the animals. After a tree has fallen down, they then gnaw off the wood into proper lengths for their work. They carry the wood together, and nearly all the inhabitants of the New Netherlands know that many skins are sold from which the outside wind hairs are worn off on the back, which are called wood-carriers' skins, because they carried wood for the construction of their houses; this is not done as the ancients relate, between their legs, as upon a sled or waggon; but the Indians who have seen the beavers labour, have frequently told me, that after the wood is cut off and ready for removal, the female places herself under the piece to be removed, which the male and the young ones support on her back to the place where it is used. In this manner every stick is carried. That the carrier is dragged by its tail with the wood, lying on its back, by the other beavers, is a fabulous tale. The tail of a beaver is not large and long, as the ancients remark. The largest are not larger and broader than a man's hand, without the thumb. Their tails also are tender and would not bear pulling by the same with the sharp teeth of another beaver.

The beaver tails are flattish, without hair, coated with a skin which appears as if set with fish scales, and when chopped up with the flesh of the beaver, it is a delicate food, and is always preserved for the Emperor's table, whenever a beaver is caught in Germany, which seldom happens. The beaver tails excel all other flesh taken on land and in the water. Wherefore the Indians deem it a special favour to permit us to partake with them of a part of a beaver's tail; and they will seldom part with any beaver flesh. The most of the settlers in the New Netherlands have never tasted it—but the best and most excellent part of a beaver is its tail. The Indians will seldom part with it, unless on an extraordinary occasion as a present.

The beaver like the swine goes with young sixteen weeks; they bear once a year and in summer, some earlier than others, and have four in a litter, except at the first, when they sometimes have but two or three. The young beavers, whenever they are brought forth, cry like children, so that a person coming to a place where there is a young beaver, if he did not know to the contrary, would suppose a child was at hand. The beavers have two paps between the forelegs at the breast, resembling the paps of a woman, and no more. She suckles her young sitting and permits two to suckle at the same time, like children standing at the breast. Meanwhile the others lay, as if they were crying, in their nest—they are suckled in turn. A young beaver is a beautiful creature; is easily raised and will become as tame as a dog, and will feed on any food, like cats, except flesh and fish, which they will eat when boiled. When they are taken very young they require milk, which they readily learn to suck from a rag-teat, out of a horn. They are gentle to handle as a young dog, and will not get cross or bite. When grown they are fond of the water, and will sport and play in a stream with astonishing agility; and if they are not confined in locked waters, by going into streams every day they stroll away and become wild, and do not return again, like the deer, which also can be made very tame.

The doctors of medicine, as before related, ascribe many medicinal virtues to the beaver cods, which they name castorium. Aristotle, Pliny, and the writers of those days meant that the beavers seldom castrated themselves. But Olaus Magnus, Agricola, Albertus, and Sextius have not admitted this, but say much fraud was practiced in the sale of beaver cods, which is evident. And as I have been at great pains to arrive at a certainty on this subject, for which purpose I have not only examined many Indians carefully, who were most acquainted with the matter, but have also with my own hands opened many beavers, which I have examined curiously; the result of which, friendly reader, on this occasion will not be witheld from you.

I have heard that for medicinal purposes small kegs of dried and salted cods have been shipped to be sold by druggists, but for the most those were beaver kidneys, dugs, or not the real castor cods, therefore the article did not sell well. Several persons also have left the New Netherlands for Holland, who took with them, as they supposed, the real cods, which they had obtained from the Indians; but on their arrival, they were found to be a spurious article. Having heard of this several times, my curiosity became excited, and I even doubted whether I had seen real castor cods. All I had seen were round, some larger than others, but as long as they hung to smoke or dry, the fat dropped out as from pork hung in the sun. Finally I observed one somewhat long, like a preserved pear, shrivelled and a little musky. This I presented to an experienced physician in the New Netherlands, who pronounced it to be a true beaver cod, of the proper kind, and as the article should be. It happened at this time that beavers were found not far from my residence, and several were brought to me by the Indian hunters, unopened and fresh; these I opened and examined with great care for the real castor cods, but to no purpose. I found deep in the body, under the *os pubis*, or *eys* bone, small ballats like a *fleur-de-lis*, which in Holland were pronounced spurious. At last, a discreet Indian hunter, who had assisted me in my experimental dissections, after I had represented to him that the subjects sought for were flattish, and in form somewhat resembled a pear, advised the opening of a female beaver. We took in hand a female which was with young, to see how the young lay; upon which I found against the back bone two *testiculos*, of the form which I sought after, flattish like some pears, resembling young calves' testes, and yellowish, covered with a tolerable tough fleece or skin. I took them out, and for further certainty and assurance, that it was a female beaver, I removed four young from the body. After some time I presented those testicles to the doctor before mentioned, at the Governor's house, before much company. The doctor and all present pronounced the articles real beaver testicles. After I had related to them the whole procedure, they were amazed, but adhered to their first opinion, and that the same were the real beaver castor cods. Afterwards I have opened more beavers with the like result; therefore, without prejudice to the feelings of any person, I am decidedly of opinion, that the real *castorium* is found in the females and not in the males. The round balls of the males the Indians carve fine, and suck much with their tobacco it is healthy and well tasted. The fat or pork around the body of a beaver is frequently two or three fingers thick, of which the Indians are very fond. It resembles fed pork. The tails are great delicacies. The Indians always burn the beaver bones, and never permit their dogs to gnaw the same; alleging that afterwards they will be unlucky in the chase.

The beavers are usually all of the same colour; a few are a little browner than others. Among all the beaver skins I have seen, no more than one was of a different colour, and that was white. The outer wind hairs were golden yellow. This skin was shipped on board the ship *Princess*, with Director Kieft, which was lost at sea.

II. THE NATIVE AMERICANS

The Indian cultures of the New World were often as strange and forbidding to the early settlers as its environment. Why did European visitors feel uneasy around Indians? What in the Indian way of life was threatening to white men? How did the Indians treat the white men who came to their country? Did they treat different white men differently? Why? How do you think the Indians felt in the presence of white men? What in the European way of life was threatening to the Indians? How did the white men treat the Indians when they came to their settlements? Did they treat different Indians differently? What benefits did the Indians derive from contact with the Europeans? What benefits did the Europeans derive from contact with the Indians? Which side—Indian or white—derived the greater benefit? Why were the Europeans largely unsuccessful in converting the Indians to Christianity? In what ways was the Indian way of life adapted to their environment? For what reasons did the Indians welcome the coming of the white men? Was the Indian religion "superstitious?" How does "superstition" differ from sincerely held beliefs? To what extent could Christianity be seen as "superstitious" by the Indians?

Captain John Smith, America's first authentic hero (at least on his own word), was born in 1580 in a small village in Lincolnshire. At the age of sixteen he was apprenticed to a merchant, but his father's death the following year (1596) freed him for a life of adventure. After a crowded career in the Continental wars, fighting the Turks, enslavement, and piracy, he made the first of his many voyages to the coasts of America in 1606. The following description of the Virginia Indians that he met there is taken from A Map of Virginia: With a Description of the Countrey, the Commodities, People, Government and Religion *(Oxford, 1612).*

Of the naturall Inhabitants of Virginia.

The land is not populous, for the men be fewe; their far greater number is of women and children. Within 60 miles of James Towne there are about some 5000 people, but of able men fit for their warres scarse 1500. To nourish so many together they have yet no means, because they make so smal a benefit of their land, be it never so fertill. 6 or 700 have beene the most [that] hath beene seene together, when they gathered themselves to have surprised Captaine Smyth at Pamaunke, having but 15 to withstand the worst of their furie. As small as the proportion of ground that hath yet beene discovered, is in comparison of that yet unknowne. The people differ very much in stature, especially in language, as before is expressed. Some being very great as the Sesquesahamocks, others very little as the Wighcocomocoes: but generally tall and straight, of a comely proportion, and of a colour browne, when they are of any age, but they are borne white. Their haire is generally black; but few have any beards. The men weare halfe their heads shaven, the other halfe long. For Barbers they use their women, who with 2 shels will grate away the haire, of any fashion they please. The women are cut in many fashions agreeable to their yeares, but ever some part remaineth long. They are very strong, of an able body and full of agilitie, able to endure to lie in the woods under a tree by the fire, in the worst of winter, or in the weedes and grasse, in Ambuscado in the Sommer. They are inconstant in everie thing, but what feare constraineth them to keepe. Craftie, timerous, quicke of apprehension and very ingenuous. Some are of disposition fearefull, some bold, most cautelous, all Savage. Generally covetous of copper, beads, and such like trash. They are soone moved to anger, and so malitious, that they seldome forget an injury: they seldome steale one from another, least their conjurors should reveale it, and so they be pursued and punished. That they are thus feared is certaine, but that any can reveale their offences by conjuration I am doubtfull. Their women are carefull not to bee suspected of dishonesty without the leave of their husbands. Each houshold knoweth their owne lands and gardens, and most live of their owne labours. For their apparell, they are some time covered with the skinnes of wilde beasts, which in winter are dressed with the haire, but in sommer without. The better sort use large mantels of deare skins not much differing in fashion from the Irish mantels. Some imbrodered with white beads, some with copper, other painted after their manner. But the common sort have scarce to cover their nakednesse but with grasse, the leaves of trees, or such like. We have seen some use mantels made of Turky feathers, so prettily wrought and woven with threeds that nothing could bee discerned but the feathers, that was exceeding warme and very handsome. But the women are alwaies covered about their midles with a skin and very shamefast to be seene bare. They adorne themselves most with copper beads and paintings. Their women some have their legs, hands, brests and face cunningly imbrodered with diverse workes, as beasts, serpentes, artificially wrought into their flesh with blacke spots. In each eare commonly they have 3 great holes, whereat they hange chaines, bracelets, or copper. Some of their men weare in those holes, a smal greene and yellow coloured snake, neare halfe a yard in length, which crawling and lapping her selfe about his necke often times familiarly would kiss his lips. Others wear a dead Rat tied by the tail. Some on their heads weare the wing of a bird or some large feather, with a Rattell. Those Rattels are somewhat like the chape of a Rapier but lesse, which they take from the taile of a snake. Many have the whole skinne of a hawke or some strange fowle, stuffed with the wings abroad. Others a broad peece of copper, and some the hand of their enemy dryed. Their heads and shoulders are painted red with the roote *Pocone* braied to powder mixed with oyle; this they hold in somer to preserve them from the heate, and in winter from the cold. Many other formes of paintings they use, but he is the most gallant that is the most monstrous to behould.

Their buildings and habitations are for the most part by the rivers or not farre distant from some fresh spring. Their houses are built like our Arbors of small young springs [sprigs] bowed and tyed, and so close covered with mats or the barkes of trees very handsomely, that notwithstanding either winde raine or weather, they are as warme as stooves, but very smoaky, yet at the toppe of the house there is a hole made for the smoake to goe into right over the fire.

Against the fire they lie on little hurdles of Reedes covered with a mat, borne from the ground a foote and more by a hurdle of wood. On these round about the house, they lie heads and points one by thother against the fire: some covered with mats, some with skins, and some starke naked lie on the ground, from 6 to 20 in a house. Their houses are in the midst of their fields or gardens; which are smal plots of ground, some 20 [acres], some 40, some 100, some 200, some more, some lesse. Some times from 2 to 100 of these houses togither, or but a little separated by groves of trees. Neare their habitations is little small wood, or old trees on the ground, by reason of their burning of them for fire. So that a man may gallop a horse amongst these woods any waie, but where the creekes or Rivers shall hinder.

Men women and children have their severall names according to the severall humor of their Parents. Their women (they say) are easilie delivered of childe, yet doe they love children verie dearly. To make them hardy, in the coldest mornings they wash them in the rivers, and by painting and ointments so tanne their skins, that after year or two, no weather will hurt them.

The men bestowe their times in fishing, hunting, wars, and such manlike exercises, scorning to be seene in any woman like exercise, which is the cause that the women be verie painefull and the men often idle. The women and children do the rest of the worke. They make mats, baskets, pots, morters, pound their corne, make their bread, prepare their victuals, plant their corne, gather their corne, beare al kind of burdens, and such like.

Their fire they kindle presently by chafing a dry pointed sticke in a hole of a little square peece of wood, that firing it selfe, will so fire mosse, leaves, or anie such like drie thing that will quickly burne. In March and Aprill they live much upon their fishing weares, and feed on fish, Turkies and squirrels. In May and June they plant their fieldes, and live most of Acornes, walnuts, and fish. But to mend their diet, some disperse themselves in small companies, and live upon fish, beasts, crabs, oysters, land Torteyses, strawberries, mulberries, and such like. In June, Julie, and August, they feed upon the rootes of *Tocknough*, berries, fish, and greene wheat. It is strange to see how their bodies alter with their diet; even as the deare and wild beastes, they seeme fat and leane, strong and weak. Powhatan their great king and some others that are provident, rost their fish and flesh upon hurdles as before is expressed, and keepe it till scarce times.

For fishing and hunting and warres they use much their bow and arrowes. They bring their bowes to the forme of ours by the scraping of a shell. Their arrowes are made, some of straight young sprigs, which they head with bone some 2 or 3 inches long. These they use to shoot at squirrels on trees. An other sort of arrowes they use, made of reeds. These are peeced with wood, headed with splinters of christall or some sharpe stone, the spurres of a Turkey, or the bill of some bird. For his knife, he hath the splinter of a reed to cut his feathers in forme. With this knife also, he will joint a Deare or any beast, shape his shooes, buskins, mantels, &c. To make the noch of his arrow hee hath the tooth of a Bever set in a sticke, wherewith he grateth it by degrees. His arrow head he quickly maketh with a little bone, which he ever weareth at his bracer, of any splint of a stone, or glasse in the forme of a hart, and these they glew to the end of their arrowes. With the sinewes of Deare, and the tops of Deares hornes boiled to a jelly, they make a glew that will not dissolve in cold water.

For their wars also they use Targets that are round and made of the barkes of trees, and a sworde of wood at their backs, but oftentimes they use for swords the horne of a Deare put through a peece of wood in forme of a Pickaxe. Some, a long stone sharpened at both ends used in the same manner. This they were wont to use also for hatchets, but now by trucking they have plenty of the same forme, of yron. And those are their chiefe instruments and armes.

Their fishing is much in Boats. These they make of one tree by bowing [burning] and scratching away the coles with stone and shels till they have made it in forme of a Trough. Some of them are an elne [45 inches] deepe, and 40 or 50 foot in length, and some will beare 40 men, but the most ordinary are smaller, and will beare 10, 20 or 30, according to their bignes. Instead of oares, they use paddles and sticks, with which they will row faster then our Barges. Betwixt their hands and thighes, their women use to spin the barks of trees, deare sinews, or a kind of grasse they call *Pemmenaw*; of these they make a thred very even and readily. This thred serveth for many uses, as about their housing, apparell, as also they make nets for fishing, for the quantity as formally braded as ours. They make also with it lines for angles. Their hookes are either a bone grated, as they nock their arrows, in the forme of a crooked pinne or fishhook or of the splinter of a bone tied to the clift of a litle stick and with the ende of the line, they tie on the bate. They use also long arrowes tyed in a line wherewith they shoote at fish in the rivers. But they of Accawmack use staves like unto Javelins headed with bone. With these they dart fish swimming in the water. They have also many artificiall weares in which they get abundance of fish.

In their hunting and fishing they take extreame paines; yet it being their ordinary exercise from their infancy, they esteeme it a pleasure and are very proud to be expert therein. And by their continuall ranging, and travel, they know all the advantages and places most frequented with Deare, Beasts, Fish, Foule, Rootes, and Berries. At their huntings they leave their habitations, and reduce themselves into companies, as the Tartars doe, and goe to the most desert places with their families, where they spend their time in hunting and fowling up towards the mountaines, by the heads of their rivers, where there is plentie of game. For betwixt the rivers, the grounds are so narrowe, that little commeth there which they devoure not. It is a marvel they can so directly passe these deserts some 3 or 4 daies journey without habitation. Their hunting houses are like unto Arbours covered with mats. These their women beare after them, with Corne, Acornes, Morters, and all bag and baggage they use. When they come to the place of exercise, every man doth his best to shew his dexteritie, for by their excelling in those quallities, they get their wives. Forty yards will they shoot levell, or very neare the mark, and 120 is their best at Random. At their huntings in the deserts they are commonly 2 or 300 together. Having found the Deare, they environ them with many fires, and betwixt the fires they place themselves. And some take their stands in the midst. The Deare being thus feared by the fires and their voices, they chace them so long within that circle, that many times they kill 6, 8, 10, or 15 at a hunting. They use also to drive them into some narrowe point of land, when they find that advantage, and so force them into the river, where with their boats they have Ambuscadoes to kill them. When they have shot a Deare by land, they follow him like blood hounds by the blood and straine, and oftentimes so take them. Hares, Pattridges, Turkies, or Egges, fat or leane, young or old, they devoure all they can catch in their power. In one of these huntings, they found Captaine Smith in the discoverie of the head of the river of Chickahamania, where they slew his men, and tooke him prisoner in a Bogmire; where he saw those exercises, and gathered these observations.

One Savage hunting alone, useth the skinne of a Deare slit on the one side, and so put on his arme, through the neck, so that his hand comes to the head which is stuffed, and the hornes, head, eies, eares, and every part as arteficially counterfeited as they can devise. Thus shrowding his body in the skinne, by stalking he approacheth the Deare, creeping on the ground from one tree to another. If the Deare chance to find fault, or stande at gaze, hee turneth the head with his hand to his best advantage to seeme like a Deare, also gazing and licking himselfe. So watching his best advantage to approach, having shot him, hee chaseth him by his blood and straine till he get him.

When they intend any warres, the Werowances usually have the advice of their Priests and Conjurors, and their Allies and ancient friends, but chiefely the Priestes determine their resolution. Every Werowance, or some lustie fellow, they appoint Captaine over every nation. They seldome make warre for lands or goods, but for women and children, and principally for revenge. They have many enimies, namely all their westernely Countries beyond the mountaines, and the heads of the rivers. Upon the head of the Powhatans are the Monacans, whose chiefe habitation is at Russawmeake, unto whome the Mouhemenchughes, the Massinnacacks, the Monahassanuggs, and other nations, pay tributs. Upon the head of the river of Toppahanock is a people called Mannahoacks. To these are contributers the Tauxsnitanias, the Shackaconias, the Outponcas, the Tegoneaes, the Whonkentyaes, the Stegarakes, the Hassinnungas, and diverse others, all confederats with the Monacans, though many different in language, and be very barbarous, living for most part of wild beasts and fruits. Beyond the mountaines from whence is the head of the river Patawomeke, the Savages report, inhabit their most mortall enimies, the Massawomekes upon a great salt water, which by all likelyhood is either some part of Commada [Canada], some great lake, or some inlet of some sea that falleth into the South sea. These Massawomekes are a great nation and very populous. For the heads of all those rivers, especially the Pattawomekes, the Pautuxuntes, the Sasquesahanocks, the Tockwoughes, are continually tormented by them: of whose crueltie, they generally complained, and very importunate they were with Captaine Smith and his company, to free them from these tormentors. To this purpose, they offered food, conduct, assistance, and continuall subjection. To which he concluded to effect. But the counsell then present, emulating his successe, would not thinke it fit to spare him 40 men to be hazarded in those unknowne regions, having passed (as before was spoken of) but with 12, and so was lost that opportunitie. Seaven boats full of these Massawomeks the discoverers encountred at the head of the Bay; whose Targets, Baskets, Swords, Tobaccopipes, Platters, Bowes and Arrowes, and every thing shewed, they much exceeded them of our parts: and their dexteritie in their small boats made of the barkes of trees sowed with barke, and well luted with gumme, argueth that they are seated upon some great water.

Against all these enimies the Powhatans are constrained sometimes to fight. Their chiefe attempts are by Stratagems, trecheries, or surprisals. Yet the Werowances, women and children, they put not to death, but keepe them Captives. They have a method in warre, and for our pleasures, they shewd it us, and it was in this manner performed at Mattapanient.

Having painted and disguised themselves in the fiercest manner they could devise, they divided themselves into two Companies, neare a 100 in a company. The one company called Monacans, the other Powhatans. Either army had their Captaine. These as enimies tooke their stands a musket shot one from another; ranked themselves 15 abreast, and each ranke from another 4 or 5 yards, not in fyle, but in the opening betwixt their fyles, so as the Reare could shoot as conveniently as the Front. Having thus pitched the fields; from either part went a Messenger with these conditions, that whosoever were vanquished, such as escape, upon their submission in 2 daies after, should live, but their wives and children should be prize for the Conquerers. The messengers were no sooner returned, but they approached in their orders. On each flanke a Sarjeant, and in the Reare an office for leuitenant, all duly keeping their orders, yet leaping and singing after their accustomed tune, which they use only in warres. Upon the first flight of arrowes, they gave such horrible shouts and screeches, as though so many infernall helhounds could not have made them more terrible. When they had spent their arrowes, they joined together prettily, charging and retiring, every ranke seconding other. As they got advantage, they catched their enimies by the haire of the head, and downe he came that was taken. His enimie with his wooden sword seemed to beat out his braines, and still they crept to the Reare, to maintaine the skirmish. The Monacans decreasing, the Powhatans charged them in the forme of a halfe moone: they unwilling to be inclosed, fled all in a troope to their Ambuscadoes, on whome they led them very cunningly. The Monacans disperse themselves among the fresh men, whereupon the Powhatans retired with al speed to their seconds; which the Monacans seeing, took that advantage to retire againe to their owne battell, and so each returned to their owne quarter. All their actions, voices and gestures, both in charging and retiring, were so strained to the hight of their quallitie and nature, that the strangenes thereof made it seem very delightfull.

For their musicke they use a thicke cane, on which they pipe as on a Recorder. For their warres, they have a great deepe platter of wood. They cover the mouth thereof with a skin, at each corner they tie a walnut, which meeting on the backside neere the bottome, with a small rope they twitch them togither till it be so tought and stiffe, that they may beat upon it as upon a drumme. But their chiefe instruments are Rattels made of small gourds or Pumpion shels. Of these they have Base, Tenor, Counter-tenor, Meane and Trible. These mingled with their voices sometimes 20 or 30 togither, make such a terrible noise as would rather affright then delight any man. If any great commander arrive at the habitation of a Werowance, they spread a mat as the Turkes do a carpet, for him to sit upon. Upon an other right opposite they sit themselves. Then doe all with a tunable voice of showting bid him welcome. After this, doe 2. or more of their chiefest men make an oration, testifying their love. Which they do with such vehemency and so great passions, that they sweate till they drop, and are so out of breath they can scarce speake. So that a man would take them to be exceeding angry or starke mad. Such victuall as they have, they spend freely, and at night where his lodging is appointed, they set a woman fresh painted red with *Pocones* and oile, to be his bedfellow.

Their manner of trading is for copper, beades, and such like; for which they give such commodities as they have, as skins, fowle, fish, flesh, and their country corne. But their victuall is their chiefest riches.

Every spring they make themselves sicke with drinking the juice of a root they call *wighsacan*, and water, whereof they powre so great a quantity, that it purgeth them in a very violent maner; so that in 3 qr 4 daies after, they scarce recover their former health. Sometimes they are troubled with dropsies, swellings, aches, and such like diseases; for cure wherof they build a stove in the form of a dovehouse with mats, so close that a fewe coales therein covered with a pot, will make the pacient sweate extreamely. For swellings also they use smal peeces of touchwood, in the forme of cloves, which pricking on the griefe, they burne close to the flesh, and from thence draw the corruption with their mouth. With this root *wighsacan* they ordinarily heal greene wounds: but to scarrifie a swelling or make incision, their best instruments are some splinted stone. Old ulcers or putrified hurtes are seldome seene cured amongst them. They have many professed Phisitions, who with their charmes and Rattels, with an infernall rowt of words and actions, will seeme to sucke their inwarde griefe from their navels or their grieved places; but of our Chirurgians they were so conceipted, that they beleeved any Plaister would heale any hurt.

Of their Religion.

There is yet in Virginia no place discovered to bee so Savage in which the Savages have not a religion, Deare, and Bow and Arrowes. All thinges that were able to do them hurt beyond their prevention, they adore with their kinde of divine worship; as the fire, water, lightning, thunder, our ordinance, peeces, horses, &c. But their chiefe God they worship is the Divell. Him they call *Oke* and serve him more of feare than love. They say they have conference with him, and fashion themselves as neare to his shape as they can imagine. In their temples, they have his image evill favouredly carved, and then painted and adorned with chaines, copper, and beades, and covered with a skin, in such manner as the deformity may well suit with such a God. By him is commonly the sepulcher of their kings. Their bodies are first bowelled, then dryed upon hurdles till they bee verie dry, and so about the most of their jointes and necke they hang bracelets or chaines of copper, pearle, and such like, as they use to weare: their inwards they stuffe with copper beads and cover with a skin, hatchets, and such trash. Then lappe they them very carefully in white skins, and so rowle them in mats for their winding sheetes. And in the Tombe, which is an arch made of mats, they lay them orderly. What remaineth of this kinde of wealth their kings have, they set at their feet in baskets. These Temples and bodies are kept by their Priests.

For their ordinary burials, they digge a deep hole in the earth with sharpe stakes, and the corp[s]es being lapped in skins and mats with their jewels, they lay them upon sticks in the ground, and so cover them with earth. The buriall ended, the women being painted all their faces with black cole and oile, doe sit 24 howers in the houses mourning and lamenting by turnes, with such yelling and howling as may expresse their great passions.

In every Territory of a Werowance is a Temple and a Priest 2 or 3 or more. Their principall Temple or place of superstition is at Uttamussack at Pamaunke, neare unto which is a house Temple or place of Powhatans.

Upon the top of certaine redde sandy hils in the woods, there are 3 great houses filled with images of their kings and Divels and Tombes of their Predecessors. Those houses are neare 60 foot in length, built arbor wise, after their building. This place they count so holy as that [none] but the Priestes and kings dare come into them: nor the Savages dare not go up the river in boats by it, but that they solemnly cast some peece of copper, white beads, or Pocones, into the river, for feare their *Oke* should be offended and revenged of them.

In this place commonly is resident 7 Priests. The chiefe differed from the rest in his ornaments: but inferior Priests could hardly be knowne from the common people, but that they had not so many holes in their eares to hang their jewels at. The ornaments of the chiefe Priest was certain attires for his head made thus. They tooke a dosen or 16 or more snake skins, and stuffed them with mosse; and of weesels and other vermine skins, a good many. All these they tie by their tailes, so as all their tailes meete in the toppe of their head, like a great Tassell. Round about this Tassell is as it were a crown of feathers; the skins hang round about his head necke and shoulders, and in a manner cover his face. The faces of all their Priests are painted as ugly as they can devise. In their hands, they had every one his Rattell, some base, some smaller. Their devotion was most in songs which the chiefe Priest beginneth and the rest followed him: sometimes he maketh invocations with broken sentences, by starts and strange passions, and at every pause, the rest give a short groane.

It could not bee perceived that they keepe any day as more holy then other: but only in some great distresse, of want, feare of enimies, times of triumph and gathering together their fruits, the whole country of men women and children come togither to solemnities. The manner of their devotion is sometimes to make a great fire in the house or fields, and all to sing and dance about it, with rattles and shouts togither, 4 or 5 houres. Sometimes they set a man in the midst, and about him they dance and sing, he all the whole clapping his hands as if he would keepe time. And after their songs and dauncings ended, they goe to their Feasts.

They have also divers conjurations. One they made when Captaine Smith was their prisoner (as they reported) to know if any more of his countrymen would arrive there, and what he there intended. The manner of it was thus. First they made a faire fire in a house. About this fire set 7 Priests setting him by them, and about the fire, they made a circle of meale. That done, the chiefe Priest attired as is expressed, began to shake his rattle, and the rest followed him in his song. At the end of the song, he laid downe 5 or 3 graines of wheat, and so continued counting his songs by the graines, till 3 times they incirculed the fire. Then they divide the graines by certaine numbers with little stickes, laying downe at the ende of every song a little sticke. In this manner, they sat 8, 10 or 12 houres without cease, with such strange stretching of their armes, and violent passions and gestures as might well seeme strange to him they so conjured, who but every houre expected his end. Not any meat they did eat till, late in the evening, they had finished this worke: and then they feasted him and themselves with much mirth. But 3 or 4 daies they continued this ceremony.

They have also certaine Altar stones they call *Pawcorances*: but these stand from their Temples, some by their houses, other in the woodes and wildernesses. Upon these, they offer blood, deare suet, and Tobacco. These they doe when they returne from the warres, from hunting, and upon many other occasions. They have also another superstition that they use in stormes, when the waters are rough in the rivers and sea coasts. Their Conjurers runne to the water sides, or passing in their boats, after many hellish outcries and invocations, they cast Tobacco, Copper, *Pocones*, and such trash into the water, to pacifie that God whome they thinke to be very angry in those stormes. Before their dinners and suppers, the better sort will take the first bit, and cast it in the fire, which is all the grace they are known to use.

In some part of the Country, they have yearely a sacrifice of children. Such a one was at Quiyoughcohanock, some 10 miles from

James Towne, and thus performed. Fifteene of the properest young boyes, betweene 10 and 15 yeares of age, they painted white. Having brought them forth, the people spent the forenoone in dancing and singing about them with rattles. In the afternoone, they put those children to the roote of a tree. By them, all the men stood in a guard, every one having a Bastinado in his hand, made of reeds bound together. This made a lane betweene them all along, through which there were appointed 5 young men to fetch these children. So every one of the five went through the guard, to fetch a child, each after other by turnes: the guard fearelessly beating them with their Bastinadoes, and they patiently enduring and receaving all, defending the children with their naked bodies from the unmercifull blowes they pay them soundly, though the children escape. All this while, the women weepe and crie out very passionately, providing mats, skinnes, mosse, and drie wood, as things fitting their childrens funerals. After the children were thus passed the guard, the guard tore down the tree, branches and boughs, with such violence, that they rent the body, and made wreathes for their heads, or bedecked their haire with the leaves. What else was done with the children was not seene; but they were all cast on a heape in a valley, as dead: where they made a great feast for al the company. The Werowance being demanded the meaning of this sacrifice, answered that the children were not al dead, but that the *Oke* or Divell did sucke the blood from their left breast, who chanced to be his by lot, till they were dead. But the rest were kept in the wildernesse by the yong men till nine moneths were expired, during which time they must not converse with any: and of these, were made their Priests and Conjurers. This sacrifice they held to bee so necessarie, that if they should omit it, their *Oke* or Divel and all their other *Quiyoughcosughes* (which are their other Gods) would let them have no Deare, Turkies, Corne nor fish: and yet besides, hee would make great slaughter amongst them.

They thinke that their Werowances and Priestes, which they also esteeme *Quiyoughcosughes*, when they are dead, doe goe beyond the mountaines towardes the setting of the sun, and ever remaine there in forme of their Oke, with their heads painted with oile and *Pocones*, finely trimmed with feathers, and shal have beades, hatchets, copper, and tobacco, doing nothing but dance and sing with all their Predecessors. But the common people, they suppose shall not live after death.

To divert them from this blind idolatrie, many used their best indeavours, chiefly with the Werowances of Quiyoughcohanock, whose devotion, apprehension, and good disposition much exceeded any in those Countries: who though we could not as yet prevaile with-all to forsake his false Gods, yet this he did beleeve, that our God as much exceeded theirs, as our Gunnes did their Bowes and Arrows, and many times did send to the President, at James Towne, men with presents, intreating them to pray to his God for raine, for his Gods would not send him any. And in this lamentable ignorance doe these poore soules sacrifice themselves to the Divell, not knowing their Creator.

Of the manner of the Virginians governement.

Although the countrie people be very barbarous; yet have they amongst them such governement, as that their Magistrats for good commanding, and their people for du subjection and obeying, excell many places that would be counted very civill.

The forme of their Common wealth is a monarchicall governement. One as Emperour ruleth over many kings or governours. Their chiefe ruler is called Powhatan, and taketh his name of the principall place of dwelling called Powhatan. But his proper name is Wahunsonacock. Some countries he hath, which have been his ancestors, and came unto him by inheritance, as the countrie called Powhatan, Arrohateck, Appamatuke, Pamaunke, Youghtanud, and Mattapanient. All the rest of his Territories expressed in the Map, they report have beene his severall conquests. In all his ancient inheritances, hee hath houses built after their manner like arbours, some 30, some 40 yardes long, and at every house, provision for his entertainment, according to the time. At Werowcomoco, he was seated upon the North side of the river Pamaunke, some 14 miles from James Towne, where for the most part, hee was resident, but he tooke so little pleasure in our neare neighbourhood, that were able to visit him against his will in 6 or 7 houres, that he retired himself [in Jan. 1609] to a place in the deserts at the top of the river Chickahamania betweene Youghtanund and Powhatan. His habitation there is called Orapacks, where he ordinarily now resideth. He is of parsonage a tall well pro-portioned man, with a sower looke, his head somwhat gray, his beard so thinne that it seemeth none at al. His age neare 60; of a very able and hardy body to endure any labour. About his person ordinarily attendeth a guard of 40 or 50 of the tallest men his Country doth afford. Every night upon the 4 quarters of his house are 4 Sentinels, each standing from other a flight shoot: and at every halfe houre, one from the Corps du guard doth hollowe, unto whom every Sentinell doth answer round from his stand. If any faile, they presently send forth an officer that beateth him extreamely.

A mile from Orapakes in a thicket of wood, hee hath a house, in which he keepeth his kind of Treasure, as skinnes, copper, pearle, and beades, which he storeth up against the time of his death and buriall. Here also is his store of red paint for ointment, and bowes and arrowes. This house is 50 or 60 yards in length, frequented only by Priestes. At the 4 corners of this house stand 4 Images as Sentinels, one of a Dragon, another a Beare, the 3 like a Leopard, and the fourth like a giantlike man: all made evill favordly, according to their best workmanship.

He hath as many women as he will: whereof when hee lieth on his bed one sitteth at his head, and another at his feet, but when he sitteth, one sitteth on his right hand, and another on his left. As he is wearie of his women, hee bestoweth them on those that best deserve them at his hands. When he dineth or suppeth, one of his women, before and after meat, bringeth him water in a wo[o]den platter to wash his hands. Another waiteth with a bunch of feathers to wipe them insteed of a Towell, and the feathers when he hath wiped are dryed againe. His kingdome descendeth not to his sonnes nor children: but first to his brethren, whereof he hath 3. namely Opitchapan, Opechancanough, and Catataugh, and after their decease to his sisters. First to the eldest sister, then to the rest: and after them to the heires male and female of the eldest sister, but never to the heires of the males.

He nor any of his people understand any letters wherby to write or read, only the lawes whereby he ruleth is custome. Yet when he listeth, his will is a law and must bee obeyed: not only as a king, but as halfe a God they esteeme him. His inferiour kings whom they cal Werowances are tyed to rule by customes, and have power of life and death as their command in that nature. But this word Werowance which we call and conster [translate] for a king, is a common worde whereby they call all commanders: for they have but fewe words in their language and but few occasions to use anie officers more then one commander, which commonly they call Werowances. They all knowe their severall landes, and habitations, and limits to fish, fowle, or hunt in, but they hold all of their great Werowances Powhatan, unto whome they pay tribute of skinnes, beades, copper, pearle, deare, turkies, wild beasts, and corne. What he commandeth they dare not disobey in the least thing. It is strange to see with what great feare and adoration all these people doe obay this Powhatan. For at his feet, they present whatsoever he commandeth, and at the least frowne of his browe, their greatest spirits will tremble with feare: and no marvell, for he is very terrible and tyrannous in punishing such as offend him. For example, hee caused certaine malefactors to be bound hand and foot, then having of many fires gathered great store of burning coles, they rake these coles round in the forme of a cockpit, and in the midst they cast the offenders to broyle to death. Sometimes he causeth the heads of them that offend him, to be laid upon the altar or sacrificing stone, and one with clubbes beates out their braines. When he would punish any notorious enimie or malefactor, he causeth him to be tied to a tree, and, with muscle shels or reeds, the executioner cutteth of[f] his joints one after another, ever casting what they cut of[f] into the fire; then doth he proceed with shels and reeds to case the skinne from his head and face; then doe they rip his belly, and so burne him with the tree and all. Thus themselves reported they executed George Cassen. Their ordinary correction is to beate them with cudgels. Wee have seene a man kneeling on his knees, and at Powhatans command, two men have beat him on the bare skin, till he hath fallen senselesse in a s[w]ound, and yet never cry nor complained.

In the yeare 1608, hee surprised the people of Payankatank, his neare neighbours and subjects. The occasion was to us unknowne, but the manner was thus. First he sent diverse of his men as to lodge amongst them that night, then the Ambuscadoes invironed al their houses, and at the houre appointed, they all fell to the spoile; 24 men they slewe, the long haire of the one side of their heades with the skinne cased off with shels or reeds, they brought away. They surprised also the women and the children and the Werowance. All these they present to Powhatan. The Werowance, women and children became his prisoners, and doe him service. The lockes of haire with their skinnes he hanged on a line unto two trees. And thus he made ostentation as of a great triumph at Werowocomoco, shewing them to the English men that then came unto him, at his appointment: they expecting provision; he, to betray them, supposed to halfe conquer them, by this spectacle of his terrible crueltie.

Among the earliest visitors to North America were Christian minis-ters and priests seeking to convert the Indians from "superstitious" observances and beliefs to their own "civilized" brand of religion. One of these zealous apostles was the Dutch Protestant minister, Jonas Jansen Michielse, or, as he Latinized it, Jonas Johannis Michaelius. Born in North Holland in 1577, he entered the University of Leyden as a student of divinity in 1600 and became a minister twelve years later. In 1624 he went to San Salvador and after brief service there to one of the Dutch West India Company's posts in West Africa. By April 1628 he was in Manhattan where he probably spent the next three years vainly trying to change the Indians' religious beliefs. The following excerpt from a letter written four months after his arrival to a colleague in Amsterdam is taken from Ecclesiastical Records, State of New York *(Albany, 1901-1905), vol. 1, pp. 49-68.*

As to the natives of this country, I find them entirely savage and wild, strangers to all decency, yea, uncivil and stupid as garden poles, proficient in all wickedness and godlessness; devilish men, who serve nobody but the Devil, that is, the spirit which in their language they call Menetto; under which title they comprehend everything that is subtle and crafty and beyond human skill and power. They have so much witchcraft, divination, sorcery and wicked arts, that they can hardly be held in by any bands or locks. They are as thievish and treacherous as they are tall; and in cruelty they are altogether inhuman, more than barbarous, far exceeding the Africans.

I have written concerning this matter to several persons elsewhere, not doubting that Brother Crol will have written sufficient to your Reverence, or to the Honorable Directors; as also of the base treachery and the murders which the Mohicans, at the upper part of this river had planned against Fort Orange, but which failed through the gra-cious interposition of the Lord, for our good—who, when it pleases Him, knows how to pour, unexpectedly, natural impulses into these unnatural men, in order to prevent them. How these people can best be led to the true knowledge of God and of the Mediator Christ, is hard to say. I cannot myself wonder enough who it is that has imposed so much upon your Reverence and many others in the Fatherland, concerning the docility of these people and their good nature, the proper *principia religionis* [principles of religion] and *vestigia legis naturae* [vestiges of natural law] which are said to be among them; in whom I have as yet been able to discover hardly a single good point, except that they do not speak so jeeringly and so scoffingly of the godlike and glorious majesty of their Creator as the Africans dare to do. But it may be because they have no certain knowledge of Him, or scarcely any. If we speak to them of God, it appears to them like a dream; and we are compelled to speak of him, not under the name of Menetto, whom they know and serve—for that would be blasphemy—but of one great, yea, most high, *Sackiema*, by which name they—living without a king—call him who has the command over several hundred among them, and who by our people are called *Sackemakers*; and as the people listen, some will begin to mutter and shake their heads as if it were a silly fable; and others, in order to express regard and friendship for such a proposition, will say *Orith* (That is good). Now, by what means are we to lead this people to salvation, or to make a salutary breach among them? I take the liberty on this point of enlarging somewhat to your Reverence.

Their language, which is the first thing to be employed with them, methinks is entirely peculiar. Many of our common people call it an easy language, which is soon learned, but I am of a contrary opinion. For those who can understand their words to some extent and repeat them, fail greatly in the pronunciation, and speak a broken language, like the language of Ashdod. [Nehemiah xiii.24] For these people have difficult aspirates and many guttural letters, which are formed more in the throat than by the mouth, teeth and lips, to which our people not being accustomed, make a bold stroke at the thing and imagine that they have accomplished something wonderful. It is true one can easily learn as much as is sufficient for the purposes of trading, but this is done almost as much by signs with the thumb and fingers as by speaking; and this cannot be done in religious matters. It also seems to us that they rather design to conceal their language from us than to properly communicate it, except in things which happen in daily trade; saying that it is sufficient for us to understand them in that; and then they speak only half sentences, shortened words, and frequently call out a dozen things and even more; and all things which have only a rude resemblance to each other, they frequently call by the same name. In truth it is a made-up, childish language; so that even those who can best of all speak with the savages, and get along well in trade, are nevertheless wholly in the dark and bewildered when they hear the savages talking among themselves.

It would be well then to leave the parents as they are, and begin with the children who are still young. So be it. But they ought in youth to be separated from their parents; yea, from their whole nation. For, without this, they would forthwith be as much accustomed as their parents to the heathenish tricks and deviltries, which are kneaded naturally in their hearts by themselves through a just judgment of God; so that having once, by habit, obtained deep root, they would with great difficulty be emancipated therefrom. But this separation is hard to effect. For the parents have a strong affection for their children, and are very loth to part with them; and when they are separated from them, as we have already had proof, the parents are never contented, but take them away stealthily, or induce them to run away. Nevertheless, although it would be attended with some expense, we ought, by means of presents and promises, to obtain the children, with the gratitude and consent of the parents, in order to place them under the instruction of some experienced and godly schoolmaster, where they may be instructed not only to speak, read, and write in our language, but also especially in the fundamentals of our Christian religion; and where, besides, they will see nothing but good examples of virtuous living; but they must sometimes speak their native tongue among themselves in order not to forget it, as being evidently a principal means of spreading the knowledge of religion through the whole nation. In the meantime we should not forget to beseech the Lord, with ardent and continual prayers, for His blessing; who can make things which are unseen suddenly and opportunely to appear; who gives life to the dead; calls that which is not as though it were; and being rich in mercy has pity on whom He will; as He has compassionated us to be His people; and has washed us clean, sanctified us and justified us, when we were covered with all manner of corruption, calling us to the blessed knowledge of His Son, and out of the power of darkness to His marvellous light. And this I regard so much the more necessary, as the wrath and curse of God, resting upon this miserable people, is found to be the heavier. Perchance God may at last have mercy upon them, that the fulness of the heathen may be gradually brought in and the salvation of our God may be here also seen among these wild savage men. I hope to keep a watchful eye over these people, and to learn as much as possible of their language, and to seek better opportunities for their instruction than hitherto it has been possible to find.

Of all the tribes encountered by the first European settlers, the Iroquois nations (Mohawk, Oneida, Onondaga, Cayuga, and Seneca) of what is now New York State commanded the most respect. So great was their reputation for ferocity and courage that no Dutchman visited their homeland until the winter of 1634-35, when a well-educated member of the Dutch West India Company—perhaps Harmen Meyndertsz van den Bogaert, the surgeon of Fort Orange (Albany)—ventured to Onondaga, their capitol, to cement trade relations. The complete journal of his visit is given below from the translation by Gen. James Grant Wilson published in the Annual Report of the American Historical Association *for 1895, pp. 81-104.*

Praise the Lord above all—Fort Orange, 1634.

December 11. JOURNAL kept of the principal events that happened during the journey to the Maquas and Sinnekens [Mohawks and Senecas (actually Oneidas)] Indians. First, the reasons why we went on this journey were these, that the Maquas and Sinnekens very often came to our factor Marten Gerritsen and me stating that there were French Indians in their land, and that they had made a truce with them so that they, namely, the Maquas, wished to trade for their skins, because the Maquas Indians wanted to receive just as much for their skins as the French Indians did. So I proposed to Mr. Marten Gerritsen to go and see if it was true, so soon to run counter to their High Mightinesses; and, besides, trade was doing very badly, therefore I went as above with Jero[ni]mus [de] la Croex and Willem Tomassen. May the Lord bless my voyage! We went between nine and ten o'clock with five Maquas Indians, mostly northwest above eight leagues, and arrived at half-past twelve in the evening at a hunter's cabin, where we slept for the night, near the stream that runs into their land and is named Oyoge. The Indians here gave us venison to eat. The land is mostly full of fir trees, and the flat land is abundant. The stream runs through their land near their (Maquas) castle, but we could not ascend it on account of the heavy freshet.

December 12. At three hours before daylight, we proceeded again, and the savages that went with us would have left us there if I had not noticed it; and when we thought of taking our meal we perceived that their dogs had eaten our meat and cheese. So we had then only dry bread and had to travel on that; and, after going for an hour, we came to the branch [the Mohawk River] that runs into our river [the Hudson River] and past the Maquas villages, where the ice drifted very fast. Jeronimus crossed first, with one savage in a canoe made of the bark of trees, because there was only room for two; after that Willem and I went over; and it was so dark that we could not see each other if we did not come close together. It was not without danger. When all of us had crossed, we went another league and a half and came to a hunter's cabin, which we entered to eat some venison, and hastened farther, and after another half league we saw some Indians approaching; and as soon as they saw us they ran off and threw their sacks and bags away, and fled down a valley behind the underwood, so that we could not see them. We looked at their goods and bags, and took therefrom a small [loaf of] bread. It was baked with beans, and we ate it. We went farther, and mostly along the aforesaid kill that ran very swiftly because of the freshet. In this kill there are a good many islands, and on the sides upward of 500 or 600 morgen [1000 or 1200 acres] of flat land; yes, I think even more. And after we had been marching about eleven leagues, we arrived at one o'clock in the evening half a league from the first castle at a little house. We found only Indian women inside. We should have gone farther, but I could hardly move my feet because of the rough road, so we slept there. It was very cold, with northerly wind.

December 13. In the morning we went together to the castle over the ice that during the night had frozen on the kill, and, after going half a league, we arrived in their first castle, which is built on a high hill. There stood but 36 houses, in rows like streets, so that we could pass nicely. The houses are made and covered with bark of trees, and mostly are flat at the top. Some are 100, 90, or 80 paces long and 22 and 23 feet high. There were some inside doors of hewn boards, furnished with iron hinges. In some houses we saw different kinds of iron work, iron chains, harrow irons, iron hoops, nails —which they steal when they go forth from here. Most of the people were out hunting deer and bear. The houses were full of corn that they call *onersti*, and we saw maize; yes, in some of the houses more than 300 bushels. They make canoes and barrels of the bark of trees, and sew with bark as well. We had a good many pumpkins cooked and baked that they called *anansira*. None of the chiefs were at home, but the principal chief is named Adriochten, who lived a quarter of a mile from the fort in a small house, because a good many savages here in the castle died of smallpox. I sent him a message to come and see us, which he did; he came and bade me welcome, and said that he wanted us very much to come with him. We should have done so, but when already on the way another chief called us, and so we went to the castle again. This one had a big fire lighted, and a fat haunch of venison cooked, of which we ate. He gave us two bearskins to sleep upon, and presented me with three beaver skins. In the evening Willem Tomassen, whose legs were swollen from the march, had a few cuts made with a knife therein, and after that had them rubbed with bear grease. We slept in this house, ate heartily of pumpkins, beans and venison, so that we were not hungry, but were treated as well as is possible in their land. We hole that all will succeed.

December 14. Jeronimus wrote a letter to our *commis* (factor), Marten Gerritsen, and asked for paper, salt, and *atsochwat*—that means tobacco for the savages. We went out to shoot turkeys with the chief, but could not get any. In the evening I bought a very fat one for two hands of seewan [wampum]. The chief cooked it for us, and the grease he mixed with our beans and maize. This chief showed me his idol; it was a male cat's head, with the teeth sticking out; it was dressed in duffel cloth. Others have a snake, a turtle, a swan, a crane, a pigeon, or the like for their idols, to tell the fortune; they think they will always have good luck in doing so. From here two savages went with their skins to Fort Orange.

December 15. I went again with the chief to hunt turkeys, but could not get any; and in the evening the chief again showed us his idol, and we resolved to stay here for another two or three days till there should be an opportunity to proceed, because all the footpaths had disappeared under the heavy snowfalls.

December 16. After midday a famous hunter came here named Sickarus, who wanted very much that we should go with him to his castle. He offered to carry our goods and to let us sleep and remain in his house as long as we liked; and because he was offering us so much I gave him a knife and two awls as a present, and to the chief in whose house we had been I presented a knife and a pair of scissors; and then we took our departure from this castle, named Onekagoncka, and after going for half a league over the ice we saw a village with only six houses, of the name Canowarode; but we did not enter it, because he said it was not worth while, and after another half league we passed again a village where twelve houses stood. It was named Schatsyerosy. These were like the others, he saying they likewise were not worth while entering; and after passing by great stretches of flat land, for another league or league and a half, we came into this castle, at two good hours after dark. I did not see much besides a good many graves. This castle is named Canagere. It is built on a hill, without any palisades or any defense. We found only seven men at home, besides a party of old women and children. The chiefs of this castle, named Tonnosatton and Tonewerot, were hunting; so we slept in the house of Sickarus, as he had promised us; and we counted in his house 120 pieces of salable beaver skins that he captured with his own dogs. Every day we ate beaver meat here. In this castle are sixteen houses, 50, 60, 70, or 80 paces long, and one of sixteen paces, and one of five paces, containing a bear to be fattened. It had been in there upward of three years, and was so tame that it took everything that was given to it to eat.

December 17. Sunday we looked over our goods, and found a paper filled with sulphur, and Jeronimus took some of it and threw it in the fire. They saw the blue flame and smelled the smoke, and told us they had the same stuff; and when Sickarus came they asked us to let them take a look at it, and it was the same; and we asked him where he obtained it. He told us they obtained it from the stranger savages, and that they believed it to be good against many maladies, but principally for their legs when they were sore from long marching and were very tired.

December 18. Three women of the Sinnekens came here with dried and fresh salmon; the latter smelled very bad. They sold each salmon for one florin or two hands of seawan. They brought, also, a good quantity of green tobacco to sell; and had been six days on the march.

They could not sell all their salmon here, but went farther on to the first castle; and when they returned we were to go with them, and in the evening Jeronimus told me that a savage tried to kill him with a knife.

December 19. We received a letter from Marten Gerritsen dated December 18, and with it we received paper, salt, tobacco for the savages, and a bottle of brandy, and secured an Indian that was willing to be our guide to the Sinnekens. We gave him half a yard of cloth, two axes, two knives, and two awls. If it had been summer, many Indians would have gone with us, but as it was winter they would not leave their land, because it snowed very often up to the height of a man. To-day we had a great rainfall, and I gave the guide a pair of shoes. His name was Sqorhea.

December 20. We took our departure from the second castle, and, after marching a league, our savage, Sqorhea, came to a stream that we had to pass. This stream ran very fast; besides, big cakes of ice came drifting along, for the heavy rainfall during yesterday had set the ice drifting. We were in great danger, for if one of us had lost his footing it had cost us our lives; but God the Lord preserved us, and we came through safely. We were wet up to above the waist, and after going for another half league we came thus wet, with our clothes, shoes and stockings frozen to us, to a very high hill on which stood 32 houses, like the other ones. Some were 100, 90, or 80 paces long; in every house we saw four, five, or six fireplaces where cooking went on. A good many savages were at home, so we were much looked at by both the old and the young; indeed, we could hardly pass through. They pushed each other in the fire to see us, and it was more than midnight before they took their departure. We could not absent ourselves to go to stool; even then they crawled around us without any feeling of shame. This is the third castle and is named Schanidisse. The chief's name is Tewowary. They lent me this evening a lion [cougar] skin to cover myself; but in the morning I had more than a hundred lice. We ate much venison here. Near this castle there is plenty of flat land, and the wood is full of oaks and nut trees. We exchanged here one beaver skin for one awl.

December 21. We started very early in the morning, and thought of going to the fourth castle, but after a half league's marching we came to a village with only nine houses, of the name of Osquage; the chief's name was Oquoho—that is, wolf. And here we saw a big stream that our guide did not dare to cross, as the water was over one's head because of the heavy rainfall; so we were obliged to postpone it till the next day. The chief treated us very kindly; he did us much good and gave us plenty to eat, for everything to be found in his houses was at our service. He said often to me that I was his brother and good friend; yes, he told me even how he had been travelling overland for thirty days, and how he met there an Englishman, to learn the language of the Minquase [Conestogas] and to buy the skins. I asked him whether there were any French savages there with the Sinnekens. He said yes; and I felt gratified and had a good hope to reach my aim. They called me here to cure a man that was very sick.

December 22. When the sun rose, we waded together through the stream; the water was over the knee, and so cold that our shoes and stockings in a very short time were frozen as hard as armor. The savages dared not go through, but went two by two, with a stick and hand in hand; and after going half a league we came to a village named Cawaoge. There stood fourteen houses, and a bear to fatten. We went in and smoked a pipe of tobacco, because the old man who was our guide was very tired. Another old man approached us, who shouted, "Welcome, welcome! you must stop here for the night"; but we wanted to be on the march and went forward. I tried to buy the bear, but they would not let it go. Along these roads we saw many trees much like the savin, with a very thick bark. This village likewise stood on a very high hill, and after going for another league we came into the fourth castle by land whereon we saw only a few trees. The name is Tenotoge. There are 55 houses, some one hundred, others more or fewer paces long. The kill we spoke about before runs past here, and the course is mostly north by west and south by east. On the other bank of the kill there are also houses; but we did not go in, because they were most of them filled with corn and the houses in this castle are filled with corn and beans. The savages here looked much surprised to see us, and they crowded so much around us that we could hardly pass through, for nearly all of them were at home. After awhile one of the savages came to us and invited us to go with him to his house, and we entered. This castle had been surrounded by three rows of palisades, but now there were none save six or seven pieces so thick that it was quite a wonder that savages should be able to do that. They crowded each other in the fire to see us.

December 23. A man came calling and shouting through some of the houses, but we did not know what it meant, and after awhile Jeronimus de la Croix came and told us what this was—that the savages are preparing and arming. I asked them what all this was about, and they said to me: "Nothing, we shall play with one another," and there were four men with clubs and a party with axes and sticks. There were twenty people armed, nine on one side and eleven on the other; and they went off against each other, and they fought and threw each other. Some of them wore armor and helmets that they themselves make of thin reeds and strings braided upon each other so that no arrow or axe can pass through to wound them severely; and after they had been playing thus a good while the parties closed and dragged each other by the hair, just as they would have done to their enemies after defeating them and before cutting off their scalps. They wanted us to fire our pistols, but we went off and left them alone. This day we were invited to buy bear meat, and we also got half a bushel of beans and a quantity of dried strawberries, and we bought some bread, that we wanted to take on our march. Some of the loaves were baked with nuts and cherries and dry blueberries and the grains of the sunflower.

December 24. It was Sunday. I saw in one of the houses a sick man. He had invited two of their doctors that could cure him—they call them *simachkoes*; and as soon as they came they began to sing and to light a big fire. They closed the house most carefully everywhere, so that the breeze could not come in, and after that each of them wrapped a snake-skin around his head. They washed their hands and faces, lifted the sick man from his place, and laid him alongside the big fire. Then they took a bucket of water, put some medicine in it, and washed in this water a stick about half a yard long, and kept sticking it in their throats so that no end of it was to be seen; and then they spat on the patient's head, and over all his body; and after that they made all sorts of farces, as shouting and raving, slapping of the hands; so are their manners; with many demonstrations upon one thing and another till they perspired so freely that their perspiration ran down on all sides.

December 25—being Christmas. We rose early in the morning and wanted to go to the Sinnekens; but, as it was snowing steadily, we could not go, because nobody wanted to go with us to carry our goods.

I asked them how many chiefs there were in all, and they told me thirty.

December 26. In the morning I was offered two pieces of bear's bacon to take with us on the march; and we took our departure, escorted by many of them that walked before and after us. They kept up shouting: *"Allesa rondade!"* that is, to fire our pistols; but we did not want to do so, and at last they went back. This day we passed over many a stretch of flat land, and crossed a kill where the water was knee-deep; and I think we kept this day mostly the direction west and northwest. The woods that we traversed consisted in the beginning mostly of oaks, but after three or four hours' marching it was mostly birch trees. It snowed the whole day, so it was very heavy marching over the hills; and after seven leagues, by guess, we arrived at a little house made of bark in the forest, where we lighted a fire and stopped for the night to sleep. It went on snowing, with a sharp, northerly wind. It was very cold.

December 27. Early in the morning again on our difficult march, while the snow lay 2-1/2 feet in some places. We went over hills and through underwood. We saw traces of two bears, and elks, but no savages. There are beech trees; and after marching another seven or eight leagues, at sunset we found another little cabin in the forest, with hardly any bark, but covered with the branches of trees. We made a big fire and cooked our dinner. It was so very cold during this night that I did not sleep more than two hours in all.

December 28. We went as before, and after marching one or two leagues we arrived at a kill that, as the savages told me, ran into the land of the Minquaass, and after another mile we met another kill that runs into the South River, as the savages told me, and here a good many otter and beaver are caught. This day we went over many high hills. The wood was full of great trees, mostly birches; and after seven or eight leagues' marching we did the same as mentioned above. It was very cold.

December 29. We went again, proceeding on our voyage; and after marching a while we came on a very high hill, and as we nearly had mounted it I fell down so hard that I thought I had broken my ribs, but it was only the handle of my cutlass that was broken. We went through a good deal of flat land, with many oaks and handles for axes, and after another seven leagues we found another hut, where we rested ourselves. We made a fire and ate all the food we had, because the savages told us that we were still about four leagues distant from the castle. The sun was near setting as still another of the savages went on to the castle to tell them we were coming. We would have gone with him, but because we felt so very hungry the savages would not take us along with them. The course northwest.

December 30. Without anything to eat we went to the Sinnekens' castle, and after marching awhile the savages showed me the branch of the river that passes by Fort Orange and past the land of the Maquas. A woman came to meet us, bringing us baked pumpkins to eat. This road was mostly full of birches and beautiful flat land for sowing. Before we reached the castle we saw three graves, just like our graves in length and height; usually their graves are round. These graves were surrounded with palisades that they had split from trees, and they were closed up so nicely that it was a wonder to see. They were painted with red and white and black paint; but the chief's grave had an entrance, and at the top of that was a big wooden bird, and all around were painted dogs, and deer, and snakes, and other beasts. After four or five leagues' marching the savages still prayed us to fire our guns, and so we did, but loaded them again directly and went on to the castle. And we saw to the northwest of us, a large river, and on the other side thereof tremendously high land that seemed to lie in the clouds. Upon inquiring closely into this, the savages told me that in this river the Frenchmen came to trade. And then we marched confidently to the castle, where the savages divided into two rows, and so let us pass through them by the gate, which was—the one we went through—3-1/2 feet wide, and at the top were standing three big wooden images, carved like men, and with them I saw three scalps fluttering in the wind, that they had taken from their foes as a token of the truth of their victory. This castle has two gates, one on the east and one on the west side. On the east side a scalp was also hanging; but this gate was 1-1/2 feet smaller than the other one. When at last we arrived in the chief's house, I saw there a good many people that I knew; and we were requested to sit down in the chief's place where he was accustomed to sit, because at the time he was not at home, and we felt cold and were wet and tired. They at once gave us to eat, and they made a good fire. This castle likewise is situated on a very high hill, and was surrounded with two rows of palisades. It was 767 paces in circumference. There are 66 houses, but much better, higher, and more finished than all the others we saw. A good many houses had wooden fronts that are painted with all sorts of beasts. There they sleep mostly on elevated boards, more than any other savages. In the afternoon one of the council came to me, asking the reason of our coming into his land, and what we brought for him as a present. I told him that we did not bring any present, but that we only paid him a visit. He told us that we were not worth anything, because we did not bring him a present. Then he told us how the Frenchmen had come thither to trade with six men, and had given them good gifts, because they had been trading in this river with six men in the month of August of this year. We saw very good axes to cut the underwood, and French shirts and coats and razors; and this member of the council said we were scoundrels, and were not worth anything because we paid not enough for their beaver skins. They told us that the Frenchmen gave six hands of seawan for one beaver, and all sorts of things more. The savages were pressing closely upon us, so that there was hardly room for us to sit. If they had desired to molest us, we could hardly have been able to defend ourselves; but there was no danger. In this river here spoken of, often six, seven, or eight hundred salmon are caught in a single day. I saw houses where 60, 70 and more dried salmon were hanging.

December 31. On Sunday the chief of this castle came back (his name is Arenias), and one more man. They told us that they returned from the French savages, and some of the savages shouted "*Jawe Arenias!*" which meant that they thanked him for having come back. And I told him that in the night we should fire three shots; and he said it was all right; and they seemed very well contented. We questioned them concerning the situation [of the places] in their castle and their names, and how far they were away from each other. They showed us with stones and maize grains, and Jeronimus then made a chart of it. And we counted all in leagues how far each place was away from the next. The savages told us that on the high land which we had seen by that lake there lived men with horns on their heads; and they told us that a good many beavers were caught there, too, but they dared not go so far because of the French savages; therefore they thought best to make peace. We fired three shots in the night in honor of the year of our Lord and Redeemer, Jesus Christ.

Praise the Lord above all! In the castle Onneyuttehage, or Sinnekens, January 1, 1635.

January 1, 1635. Another savage scolded at us. We were scoundrels, as told before; and he looked angry. Willem Tomassen got so excited that the tears were running along his cheeks, and the savages, seeing that we were not at all contented, asked us what was the matter, and why we looked so disgusted at him. There were in all 46 persons seated near us; if they had intended to do mischief, they could easily have caught us with their hands and killed us without much trouble; when I had listened long enough to the Indian's chatter I told him that he was a scoundrel himself and he began to laugh, said he was not angry and said: "You must not grow so furious, for we are very glad that you came here." And after that Jeronimus gave the chief two knives, two pairs of scissors, and a few awls and needles that we had with us. And in the evening the savages suspended a band of seawan, and some other stringed seawan that the chief had brought with him from the French savages as a sign of peace and that the French savages were to come in confidence to them, and he sang: "*Ho schene jo ho ho schene I atsiehoewe atsihoewe,*" after which all the savages shouted three times: "*Netho, netho, netho!*" and after that another band of seawan was suspended and he sang then: "*Katon, katon, katon, katon!*" and all the savages shouted as hard as they could: "*Hy, hy, hy!*" After long deliberation they made peace for four years, and soon after everyone returned to his home.

January 2. The savages came to us and told us that we had better stop another four or five days. They would provide for all our needs and have us treated nicely; but I told them we could not wait so long as that. They replied that they had sent a message to the Onondagas—that is, the castle next to theirs—but I told them they nearly starved us. Then they said that in future they would look better after us, and twice during this day we were invited to be their guests, and treated to salmon and bear's bacon.

January 3. Some old men came to us and told us they wanted to be our friends, and they said we need not be afraid. And I replied we were not afraid, and in the afternoon the council sat here—in all, 24 men—and after consulting for a long while an old man approached me and laid his hand upon my heart to feel it beat; and then he shouted we really were not afraid at all. After that six more members of the council came, and after that they presented me a coat made of beaver skin, and told me they gave it to me because I came here and ought to be very tired, and he pointed to his and my legs; and besides, it is because you have been marching through the snow. And when I took the coat they shouted three times: *"Netho, netho, netho!"* which means, "This is very well." And directly after that they laid five pieces of beaver skins on my feet, at the same time requesting me that in the future they should receive four hands of seawan and four handbreadths of cloth for every big beaver skin, because we have to go so far with our skins; and very often when we come to your places we do not find any cloth or seawan or axes or kettles, or not enough for all of us, and then we have had much trouble for nothing, and have to go back over a great distance, carrying our goods back again. After we sat for a considerable time, an old man came to us, and translated it to us in the other language, and told us that we did not answer yet whether they were to have four hands of seawan or not for their skins. I told him that we had not the power to promise that, but that we should report about it to the chief at the Manhatans, who was our commander, and that I would give him a definite answer in the spring, and come myself to their land. Then they said to me *"Welsmachkoo,"* you must not lie, and surely come to us in the spring, and report to us about all. And if you will give us four hands of seawan we will not sell our skins to anyone but you; and after that they gave me the five beaver skins, and shouted as hard as they could: *"Netho, netho, netho!"* And then, that everything should be firmly binding, they called or sang: *"Ha assironi atsimach koo kent oya kayuig wee Onneyatte Onaondaga Koyocke hoo hanoto wany agweganne hoo schene ha caton scahten franosoni yndicho."* That means that I could go in all these places—they said the names of all the castles—freely and everywhere. I should be provided with a house and a fire and wood and everything I needed; and if I wanted to go to the Frenchmen they would guide me there and back; and after that they shouted again: *"Netho, netho, netho!"* and they made a present of another beaver skin to me, and we ate to-day bear meat that we were invited to. In this house, belonging to the chief, there were three or four meals a day, and they did not cook in it, as everything was brought in from the other houses in large kettles; for it was the council that took their meals here every day. And whoever then happens to be in the house receives a bowlful of food; for it is the rule here that everyone that comes here has his bowl filled; and if they are short of bowls they bring them and their spoons with them. They go thus and seat themselves side by side; the bowls are then fetched and brought back filled, for a guest that is invited does not rise before he has eaten. Sometimes they sing, and sometimes they do not, thanking the host before they return home.

January 4. Two savages came, inviting us to come and see how they used to drive away the devil. I told them that I had seen it before; but they did not move off, and I had to go; and because I did not choose to go alone I took Jeronimus along. I saw a dozen men together who were going to drive him off. After we arrived the floor of the house was thickly covered with the bark of trees for the hunters of the devil to walk upon. They were mostly old men, and they had their faces all painted with red paint—which they always do when they are going to do anything unusual. Three men among them had a wreath on their heads, on which stuck five white crosses. These wreaths are made of deer hair that they had braided with the roots of a sort of green herb. In the middle of the house they then put a man who was very sick, and who was treated without success during a considerable time. Close by sat an old woman with a turtle shell in her hands. In the turtle shell were a good many beads. She kept clinking all the while, and all of them sang to the measure; then they would proceed to catch the devil and trample him to death; they trampled the bark to atoms so that none of it remained whole, and wherever they saw but a little cloud of dust upon the maize, they beat at it in great amazement and then they blew that dust at one another and were so afraid that they ran as if they really saw the devil; and after long stamping and running one of them went to the sick man and took away an otter that he had in his hands; and he sucked the sick man for awhile in his neck and on the back, and after that he spat in the otter's mouth and threw it down; at the same time he ran off like mad through fear. Other men then went to the otter, and then there took place such foolery that it was quite a wonder to see. Yes; they commenced to throw fire and eat fire, and kept scattering hot ashes and red-hot coal in such a way that I ran out of the house. To-day another beaver skin was presented to me.

January 5. I bought four dried salmon and two pieces of bear bacon that was about nine inches thick; and we saw thicker, even. They gave us beans cooked with bear bacon to eat to-day, and further nothing particular happened.

January 6. Nothing particular than that I was shown a parcel of flint stones wherewith they make fire when they are in the forest. Those stones would do very well for firelock guns.

January 7.—We received a letter from Marten Gerritsen, dated from the last of December; it was brought by a Sinneken that arrived from our fort. He told us that our people grew very uneasy about our not coming home, and that they thought we had been killed. We ate fresh salmon only two days caught, and we were robbed to-day of six and a half hands of seawan that we never saw again.

January 8. Arenias came to me to say that he wanted to go with me to the fort and take all his skins to trade. Jeronimus tried to sell his coat here, but he could not get rid of it.

January 9. During the evening the Onondagas came. There were six old men and four women. They were very tired from the march, and brought with them some bear skins. I came to meet them, and thanked them that they came to visit us; and they welcomed me, and because it was very late I went home.

January 10. Jeronimus burned the greater part of his pantaloons, that dropped in the fire during the night, and the chief's mother gave him cloth to repair it, and Willem Tomassen repaired it.

January 11. At ten o'clock in the morning the savages came to me and invited me to come to the house where the Onondagans sat in council. "They will give you presents"; and I went there with Jeronimus; took our pistols with us and sat alongside of them, near an old man of the name of Canastogeera, about 55 years of age; and he said: "Friends, I have come here to see you and to talk to you;" wherefore we thanked him, and after they had sat in council for a long time an interpreter came to me and gave me five pieces of beaver skin because we had come into their council. I took the beaver skins and thanked them, and they shouted three times *"Netho!"* And after that another five beaver skins that they laid upon my feet, and they gave them to me because I had come into their council-house. We should have been given a good many skins as presents if we had come into his land; and they earnestly requested me to visit their land in the summer, and after that gave me another four beaver skins and asked at the same time to be better paid for their skins. They would bring us a great quantity if we did; and if I came back in the summer to their land we should have three or four savages along with us to look all around that lake and show us where the Frenchmen came trading with their shallops. And when we gathered our fourteen beavers they again shouted as hard as they could, *"Zinae netho!"* and we fired away with our pistols and gave the chief two pairs of knives, some awls, and needles; and then we were informed we might take our departure. We had at the time five pieces of salmon and two pieces of bear bacon that we were to take on the march, and here they gave a good many loaves and even flour to take with us.

January 12. We took our departure; and when we thought everything was ready the savages did not want to carry our goods—twenty-eight beaver skins, five salmon, and some loaves of bread—because they all had already quite enough to carry; but after a good deal of grumbling and nice words they at last consented and carried our goods. Many savages walked along with us and they shouted, *"Alle sarondade!"* that is, to fire the pistols; and when we came near the chief's grave we fired three shots, and they went back. It was about nine o'clock when we left this place and walked only about five leagues through 2-1/2 feet of snow. It was a very difficult road, so that some of the savages had to stop in the forest and sleep in the snow. We went on, however, and reached a little cabin, where we slept.

January 13. Early in the morning we were on our journey again, and after going seven or eight leagues we arrived at another hut, where we rested awhile, cooked our dinner, and slept. Arenias pointed out to me a place on a high mountain, and said that after ten days' marching we could reach a big river there where plenty of people are living, and where plenty of cows and horses are; but we had to cross the river for a whole day and then to proceed for six days more in order to reach it. This was the place which we passed on the 29th of December. He did us a great deal of good.

January 14. On Sunday we made ready to proceed, but the chief wished to go bear hunting and wanted to stop here but, because it was fine weather, I went alone with two or three savages. Here two Maquas Indians joined us, as they wanted to go and trade elk skins and *satteeu*.

January 15. In the morning, two hours before daylight, after taking breakfast with the savages, I proceeded on the voyage, and when it was nearly dark again the savages made a fire in the wood, as they did not want to go farther, and I came about three hours after dark to a hut where I had slept on the 26th of December. It was very cold. I could not make a fire, and was obliged to walk the whole night to keep warm.

January 16. In the morning, three hours before dawn, as the moon rose, I searched for the path, which I found at last; and because I marched so quickly I arrived about nine o'clock on very extensive flat land. After having passed over a high hill I came to a very even footpath that had been made through the snow by the savages who had passed this way with much venison, because they had come home to their castle after hunting; and about ten o'clock I saw the castle and arrived there about twelve o'clock. Upward of one hundred people came out to welcome me, and showed me a house where I could go. They gave me a white hare to eat that they caught two days ago. They cooked it with walnuts, and they gave me a piece of wheaten bread a savage that had arrived here from Fort Orange on the fifteenth of this month had brought with him. In the evening more than forty fathoms of seawan were divided among them as the last will of the savages that died of the smallpox. It was divided in the presence of the chief and the nearest friends. It is their custom to divide among the chief and nearest friends. And in the evening the savages gave me two bear skins to cover me, and they brought rushes to lay under my head, and they told us that our kinsmen wanted us very much to come back.

January 17. Jeronimus and Tomassen, with some savages, joined us in this castle, Tenotogehage, and they still were all right; and in the evening I saw another hundred fathoms of seawan divided among the chief and the friends of the nearest blood.

January 18. We went again to this castle, I should say from this castle on our route, in order to hasten home. In some of the houses we saw more than forty or fifty deer cut in quarters and dried; but they gave us very little of it to eat. After marching half a league we passed through the village of Kawaoge, and after another half league we came to the village of Osquage. The chief, Ohquahoo, received us well, and we waited here for the chief, Arenias, whom we had left in the castle Te Notooge.

January 19. We went as fast as we could in the morning, proceeding on the march; and after going half a league we arrived at the third castle, named Schanadisse, and I looked around in some of the houses to see whether there were any skins. I met nine Onondagas there with skins, that I told to go with me to the second castle, where the chief, Taturot, I should say Tonewerot, was at home, who welcomed us at once, and gave us a very fat piece of venison, which we cooked; and when we were sitting at dinner we received a letter from Marten Gerritsen, brought us by a savage that came in search of us, and was dated January 18. We resolved to proceed at once to the first castle, and to depart on the morrow for Fort Orange, and a good three hours before sunset we arrived at the first castle. We had bread baked for us again, and packed the three beavers we had received from the chief when we had first come here. We slept here this night and ate here.

January 20. In the morning, before daylight, Jeronimus sold his coat for four beaver skins to an old man. We set forth at one hour before daylight, and after marching by guess two leagues the savages pointed to a high mountain where their castle stood nine years before. They had been driven out by the Mahicans, and after that time they did not want to live there. After marching seven or eight leagues we found that the hunters' cabins had been burned, so we were obliged to sleep under the blue sky.

January 21. We proceeded early in the morning, and after a long march we took a wrong path that was the most walked upon; but as the savages knew the paths better than we did they returned with us, and after eleven leagues' marching we arrived, the Lord be praised and thanked, at Fort Orange, January 21, anno 1635.

The Indians' contact with the white man was not always salutary. New diseases to which they had no immunity, powerful alcohol for which their culture had no sanctions, and a perplexing system of commercial values to which they were strangers often left them much worse off than they had been before their introduction to "civilization." The following observations of two Dutch visitors in 1679-80 expose some of the effects of white contact upon the natives of New York. Jaspar Dankers and Peter Sluyter were sent by their religious sect, the Labadists of Friesland, to find a suitable place in America to plant a colony where its members might worship God in their own way, free from persecution by the state or contamination by the things of this world. The passages below are taken from Henry C. Murphy's translation of Journal of a Voyage to New York and a Tour in Several of the American Colonies in 1679-80, *published in the* Memoirs of the Long Island Historical Society, *vol. 1 (1867), pp. 149-153, 267-268, 273-274*.

16 October 1679: In the morning there came an Indian to our house, a man about eighty years of age, whom our people called Jasper, who lived at *Ahakinsack* or at *Akinon*. Concerning this Indian our old people related that when they lived on Long Island, it was once a very dear time; no provisions could be obtained, and they suffered great want, so that they were reduced to the last extremity; that God the Lord then raised up this Indian, who went out a fishing daily in order to bring fish to them every day when he caught a good mess, which he always did. If, when he came to the house, he found it alone, and they were out working in the fields, he did not fail, but opened the door, laid the fish on the floor, and proceeded on his way. For this reason these people possess great affection for him and have given him the name of Jasper, and also my *nitap*, that is, my great friend. He never comes to the *Manhatans* without visiting them and eating with them, as he now did, as among his old friends. We asked him why he had done so much kindness to these people. "I have always been inclined," he answered, "from my youth up to do good, especially to good people, known to me. I took the fish to them because *Maneto* (the devil) said to me, you must take fish to these people, whispering ever in my ear 'you must take fish to them.' I had to do it, or *Maneto* would have killed me." Our old woman telling us he sometimes got drunk, we said to him he should not do so any more, that the great *Sakemacker* (the Lord) who is above, was offended at such conduct and would kill him. "No," said he, laughing as if that were a mistake of ours, "it is *Maneto* who kill those who do evil, and leaves those who do good at peace." "That is only" we replied, "because *Maneto* is the slave and executioner of the great Sakemacker above;" and we then asked him if he believed there was such a great and good Sakemacker there? "Undoubtedly," he said, "but he remains above, and does not trouble himself with the earth or earthly things, because he does nothing except what is good; but *Maneto*, who also is a Sakemacker, and is here below, and governs all, and punishes and torments those men who do evil and drink themselves drunk." Hereupon we inquired of him why he did so then.

"Yes," he said, "I had rather not, but my heart is so inclined that it causes me to do it, although I know it is wrong. The Christians taught it to us, and give us or sell us the drink, and drink themselves drunk." We said to him: "Listen! if we came to live near you, you would never see us drunk, nor would we give or sell you or your people any rum." "That," he replied, "would be good." We told him he must not make such a difference between himself and a Christian, because one was white and the other red, and one wore clothes and the other went almost naked, or one was called a Christian and the other an Indian, that this great and good Sakemacker was the father of us all, and had made us all, and that all who did not do good would be killed by *Maneto* whether they were called Christians or Indians; but that all who should do good would go to this good *Sakemacker* above. "Yes," said he, "we do not know or speak to this Sakemacker, but *Maneto* we know and speak to, but you people, who can read and write, know and converse with this *Sakemacker*."

We asked him, where he believed he came from? He answered from his father. "And where did your father come from?" we said, "and your grand-father and great grand-father, and so on to the first of the race?" He was silent for a little while, either as if unable to climb up at once so high with his thoughts, or to express them without help, and then took a piece of coal out of the fire where he sat, and began to write upon the floor. He first drew a circle, a little oval, to which he made four paws or feet, a head and a tail. "This," said he, "is a tortoise, lying in the water around it," and he moved his hand round the figure, continuing, "this was or is all water, and so at first was the world or the earth, when the tortoise gradually raised its round back up high, and the water ran off of it, and thus the earth became dry." He then took a little straw and placed it on end in the middle of the figure, and proceeded, "the earth was now dry, and there grew a tree in the middle of the earth, and the root of this tree sent forth a sprout beside it and there grew upon it a man, who was the first male. This man was then alone, and would have remained alone; but the tree bent over until its top touched the earth, and there shot therein another root, from which came forth another sprout, and there grew upon it the woman, and from these two are all men produced." We gave him four fish-hooks with which he was much pleased, and immediately calculated how much in money he had obtained. "I have got twenty four stuivers worth," he said. He then inquired our names, which we gave him, and wished to know why he asked for them? "Well," he replied, "because you are good people and are true *nitaps*; and in case you should come into the woods and fall into the hands of the Indians, and they should wish to kill or harm you, if I know or hear of it I might help you, for they will do you no injury when they know me." For he was the brother of a Sackemaker. We told him that we did not give them to him on that account, but only from regard because he was a good person, although the good will or thankfulness which he wished to show thereby was good. "Well," he said, "that is good, that is good," with which, after eating something, he departed.

But at noon he returned with a young Indian, both of them so drunk they could not speak, and having a calabash of liquor with them. We chided him, but to no purpose, for he could neither use his reason nor speak so as to be understood. The young Indian with him was a Sackemaker's son, and was bold. He wanted to have a piece of meat that was on the table, and on which we all had to make our dinner, when we told him it was not for him. "Yes," said he, "I see it is so;" nevertheless, and although we offered him something else to eat, he was evilly disposed and dissatisfied, and would take nothing except the piece of meat alone; but that was not given to him. Whereupon Jasper told him he must be quiet, that the old people and we were all his *nitaps*, and by degrees quieted him, they sitting together by the fire and drinking their rum. They left afterwards for Long Island. . . .

18 October 1679: In the afternoon Jasper, the Indian, came back again, and proceeded confidently to our room in the rear of the house, but sober and in his senses. He told us how he had been with his nephew, the Sackemaker's son to Long Island, among the other Indians; and that he had given away, not only his fish-hooks, but also his shoes and stockings. We found fault with him at first for having become so drunk, contrary to his promise, and when he well knew it was wrong. To which he said he had to buy some nails for an Englishman who lived near him, from another Englishman here, who had sold and given him the rum.

I must here remark, in passing, that the people in this city, who are most all traders in small articles, whenever they see an Indian enter the house, who they know has any money, they immediately set about getting hold of him, giving him rum to drink, whereby he is soon caught and becomes half a fool. If he should then buy any thing, he is doubly cheated, in the wares, and in the price. He is then urged to buy more drink, which they now make half water, and if he cannot drink it, they drink it themselves. They do not rest until they have cajoled him out of all his money, or most of it; and if that cannot be done in one day, they keep him, and let him lodge and sleep there, but in some out of the way place, down on the ground, guarding their merchandise and other property in the meantime, and always managing it so that the poor creature does not go away before he has given them all they want. And these miserable Christians are so much the more eager in this respect, because no money circulates among themselves, and they pay each other in wares, in which they are constantly cheating and defrauding each other. Although it is forbidden to sell the drink to the Indians, yet every one does it, and so much the more earnestly, and with so much greater and burning avarice, that it is done in secret. To this extent and further, reaches the damnable and insatiable covetousness of most of those who here call themselves Christians. Truly, our hearts grieved when we heard of these things, which call so grievously upon the supreme judge for vengeance. He will not always let his name be so profaned and exposed to reproach and execration.

We asked Jasper, why he had given away his hooks and stockings. He said, it was a custom among them, for the lesser to give to the greater. We replied the Sackemaker was richer than he, and he should, therefore, have kept them. "No," he said, "I did it as a mark of respect and obedience." We gave him four more fish-hooks, and told him he must take care of them for himself. "I will bring you fish as soon as I catch any," he said as he went away, promising also that he would get drunk no more.

4 March 1680 [Newark, N. J.]: We found nobody there except a negro who could speak nothing but a little broken French. We warmed ourselves, and eat from what we had brought with us, Hans, the Indian, sharing with us. In the meanwhile, we engaged in conversation with him, and he told us certain things which we had never heard any Indian or European mention, the opinion of the Indians in relation to the Godhead, the creation, and the preservation and government of all things.

We acknowledge, he said, a supreme first power, some cause of all things, which is known by all the Indians of North America, hereabouts, whether *Mahatans, Sinnekes, Maquaas, Minquaas*, southern or northern Indians, not only by the name of *Sackamacher* or *Sachamor* (which the Dutch for the sake of convenience will pervert into *Sackemacher*), that is to say, lord, captain or chief, which all persons bear who have any power or authority among them, especially any government or rule over other persons and affairs, and that name, it appeared to him, was used by others to express God, more than by themselves; but the true name by which they call this Supreme Being, the first and great beginning of all things, was *Kickeron* or *Kickerom*, who is the origin of all, who has not only once produced or made all things, but produces every day. All that we see daily that is good, is from him; and every thing he makes and does is good. He governs all things, and nothing is done without his aid and direction. "And," he continued, "I, who am a captain and *Sakemaker* among the Indians, and also a medicine-man (as was all true), and have performed many good cures among them, experience every day that all medicines do not cure, if it do not please him to cause them to work; that he will cure one and not another thereby; that sickness is bad, but he sends it upon whom he pleases, because those upon whom he visits it are bad; but we did not have so much sickness and death before the Christians came into the country, who have taught the people debauchery and excess; they are, therefore, much more miserable than they were before. The devil who is wicked, instigates and urges them on, to all kinds of evil, drunkenness and excess, to fighting and war, and to strife and violence amongst themselves, by which many men are wounded and killed. He thus does all kind of evil to them." I told him I had conversed with Jasper or *Tantaqué*, another old Indian, on the subject, from whence all things had come, and he had told me they came from a tortoise; that this tortoise had brought forth the world, or that all things had come from it; that from the middle of the tortoise there had sprung up a tree, upon whose branches men had grown. That was true, he replied, but *Kicheron* made the tortoise, and the tortoise had a power and a nature to produce all things, such as earth, trees, and the like, which God wished through it to produce, or have produced.

6 March 1680: I had asked Hans, our Indian, what Christians they, the Indians, had first seen in these parts. He answered the first were Spaniards or Portuguese, from whom they obtained the maize or Spanish or Turkish wheat, but they did not remain here long. Afterwards

the Dutch came into the South river and here, on Noten island, a small island lying directly opposite the fort at New York, and to Fort Orange or Albany, and after them the English came for the first, who, nevertheless, always disputed the first possession. But since the country has been taken several times by the one and the other, the dispute is ended in regard to the right of ownership, as it is now a matter of conquest.

When we arrived at Gouanes, we heard a great noise, shouting and singing in the huts of the Indians, who as we mentioned before, were living there. They were all lustily drunk, raving, striking, shouting, jumping, fighting each other, and foaming at the mouth like raging wild beasts. Some who did not participate with them, had fled with their wives and children to Simon's house, where the drunken brutes followed, bawling in the house and before the door, which we finally closed. And this was caused by Christians. It makes me blush to call by that holy name those who live ten times worse than these most barbarous Indians and heathen, not only in the eyes of those who can discriminate, but according to the testimony of these poor Indians themselves. What do I say, the testimony of the Indians! Yes, I have not conversed with an European or a native born, the most godless and the best, who has not fully and roundly acknowledged it, but they have not acknowledged it salutarily, and much less desisted, disregarding all convictions external and internal, notwithstanding all the injury which springs therefrom, not only among the Indians, but others, as we will show in its proper place. How will they escape the terrible judgment of God; how evade the wrath and anger of the Lord and King, Jesus, whom they have so dishonored and defamed, and caused to be defamed among the heathen? Just judgment is their damnation. But I must restrain myself, giving God all judgment and wrath, and keeping only what he causes us to feel therefor. Such are the fruits of the cursed cupidity of those who call themselves Christians for the very little that these poor naked people have. Simon and his wife also do their best in the same way, although we spoke to them severely on the subject. They brought forward this excuse, that if they did not do it, others would, and then they would have the trouble and others the profit; but if they must have the trouble, they ought to have the profit, and so they all said, and for the most part falsely, for they all solicit the Indians as much as they can, and after begging their money from them, compel them to leave their blankets, leggings, and coverings of their bodies in pawn, yes, their guns and hatchets, the very instruments by which they obtain their subsistence. This subject is so painful and so abominable, that I will forbear saying any thing more for the present.

III.   THE BIBLE COMMONWEALTH: NEW ENGLAND

New England's double origins as a religious haven for persecuted believers and as an economic opportunity for adventurous entrepreneurs gave it a dual character in the eyes of 17th-century visitors. What were their criticisms of the country and its inhabitants, animal and human? Was Maine any different from the Massachusetts Bay colony? To judge from their observations, were any of the visitors Puritans or sympathetic to the Puritan mission? Of what character traits of the Massachusetts Puritans were the visitors most critical? How accurate or balanced a picture of the Puritans do they give? Upon what quantity of evidence were their generalizations based? Why were visiting Englishmen largely critical of the Puritan colony? Why do you think they singled out the several Puritan laws they did? How were non-English visitors regarded in Massachusetts? Why?

According to William Wood, New England had some drawbacks as well as prospects. New Englands Prospect *(London, 1634), reprinted by the Prince Society (Boston, 1865), pp. 49-54.*

Of the evills, and such things as are hurtfull in the Plantation.

I have informed you of the Country in generall and of every plantation in particular, with their commodities and wherein one excelleth another. Now that I may be every way faithfull to my reader in this worke, I will as fully and truely relate to you what is evill, and of most annoyance to the inhabitants. First those which bring most prejudice to their estates are the ravenous Woolves, which destroy the weaker Cattell, but of these you have heard before: that which is most injurious to the person and life of man is a rattle snake which is generally a yard and a halfe long, as thicke in the middle as the small of a mans legge, she hath a yellow belly, her backe being spotted with blacke, russet, yellow, and greene colours, placed like scales; at her taile is a rattle, with which she makes a noyse when she is molested, or when she seeth any approach neere her, her necke seemes to be no thicker than a mans thumbe yet can she swallow a Squerill, having a great wide mouth, with teeth as sharpe as needles, wherewith she biteth such as tread upon her: her poyson lyeth in her teeth, for she hath no sting. When any man is bitten by any of these creatures, the poyson spreads so suddenly through the veines & so runs to the heart, that in one houre it causeth death, unlesse he hath the Antidote to expell the poyson, which is a root called snakeweed, which must be champed, the spittle swallowed, and the root applyed to the sore; this is present cure against that which would be present death without it: this weed is ranck poyson, if it be taken by any man that is not bitten: whosoever is bitten by these snakes his flesh becomes as spotted as a Leaper untill hee be perfectly cured. It is reported that if the party live that is bitten, the snake will dye, and if the partie die, the snake will live. This is a most poysonous and dangerous creature, yet nothing so bad as the report goes of him in *England*. For whereas he is sayd to kill a man with his breath, and that he can flye, there is no such matter, for he is naturally the most sleepie and unnimble creature that lives, never offering to leape or bite any man, if he be not troden on first, and it is their desire in hot weather to lye in pathes, where the sunne may shine on them, where they will sleepe so soundly that I have knowne foure men stride over one of them, and never awake her: 5 or 6 men have beene bitten by them, which by using of snakeweede were all cured, never any yet losing his life by them. Cowes have beene bitten, but being cut in divers places, and this weede thrust into their flesh were cured. I never heard of any beast that was yet lost by any of them, saving one Mare. A small switch will easily kill one of these snakes. In many places of the Countrie there bee none of them, as at *Plimouth, Newtowne, Igowamme, Nahant,* &c. In some places they will live on one side of the river, and swimming but over the water, as soone as they be come into the woods, they turne up their yellow bellies and dye. Up into the Countrey westward from the plantations is a high hill, which is called rattlesnake hill, where there is great store of these poysonous creatures. There be divers other kinde of snakes, one whereof is a great long blacke snake, two yards in length which will glide through the woods very swiftly; these never doe any hurt, neither doth any other kinde of snakes molest either man or beast. These creatures in the winter time creepe into clifts of rockes and into holes under ground, where they lie close till May or June. Here likewise bee great store of frogs, which in the Spring doe chirpe and whistle like a bird, and at the latter end of summer croake like our English frogges. Heere be also toades which will climbe the topes of high trees where they will sit croaking, to the wonderment of such as are not acquainted with them. I never saw any Wormes or Moles, but pismires and spiders be there. There are likewise troublesome flies. First there is a wilde Bee or Waspe, which commonly guards the grape, building her cobweb habitation amongst the leaves: secondly a great greene flye, not much unlike our horse flyes in *England*; they will nippe so sore that they wil fetch blood either of man or beast, and be most troublesome where most Cattle be, which brings them from out of the woods to the houses; this flye continues but for the Moneth of June. The third is a Gurnipper which is a small blacke fly no bigger than a flea; her biting causeth an itching upon the hands or face, which provoketh scratching which is troublesome to some; this fly is busie but in close mornings or evenings, and continues not above three weekes, the least winde or heate expells them. The fourth is a Musketoe which is not unlike to our gnats in *England*; In places where there is no thicke woods or Swampes, there is none or very few. In new Plantations they be troublesome for the first yeare, but the wood decaying they vanish: these Flies cannot endure winde, heate or cold, so that these are onely troublesome in close thicke weather, and against raine many that be bitten will fall a scratching, whereupon their faces and hands swell. Others are never troubled with them at all: those likewise that swell with their biting the first yere, never swell the second: for my owne part I have bin troubled as much with them or some like them, in the Fen country of *England* as ever I was there. Here be the flies that are called Chantharides, so much esteemed of Chirurgions, with divers kinds of Butterflies. Thus have you heard of the worst of the countrey: but some peradventure may

say no, and reply that they have heard that the people have beene
often driven to great wants and extremities; To which I answer, it
is true that some have lived for a certaine time with a little bread,
other without any, yet all this argues nothing against the countrey in
it selfe, but condemnes the folly and improvidence of such as would
venture into so rude and unmanaged a countrey, without so much provisions as should have comfortably maintained them in health and
strength till by their labours they had brought the land to yeeld his
fruite. I have my selfe heard some say that they heard it was a rich
land, a brave country, but when they came there they could see
nothing but a few Canvis Boothes & old houses, supposing at the
first to have found walled townes, fortifications and corne fields, as
if townes could have built themselves, or corne fields have growne
of themselves, without the husbandrie of man. These men missing
of their expectations, returned home and railed against the Country.
Others may object that of late time there hath beene great want; I
denie it not, but looke to the originall, and tell me from whence it
came. The roote of their want sprung up in *England*, for many hundreds hearing of the plenty of the Country, were so much their owne
foes and Countries hindrance, as to come without provision; which
made things both deare and scant: wherefore let none blame the Country so much as condemne the indiscreetnesse of such as will needs
runne themselves upon hardship. And I dare further assure any that
will carrie provision enough for a yeare and a halfe, shall not neede
to feare want, if he either be industrious himselfe, or have industrious
agents to mannage his estate and affaires. And whereas many doe
disparrage the land saying a man cannot live without labour, in that
they more disparage and discredit themselves, in giving the world
occasion to take notice of their droanish disposition, that would live
of the sweate of another mans browes: surely they were much
deceived, or else ill informed, that ventured thither in hope to live
in plenty and idlenesse, both at a time: and it is as much pitty as
he that can worke and will not, should eate, as it is pitty that he
that would worke and cannot, should fast. I condemne not such therefore as are now there, and are not able to worke; but I advise for
the future those men that are of weake constitutions to keepe at home,
if their estates cannot maintaine servants. For all new *England* must
be workers in some kinde: and whereas it hath beene formerly reported
that boyes of tenne or a twelve yeares of age might doe much more

than get their living, that cannot be, for he must have more than a boyes head, and no lesse than a mans strength, that intends to live comfortably; and hee that hath understanding and Industrie, with a stocke of an hundred pound, shall live better there, than he shall doe here [England] of twenty pound *per annum*. But many I know will say if it be thus, how comes it to passe then that they are so poore? To which I answere, that they are poore but in comparison, compare them with the rich Merchants or great landed men in *England*, and then I know they will seeme poore. There is no probability they should be exceeding rich, because none of such great estate went over yet; besides, a man of estate must first scatter before he gather, he must lay out monies for transporting of servants, and cattle and goods, for houses and fences and gardens, &c. This may make his purse seeme light, and to the eye of others seeme a leaking in his estate, whereas these disbursments are for his future enrichments: for he being once well seated and quietly setled, his increase comes in double; and howsoever they are accounted poore, they are well contented, and looke not so much at abundance, as a competencie; so little is the poverty of the Country, that I am perswaded if many in *England* which are constrained to begge their bread were there, they would live better than many doe here, that have money to buy it. Furthermore when corne is scarse, yet may they have either fish or flesh for their labour: and surely that place is not miserably poore to them that are there, where foure Egges may be had for a Penny, and a quart of new Milke at the same rate: Where Butter is sixe-pence a pound, and Cheshire-Cheese at five pence; sure *Middlesex* affoords *London* no better penny-worths. What though there be no such plenty, as to cry these things in the streetes? yet every day affords these penny-worths to those that neede them in most places. I dare not say in all: Can they be very poore, where for foure thousand soules, there are fifteene hundred head of Cattle, besides foure thousand Goates, and Swine innumerable? In an ill sheepe-yeare I have knowne Mutton as deere in *Old-England*, and deerer than Goates-flesh is in *New Eng-land*, which is altogether as good if fancy be set aside.

Some visitors to America were interested enough to make a second visit. John Josselyn, the son of Sir Thomas Josselyn of Kent, made his first trip in 1638, stayed fifteen months, and then returned for eight years in 1663. On both occasions he spent most of his time on his brother's estate at Scarborough, Maine, the colony their father had helped to found with Sir Ferdinando Gorges. A bachelor and a man of some learning, Josselyn recorded his frank impressions of New England in An Account of Two Voyages to New England *(London, 1674; 2nd ed. 1675). The following excerpts are taken from the reprint of the first edition published by W. Veazie in Boston in 1865, pp. 137-140, 158-162.*

The Governments of their Churches are Independent and Presbyterial, every Church (for so they call their particular Congregations) have one Pastor, one Teacher, Ruling Elders and Deacons.

They that are members of their Churches have the Sacraments administred to them, the rest that are out of the pale as they phrase it, are denyed it. Many hundred Souls there be amonst them grown up to men & women estate that were never Christened.

They judge every man and woman to pay Five shillings *per* day, who comes not to their Assemblies, and impose fines of forty shillings and fifty shillings on such as meet together to worship God.

Quakers they whip, banish, and hang if they return again.

Anabaptists they imprison, fine and weary out.

The Government both Civil and Ecclesiastical is in the hands of the thorow-pac'd Independents and rigid Presbyterians.

The grose *Goddons*, or great masters, as also some of their Merchants are damnable rich; generally all of their judgement, inexplicably covetous and proud, they receive your gifts but as an homage or tribute due to their transcendency, which is a fault their Clergie are also guilty of, whose living is upon the bounty of their hearers. On Sundays in the afternoon when Sermon is ended the people in the Galleries come down and march two a breast up one Ile and down the other, until they come before the desk, for Pulpit they have none: before the desk is a long pue where the Elders and Deacons sit, one of them with a mony box in his hand, into which the people as they pass put their offering, some a shilling, some two shillings, half a Crown, five shillings according to their ability and good will, after this they conclude with a Psalm; but this by the way.

The chiefest objects of discipline, Religion, and morality they want, some are of a *Linsie-woolsie* disposition, of several professions in Religion, all like *Ethiopians* white in the Teeth only, full of ludification and injurious dealing, and cruelty the extreamest of all vices. The chiefest cause of *Noah's* floud, Prov. 27. 26. *Agni erant ad vestitum tuum*, is a frequent Text among them, no trading for a stranger with them, but with a *Grecian* faith, which is not to part with your ware without ready money, for they are generally in their payments recusant and slow, great Syndies, or censors, or controllers of other mens manners, and savagely factious amongst themselves.

There are many strange women too, (in *Salomon's* sence) more the pitty, when a woman hath lost her Chastity, she hath no more to lose.

But mistake me not to general speeches, none but the guilty take exceptions, there are many sincere and religious people amongst them, descryed by their charity and humility (the true Characters of Christianity) by their Zenodochie or hospitality, by their hearty submission to their Soveraign the King of *England*, by their diligent and honest labour in their callings, amongst these we may account the Royalists, who are lookt upon with an evil eye, and tongue, boulted or punished if they chance to lash out; the tame *Indian* (for so they call those that are born in the Countrey) are pretty honest too, and may in good time be known for honest Kings men.

They have store of Children, and are well accommodated with Servants; many hands make light work, many hands make a full fraught, but many mouths eat up all, as some old planters have experimented; of these some are *English*, others *Negroes*: of the *English* there are can eat till they sweat, and work till they freeze; & and of the females that are like Mrs. *Winters* paddocks, very tender fingerd in cold weather.

There are none that beg in the Countrey, but there be Witches too many, bottle-bellied Witches amongst the Quakers, and others that produce many strange apparitions if you will believe report, of a *Shallop* at Sea man'd with women; of a Ship, and a great red Horse standing by the main-mast, the Ship being in a small *Cove* to the East-ward vanished of a suddain. Of a Witch that appeared aboard of a Ship twenty leagues to Sea to a Mariner who took up the Carpenters broad Axe and cleft her head with it, the Witch dying of the wound at home, with such like bugbears and *Terriculamentaes* [bogeymen].

It is published in print, that there are not much less than Ten hundred thousand souls *English*, *Scotch* and *Irish* in *New-England*.

Most of their first Magistrates are dead, not above two left in the *Massachusets*, but one at *Plimouth*, one at *Connecticut*, and one at *New-haven*, they having done their generation work are laid asleep in their beds of rest till the day of doom, there and then to receive their reward according as they have done be it good or evil.

The people in the province of *Main* may be divided into Magistrates, Husbandmen, or Planters, and fishermen; of the Magistrates some be Royalists, the rest perverse Spirits, the like are the planters and fishers, of which some be planters and fishers both, others meer fishers.

Handicrafts-men there are but few, the Tumelor or Cooper, Smiths and Carpenters are best welcome amongst them, shop-keepers there are none, being supplied by the *Massachusets* Merchants with all things they stand in need of, keeping here and there fair Magazines stored with *English* goods, but they set excessive prices on them, if they do not gain *Cent per Cent*, they cry out that they are losers, hence *English* shooes are sold for Eight and Nine shillings a pair, worsted stockins of Three shillings six pence a pair, for Seven and Eight shillings a pair, Douglass that is sold in *England* for one or two and twenty pence an ell, for four shillings a yard, Serges of two shillings or three shillings a yard, for Six and Seven shillings a yard, and so all sorts of Commodities both for planters and fishermen, as Cables, Cordage, Anchors, Lines, Hooks, Nets, Canvas for sails, &c. Bisket twenty five shillings a hundred, Salt at an excessive rate, pickled-herrin for winter bait Four and five pound a barrel (with which they speed not so well as the waggish lad at *Cape-porpus*, who baited his hooks with the drown'd *Negro's* buttocks) so for Pork and Beef.

The planters are or should be restless pains takers, providing for their Cattle, planting and sowing of Corn, fencing their grounds, cutting and bringing home fuel, cleaving of claw-board and pipe-staves, fishing for fresh water fish and fowling takes up most of their time, if not all; the diligent hand maketh rich, but if they be of a droanish disposition as some are, they become wretchedly poor and miserable, scarce able to free themselves and family from importunate famine, especially in the winter for want of bread.

They have a custom of taking Tobacco, sleeping at noon, sitting long at meals some-times four times in a day, and now and then drinking a dram of the bottle extraordinarily: the smoaking of Tobacco, if moderately used refresheth the weary much, and so doth sleep.

A Traveller five hours doth crave
To sleep, a Student seven will have,
And nine sleeps every Idle knave.

The Physitian allowes but three draughts at a meal, the first for need, the second for pleasure, and the third for sleep; but little observed by them, unless they have no other liquor to drink but water. In some places where the springs are frozen up, or at least the way to their springs made unpassable by reason of the snow and the like, they dress their meat in *Aqua Celestis*, i.e. melted snow, at other times it is very well cook't, and they feed upon (generally) as good flesh, Beef, Pork, Mutton, Fowl and fish as any is in the whole world besides.

Their Servants which are for the most part *English*, when they are out of their time, will not work under half a Crown a day, although it be for to make hay, and for less I do not see how they can, by reason of the dearness of clothing. If they hire them by the year, they pay them Fourteen or Fifteen pound, yea Twenty pound at the years end in Corn, Cattle and fish: some of these prove excellent fowlers, bringing in as many as will maintain their masters house; besides the profit that accrews by their feathers. They use (when it is to be had) a great round shot, called *Barstable* shot, (which is best for fowl) made of a lead blacker than our common lead, to six pound of shot they allow one pound of powder, Cannon powder is esteemed best.

The fishermen take yearly upon the coasts many hundred kentals of Cod, hake, haddock, polluck &c. which they split, salt and dry at their stages, making three voyages in a year. When they share their fish (which is at the end of every voyage) they separate the best from the worst, the first they call Merchantable fish, being sound, full grown fish and well made up, which is known when it is clear like a Lanthorn horn and without spots; the second sort they call refuse fish, that is such as is salt burnt, spotted, rotten, and carelessly ordered: these they put off to the *Massachusets* Merchants; the merchantable for thirty and two and thirty ryals a kental, (a kental is an hundred and twelve pound weight) the refuse for Nine shillings and Ten shillings a kental, the Merchant sends the merchantable fish to *Lisbonne, Bilbo, Burdeaux, Marsiles, Talloon, Rochel, Roan*, and other Cities of *France*, to the *Canaries* with claw-board and pipe-staves which is there and at the *Charibs* a prime Commodity: the refuse fish they put off at the *Charib-Islands*, *Barbadoes*, *Jamaica*, &c. who feed their *Negroes* with it.

To every Shallop belong four fishermen, a Master or Steersman, a Midship-man, and a Foremast-man, and a shore man who washes it out of the salt, and dries it upon hurdles pitcht upon stakes breast high and tends their Cookery; these often get in one voyage Eight or Nine pound a man for their shares, but it doth some of them little good, for the Merchant to increase his gains by putting off his Commodity in the midst of their voyages, and at the end thereof comes in with a walking Tavern, a Bark laden with the Legitimate bloud of the rich grape, which they bring from *Phial, Madera, Canaries*, with *Brandy, Rhum*, the *Barbadoes strong-water*, and *Tobacco*, coming ashore he gives them a taster or two, which so charms them, that for no perswasions that their imployers can use will they go out to Sea, although fair and seasonable weather, for two or three days, nay sometimes a whole week till they are wearied with drinking, taking ashore two or three Hogsheads of *Wine* and *Rhum* to drink off when the Merchant is gone. If a man of quality chance to come where they are roystering and gulling in *Wine* with a dear felicity, he must be sociable and *Roly-poly* with them, taking off their liberal cups as freely, or else be gone, which is best for him, for when *Wine* in their guts is at full Tide, they quarrel, fight and do one another mischief, which is the conclusion of their drunken compotations. When the day of payment comes, they may justly complain of their costly sin of drunkenness, for their shares will do no more than pay the reckoning; if they have a Kental or two to buy shooes and stockins, shirts and wastcoats with, 'tis well, other-wayes they must enter into the Merchants books for such things as they stand in need off, becoming thereby the Merchants slaves, & when it riseth to a big sum are constrained to mortgage their plantation if they have any, the Merchant when the time is expired is sure to seize upon their plantation and stock of Cattle, turning them out of house and home, poor Creatures, to look out for a new habitation in some remote place where they begin the world again. The lavish planters have the same fate, partaking with them in the like bad husbandry, of these the Merchant buys Beef, Pork, Pease, Wheat and *Indian* Corn, and sells it again many times to the fishermen. Of the same nature are the people in the Dukes province, who not long before I left the Countrey petitioned the

Governour and Magistrates in the *Massachusets* to take them into their
Government, Birds of a feather will ralley together.

*Jasper Dankers and Peter Sluyter also visited New England in
1679-80.* Journal of a Voyage to New York, *in* Memoirs of the Long
Island Historical Society, *vol. 1 (1867), pp. 382-389, 392-395.*

7 July 1680 [Boston]: We heard preaching in three churches, by
persons who seemed to possess zeal, but no just knowledge of Christianity. The auditors were very worldly and inattentive. The best of
the ministers whom we have yet heard, is a very old man, named
John Eliot, who has charge of the instruction of the Indians in the
Christian religion. He has translated the Bible into their language. We
had already made inquiries of the booksellers for a copy of it, but
it was not to be obtained in Boston. They told us if one was to be
had, it would be from Mr. Eliot. We determined to go on Monday
to the village where he resided, and was the minister, called Roxbury.
Our landlord had promised to take us, but was not able to do so,
in consequence of his having too much business. We, therefore,
thought we would go alone and do what we wanted.

8 July 1680: We went accordingly, about eight o'clock in the morning, to Roxbury, which is three-quarters of an hour from the city,
in order that we might get home early, inasmuch as our captain had
informed us, he would come in the afternoon for our money, and
in order that Mr. Eliot might not be gone from home. On arriving
at his house, he was not there, and we, therefore, went to look around
the village, and the vicinity. We found it justly called *Rocksbury*, for
it was very rocky, and had hills entirely of rocks. Returning to his
house we spoke to him, and he received us politely. Although he could
speak neither Dutch nor French, and we spoke but little English, and
were unable to express ourselves in it always, we managed, by means
of Latin and English, to understand each other. He was seventy-seven
years old, and had been forty-eight years in these parts. He had
learned very well the language of the Indians, who lived about there.
We asked him for an Indian Bible. He said in the late Indian war,

all the Bibles and Testaments were carried away, and burnt or destroyed, so that he had not been able to save any for himself; but a new edition was in press, which he hoped would be much better than the first one, though that was not to be despised. We inquired whether any part of the old or new edition could be obtained by purchase, and whether there was any grammar of that language in English. Thereupon he went and brought us the Old Testament, and also the New Testament, made up with some sheets of the new edition, so that we had the Old and New Testaments complete. He also brought us two or three small specimens of the grammar. We asked him what we should pay him for them; but he desired nothing. We presented him our *Declaration* in Latin, and informed him about the persons and conditions of the church, whose declaration it was, and about Madam Schurman and others, with which he was delighted, and could not restrain himself from praising God, the Lord, that had raised up men, and reformers, and begun the reformation in Holland. He deplored the decline of the church in New England, and especially in Boston, so that he did not know what would be the final result. We inquired how it stood with the Indians, and whether any good fruit had followed his work. Yes, much, he said, if we meant true conversion of the heart; for they had in various countries, instances of conversion, as they called it, and had seen it amounted to nothing at all; that they must not endeavor, like scribes and pharisees, to make Jewish proselytes, but true Christians. He could thank God, he continued, and God be praised for it, there were Indians, whom he knew, who were truly converted of heart to God, and whose profession was sincere. It seemed as if he were disposed to know us further, and we, therefore, said to him, if he had any desire to write to our people, he could use the names which stood on the title page of the Declaration, and that we hoped to come and converse with him again. He accompanied us as far as the jurisdiction of Roxbury extended, where we parted from him.

9 July 1680: We started out to go to Cambridge, lying to the northeast of Boston, in order to see their college, and printing office. We left about six o'clock in the morning, and were set across the river at Charlestown. We followed a road which we supposed was the right one, but went full half an hour out of the way, and would have gone still further, had not a negro who met us, and of whom we inquired, disabused us of our mistake. We went back to the right road, which

is a very pleasant one. We reached Cambridge, about eight o'clock. It is not a large village, and the houses stand very much apart. The college building is the most conspicuous among them. We went to it, expecting to see something curious, as it is the only college, or would-be academy of the Protestants in all America, but we found ourselves mistaken. In approaching the house, we neither heard nor saw any thing mentionable; but, going to the other side of the building, we heard noise enough in an upper room, to lead my comrade to suppose they were engaged in disputation. We entered, and went up stairs, when a person met us, and requested us to walk in, which we did. We found there, eight or ten young fellows, sitting around, smoking tobacco, with the smoke of which the room was so full, that you could hardly see; and the whole house smelt so strong of it, that when I was going up stairs, I said, this is certainly a tavern. We excused ourselves, that we could speak English only a little, but understood Dutch or French, which they did not. However, we spoke as well as we could. We inquired how many professors there were, and they replied not one, that there was no money to support one. We asked how many students there were. They said at first, thirty, and then came down to twenty; I afterwards understood there are probably not ten. They could hardly speak a word of Latin, so that my comrade could not converse with them. They took us to the library where there was nothing particular. We looked over it a little. They presented us with a glass of wine. This is all we ascertained there. The minister of the place goes there morning and evening to make prayer, and has charge over them. The students have tutors or masters. Our visit was soon over, and we left them to go and look at the land about there. We found the place beautifully situated on a large plain, more than eight miles square, with a fine stream in the middle of it, capable of bearing heavily laden vessels. As regards the fertility of the soil, we consider the poorest in New York, superior to the best here. As we were tired, we took a mouthful to eat, and left. We passed by the printing office, but there was nobody in it; the paper sash however being broken, we looked in; and saw two presses with six or eight cases of type. There is not much work done there. Our printing office is well worth two of it, and even more. . . .

12 July 1680: We went in the afternoon to Mr. John Taylor's, to ascertain whether he had any good wine, and to purchase some for our voyage, and also some brandy. On arriving at his house, we found

him a little cool; indeed, not as he was formerly. We inquired for
what we wanted, and he said he had good Madeira wine, but he
believed he had no brandy, though he thought he could assist us in
procuring it. We also inquired how we could obtain the history and
laws of this place. At last it came out. He said we must be pleased
to excuse him if he did not give us admission to his house; he durst
not do it, in consequence of there being a certain evil report in the
city concerning us; they had been to warn him not to have too much
communication with us, if he wished to avoid censure; they said we
certainly were Jesuits, who had come here for no good, for we were
quiet and modest, and an entirely different sort of people from themselves; that we could speak several languages, were cunning and subtle of mind and judgment, had come there without carrying on any
traffic or any other business, except only to see the place and country;
that this seemed fabulous as it was unusual in these parts; certainly
it could be for no good purpose. As regards the voyage to Europe,
we could have made it as well from New York as from Boston, as
opportunities were offered there. This suspicion seemed to have gained
more strength because the fire at Boston over a year ago was caused
by a Frenchman. Although he had been arrested, they could not prove
it against him; but in the course of the investigation, they discovered
he had been counterfeiting coin and had profited thereby, which was
a crime as infamous as the other. He had no trade or profession; he
was condemned; both of his ears were cut off; and he was ordered
to leave the country. Mr. Taylor feared the more for himself, particularly because most all strangers were addressed to him, as we
were, in consequence of his speaking several languages, French, some
Dutch, Spanish, Portuguese, Italian, &c., and could aid them. There
had also, some time ago, a Jesuit arrived here from Canada, who
came to him disguised, in relation to which there was much murmur-
ing, and they wished to punish this Jesuit, not because he was a Jesuit,
but because he came in disguise, which is generally bad and especially
for such as are the pests of the world, and are justly feared, which
just hate we very unjustly, but as the ordinary lot of God's children,
had to share. We were compelled to speak French, because we could
not speak English, and these people did not understand Dutch. There
were some persons in New York, who could speak nothing but
French, and very little English. The French was common enough in
these parts, but it seemed that we were different from them. Of all

this, we disabused Mr. Taylor, assuring him we were as great enemies of that brood, as any persons could be, and were, on the contrary, good protestants or reformed, born and educated in that faith; that we spoke only Dutch and French, except my companion, who could also speak Latin, and had not come here to trade, but to examine the country, and perhaps some morning or evening the opportunity might arrive for us to come over with our families, when affairs in Europe, and especially in Holland, might be settled, as the times there had been bad enough; that if they would be pleased to listen to Mr. Eliot, the minister at Roxbury, he could give them other testimony concerning us, as we had particularly conversed with him. This seemed in some measure to satisfy him. I think this bad report was caused by some persons who came from New York, truly worldly men, whom we had not sought when we were there, nor they us, and who, although they knew better, or at least ought to have known better, yet out of hatred to the truth, and love of sin, said of us what they conceived, and their corruption inclined them to say.

23 July 1680: After some delay the captain came on board with the rest of the passengers, accompanied by many of their friends. Weighed anchor at three o'clock in the afternoon it being most low water, and set sail with a southwest and south southwest wind. In passing the fort we fired the *salvo*, which it answered; the pilot and the company then left us and we put to sea. But before going further to sea we must give a brief description of New England, and the city of Boston in particular.

When New Netherland was first discovered by the Hollanders, the evidence is that New England was not known; because the Dutch East India Company then sought a passage by the west, through which to sail to Japan and China; and if New England had been then discovered, they would not have sought a passage there, knowing it to be the main land; just as when New Netherland and New England did become known, such a passage was sought no longer through them, but further to the north through Davis and Hudson straits. The Hollanders when they discovered New Netherland, embraced under that name and title, all the coast from Virginia or Cape *Hinloopen*, eastwardly to Cape Cod, as it was then and there discovered by them and designated by Dutch names, as sufficiently appears by the charts. The English afterwards discovered New England and settled there. They increased so in consequence of the great liberties and favorable privileges which the king granted to the Independents, that they went to live not only west of Cape Cod and Rhode Island, but also on Long Island and other places, and even took possession of the whole of the Fresh river [the Connecticut], which the Hollanders there were not able to prevent, in consequence of their small force in New Netherland, and the scanty population. The English went more readily to the west, because the land was much better there, and more accessible to vessels, and the climate was milder; and also because they could trade more conveniently with the Hollanders, and be supplied by them with provisions. New England is now described as extending from the Fresh river to Cape Cod and thence to Kennebec, comprising three provinces or colonies, Fresh river or Connecticut; Rhode Island and the other islands to Cape Cod; and Boston, which stretches from thence north. They are subject to no one, but acknowledge the king of England for their *honor* and therefore no ships enter unless they have English passports or commissions. They have free trade with all countries; but the return cargoes from there to Europe, go to England, except those which go *under the thumb* [secretly] to Holland. There is no toll or duty paid upon merchandise exported or imported, nor is there any import or excise paid upon land. Each province chooses its own governor from the magistracy, and the magistrates are chosen from the principal inhabitants, merchants or planters. They are all *Independents* in matters of religion, if it can be called religion; many of them perhaps more for the purposes of enjoying the benefit of its privileges than for any regard to truth and godliness. I observed that while the English flag or color has a red ground with a small white field in the uppermost corner where there is a red cross, they have here dispensed with this cross in their colors, and preserved the rest. They baptize no children except those of the members of the congregation. All their religion consists in observing Sunday, by not working or going into the taverns on that day; but the houses are worse than the taverns. No stranger or traveler can therefore be entertained on a Sunday, which begins at sunset on Saturday, and continues until the same time on Sunday. At these two hours you see all their countenances change. Saturday evening the constable goes round into all the taverns of the city for the purpose of stopping all noise and debauchery, which frequently causes him to stop his search, before his search causes the debauchery to stop. There is a penalty for cursing and swearing, such as they please to impose, the witnesses thereof being at liberty to insist upon it. Nevertheless, you discover little difference between this and other places. Drinking and fighting occur there not less than elsewhere; and as to truth and true godliness, you must not expect more of them than of others. When we were there, four ministers' sons were learning the silversmith's trade.

The soil is not as fertile as in the west. Many persons leave there to go to the Delaware and New Jersey. They manure their lands with heads of fish. They gain their living mostly, or very much by fish, which they salt and dry for selling; and by raising horses, oxen and cows, as well as hogs and sheep, which they sell alive, or slaughtered and salted, in the Caribbean islands and other places. They are not as good farmers as the Hollanders about New York.

As to Boston particularly, it lies in latitude 42° 20' on a very fine bay. The city is quite large, constituting about twelve companies. It has three churches, or meeting houses, as they call them. All the houses are made of thin, small cedar shingles, nailed against frames, and then filled in with brick and other stuff; and so are their churches. For this reason these towns are so liable to fires, as have already happened several times; and the wonder to me is, that the whole city has not been burnt down, so light and dry are the materials. There is a large dock in front of it constructed of wooden piers, where the large ships go to be careened and rigged; the smaller vessels all come up to the city. On the left hand side across the river, lies Charlestown, a considerable place, where there is some shipping. Upon the point of the bay, on the left hand, there is a block-house, along which a piece of water runs, called the Milk ditch. The whole place has been an island, but it is now joined to the main land by a low road to Roxbury. In front of the town there are many small islands, between which you pass in sailing in and out. On one of the middlemost stands the fort where the ships show their passports. At low tide the water in the channel between the islands is three and a half and four fathoms deep, in its shallowest part. You sail from the city southeasterly to the fort, by passing Governor's island on the larboard, and having passed the fort, you keep close to the south, then southeast, and gradually more to the east to the sea.

Being the special place that it was, New England could not expect to escape criticism, and indeed it was not disappointed. John Dunton, the bookseller whose tart observations on 17th-century Boston appear below was born in Huntingtonshire in 1659, the son of a third-generation minister. He was naturally designed for the ministry too, but he so disliked study that he was apprenticed to a London book-seller. After completing his term, he established his own business, married, and then in 1685 sailed for New England, where he landed in February 1686. The following passages occur in his Letters Written from New-England A.D. 1686, *ed. W.H. Whitmore,* Publications of the Prince Society, *vol. 4 (Boston, 1867), pp. 53, 66-74.*

We all drew near the Land with joyful hearts; and yet we durst not give too great a Loose unto those Pleasing Passions, because Extreams do equally annoy, and sometimes do infatuate our Minds. We went out into the Long-boat, and Landed near the Castle, within a mile of Boston, where we lay that Night; and tho' the Country shew'd at first but like a Barbarous Wilderness, yet by the Generous Treatment the Governour was pleas'd to give us, we found it wan't inhabited by Salvages. And now that wee were come to Land, we were not insensible of God's great Goodness in our Deliverance at Sea; tho' like men newly awaken'd out of a Dream, we had not the true Dimensions of it. We confess'd God had done Great things for us, but how great, was beyond our apprehension. We had escap'd the Sea, but yet Death might be found at Land, and therefore we shou'd moderate our Joy.

I shall next describe the Town of Boston, and shall say something of the Inhabitants, Government, Laws, and Customs of the City and Kingdom. And here, my Friend, when I come to speak of the Inhabitants of Boston, I must entreat your Candour in Distinguishing; Or else you will not know what to make of what I say; To which End, I ought to premise, That the first English that came over hither, in the latter end of Queen Elizabeth's, and the Beginning of King James's Reign, forced thereto by the severe Treatment they met with from the Bishops in England, were certainly the most Pious and Religious Men in the World, Men that had experienc'd the Power of Divine Grace upon their own Souls, and were the lively Patterns of Primitive Zeal and Integrity; and wou'd have converted all the

World, if they cou'd; especially their own Posterity: But alas! this blessed Wind of the Spirit blows where it listeth; Many of them were converted and made truly Gracious, and these walk to this Day in the steps of their Pious Fore-fathers: But there are others of them, who never knew the Power of Converting Grace, who yet retain a form of Godliness, and make a strict Profession of the out-side of Religion, tho' they never knew what the Power of Godliness was; and these are the most Profligate and Debauched Wretches in the World; their Profession of Religion teaching them only how to sin (as they think) more refinedly. Having premised thus much, you will soon know how to discern what is spoken of these Hypocrites, from what belongs to the Truly Religious; of which there are many, tho' the others are the far greater Number.

Boston is situated in the Bottom of the Massachusets Bay, in the Latitude of 42 degrees and 10 minutes, (its Longitude being 315 degrees, or, as others affirm, 322 degrees and 30 seconds.) So called from a Town in Lincolnshire. It is the Metropolis, not only of this Colony, but of the whole Country: And is built on the South-West-side of a Bay large enough for the Anchorage of 500 Sail of Ships. Situated upon a Peninsula about four miles in compass, almost Square, and inviron'd with the Sea, having one small isthmus, which gives access to other Towns by Land on the South.

The Town hath two hills of equal height on the Frontire part thereof, next the sea; the one well fortified on the Superficies with some Artillery mounted, commanding any Ship as she sails into the Harbour within the Bay: The other Hill hath a very strong Battery, built with whole Timber, and fill'd with Earth. At the Descent of the Hill, in the extreamest part thereof, betwixt these two Strong Arms, lies a large Cove or Bay, on which the chiefest part of the Town is built. To the North-west is a high Mountain that over-tops all, with its three little rising Hills on the summit, called Tramount: This is furnished with a Beacon and Great Guns: from hence you may overlook all the Islands in the Bay, and descry such ships as are upon the Coast.

The Houses are for the most part raised on the Sea-Banks, and wharfed out with great Industry and Cost; many of them standing upon Piles, close together on each side the streets, as in London, and furnished with many fair Shops; where all sorts of Comodities are sold. Their streets are many and large, paved with Pebbles; the Materials of their Houses are Brick, Stone, Lime, handsomely contrived, and when any New Houses are built, they are made conformable to our New Buildings in London since the fire. Mr. [Samuel] Shrimpton has a very stately house there, with a Brass Kettle atop, to shew his Father was not asham'd of his Original: Mr. John Usher (to the honour of our Trade) is judg'd to be worth about £20,000, and hath one of the best Houses in Boston; They have Three Fair and Large Meeting-Houses or Churches, commodiously built in several parts of the Town, which yet are hardly sufficient to receive the Inhabitants, and strangers that come in from all Parts.

Their Town-House is built upon Pillars in the middle of the Town, where their Merchants meet and confer every Day. In the Chambers above they keep their Monthly Courts. The South-side of the Town is adorned with Gardens and Orchards. The Town is rich and very populous, much frequented by strangers. Here is the Dwelling of [Mr.] [Simon] Broadstreet [Bradstreet], Esq., their present Governour. On the North-west and North-East, two constant Fairs are kept, for daily Traffick thereunto. On the South, there is a small but pleasant Common, where the Gallants a little before sunset walk with their Marmalet Madams, as we do in Moorfield, &c., till the Nine-a-Clock Bell rings them home; after which the Constables walk their Rounds to see good orders kept, and to take up loose people. In the high-street towards the Common, there are very fair Buildings, some of which are of stone. And at the East end of the Town, one amongst the rest built by the shore, by Mr. [Robert] Gibbs, a Merchant, being a very stately Edifice. But I need give you no further a Description of Boston; for I remember you have been at Bristol, which bears a very near Resemblance to Boston.

But I shall say something of the Inhabitants, as 10 months of my Life was spent amongst 'em. There is no Trading for a stranger with them but with a Grecian Faith, which is, not to part with your Ware without ready Money; for they are generally very backward in their Payments, great Censors of other Men's Manners, but extreamly careless of their own, yet they have a ready correction for every vice. As to their Religion, I cannot perfectly distinguish it; but it is such that nothing keeps 'em friends but only the fear of exposing one another's knavery. As for the Rabble, their Religion lies in cheating all they deal with. When you are dealing with 'em, you must look upon 'em as at cross purposes, and read 'em like Hebrew backward; for they seldom speak and mean the same thing, but like Water-men,

Look one Way, and Row another. The Quakers here have been a suffering Generation; and there's hardly any of the Yea-and-Nay Persuasion but will give you a severe Account of it; for the Bostonians, tho' their Forefathers fled thither to enjoy Liberty of Conscience, are very unwilling any should enjoy it but themselves: But they are now grown more moderate. Those were the Heats of some Persons among 'em whose zeal outran their knowledge, and was the effect of their Ignorance: For you and I, Mr. Larkin, are I am sure both of this Opinion, as our sufferings for it sufficiently Testifie, That Liberty of Conscience is the Birth-Right of all Men by a Charter Divine.

The Government both Civil and Ecclesiastical is in the hands of the Independents and Presbyterians, or at least of those that pretend to be such.

On Sundays in the After-noon, after Sermon is ended, the People in the Galleries come down and march two a Brest, up one Isle and down the other, until they come before the Desk, for Pulpit they have none: Before the Desk is a long Pew, where the Elders and Deacons sit, one of them with a Money-Box in his hand, into which the People as they pass put their Offerings, some a shilling, some two shillings, and some half a Crown, or five shillings, according to the Ability or Liberality of the Person giving. This I look upon to be a Praiseworthy Practice. This Money is distributed to supply the Necessities of the Poor, according to their several wants, for they have no Beggars there.

Every Church (for so they call their particular Congregations) have one Pastor, one Teacher, Ruling Elders and Deacons.

They that are Members of their Churches have the Sacrament administered to them. Those that are not actually joyned to them, may look on, but partake not thereof, till they are so joyn'd.

As to their Laws, This Colony is a Body Corporate and Politick in Fact, by the Name of, The Governour and Company of the Massachusets Bay in New-England. Their Constitution is, That there shall be one Governour and Deputy-Governour, and eighteen Assistants of the same Company, from time to time. That the Governour and Deputy-Governour, (who for this year are Esq: Broadstreet and Esq: Staughton,) Assistants and all other Officers, to be chosen from among the Freemen the last Wednesday in Easter Term, yearly, in the General Court. The Governour to take his corporal oath to be True and Faithful to the Government, and to give the same Oath to the other Officers.

They are to hold a Court once a month, and any Seven to be a sufficient Quorum. They are to have four General Courts kept in Term-Time, and one great General and Solemn Assembly, to make Laws and Ordinances; Provided, They be not contrary or repugnant to the Laws and Statutes of the Realm of England. In Anno 1646, They drew up a Body of their Laws for the benefit of the People. Every Town sends two Burgesses to their Great and Solem General Court.

Their Laws for Reformation of Manners, are very severe, yet but little regarded by the People, so at least as to make 'em better, or cause 'em to mend their manners.

For being drunk, they either Whip or impose a Fine of Five shillings: And yet notwithstanding this Law, there are several of them so addicted to it, that they begin to doubt whether it be a Sin or no; and seldom go to Bed without Muddy Brains.

For Cursing and Swearing, they bore through the Tongue with a hot Iron.

For kissing a woman in the Street, though but in way of Civil Salute, Whipping or a Fine. Their way of Whipping Criminals is by Tying them to a Gun at the Town-House, and when so Ty'd whipping them at the pleasure of the Magistrate, and according to the Nature of the Offence.

For Single Fornication, whipping or a Fine. And yet for all this Law, the Chastity of some of 'em, for I do not Condemn all the People, may be guess'd at by the Number of Delinquents in this kind: For there hardly passes a Court Day, but some are convened for Fornication; and Convictions of this Nature are very frequent: One instance lately told me, will make this matter yet more plain: There happened to be a Murder'd Infant to be found in the Town Dock: The Infant being taken up by the Magistrates Command, orders were immediately given by them for the search of all the Women of the Town, to see if thereby they cou'd find out the Murdress: Now in this Search, tho' the Murdress cou'd not be found out, yet several of the Bostonian Young Women, that went under the Denomination of Maids, were found with Child.

For Adultery they are put to Death, and so for Witchcraft; For that there are a great many Witches in this Country, the late Tryals of 20 New England Witches is a sufficient Proof.

An English Woman suffering an Indian to have carnal knowledge of her, had an Indian cut out exactly in red cloth, and sewed upon her right Arm, and enjoyed to wear it Twelve Months.

Scolds they gag, and set them at their own Doors, for certain hours together, for all comers and goers to gaze at. Were this a Law in England, and well Executed, it wou'd in a little Time prove an Effectual Remedy to cure the Noise that is in many Women's heads.

Stealing is punished with Restoring four-fold, if able; if not, they are sold for some years, and so are poor Debtors. I have not heard of many Criminals of this sort. But for Lying and Cheating, they outvye Judas, and all the false other cheats in Hell. Nay, they make a Sport of it: Looking upon Cheating as a commendable Piece of Ingenuity, commending him that has the most skill to commit a piece of Roguery; which in their Dialect (like those of our Yea-and-Nay-Friends in England [Quakers]) they call by the genteel Name of Out-Witting a Man, and won't own it to be cheating. As an Instance of what I have said, I was shewn a Man of such a Kidney as I have been speaking on, in Boston (whose Name for a Special Reason I shall here omit), who (as I was told by Mr. Gouge, Son to Charitable Divine of that Name) agreed with a Country-man for a Horse, and was to pay him Four Pounds of Massachuset Money, and that to become due upon the Day of the Election for Magistrates, which is held yearly. But our witty Bostonian understanding that the Country-man cou'd not read, makes the Bill payable under his hand, at the Day of the Resurrection of the Magistrates; willing belike to take Time enough to pay his Debts; or else possibly in good hopes that the Magistrates had no share in that Day. But he carry'd the Jest a little too far, for the Country-Man su'd him, and tho' with much Trouble and Charge recover'd his Money.

In short, These Bostonians enrich themselves by the ruine of Strangers; and like ravenous Birds of Prey, strive who shall fasten his Tallons first upon 'em. For my own share I have already trusted out £400, and know not where to get in 2*d*. of it. But all these things pass under the Notion of Self-Preservation and Christian-Policy.

I had not given you the Trouble of so large an Account of the manners of the Bostonians, nor rak'd in such a Dunghil of Filth, but that this sort of People are so apt to say, Stand off, for I am holier than Thou.

Most of the visitors to America (as opposed to permanent settlers) were well-educated men of some economic means. Edward Ward (1667-1731) was neither. This English tavernkeeper and scribbler of occasional prose was the 17th-century equivalent of "the man on the street," which gives his pungent observations special flavor. His Trip to New-England, With a Character of the Country and People, Both English and Indians *was published in London in 1699. The excerpts below are taken from the edition by George Parker Winship entitled* Boston in 1682 and 1699 *(Providence: Club for Colonial Reprints, 1905), pp. 48-59.*

Of the Country in General.

New-England is computed to begin at 40, and end at 46 *North* Latitude; Running from *De-la-Ware-Bay* to *New-found-Land*. The Country is for the most part Wilderness, being generaly *Rocky, Woody* and *Mountainous*, very rarely Beautified with *Valleys*, but those Large and Rich, wherein are *Lakes* thirty or forty Miles in compass, from whence their great Rivers have their beginnings, and are chiefly Succour'd.

There are many Plantations by the Sea-side, Situate for the advantage of the *East* and *South* Winds, which coming from Sea produceth warm Weather. The *Nor-west* blowing over Land, causeth extremity of Cold; and very often strikes both *Indian* and *English* Inhabitants with that terrible Distemper, called, the *Plague* in the *Back*.

The Country, by its Climate, is always troubled with an *Ague* and *Fever*; As soon as ever the Cold fit's over, tis attended with a Hot: And the *Natives* themselves, whose Bodys are Habituated to the suddain changes, from one Extream to another, cannot but confess, They *Freez* in Winter and *Fry* in Summer.

A Ridg of White Mountains run almost thro' the Country, whereon lies a remembrance of the past Winter, in the warmest of their weather. An *Indian* at the sight of the Snow, lodg'd upon the Shoulders of these Hills, will Quake at Midsummer: For they love Cold like a *Cricket*. At the Top there is a large Plain, ten or twelve Leages over, yielding nothing but Moss, where a Man may walk with his Mistress, in the height of his Juvenality, and not entertain one Thought of attempting her *Chastity*, it being fatally Cold, and above the

Clouds; and would have been a rare place, for the presumptious *Babilonians* to have Built their Tower on.

Plymouth Plantation was the first *English* Colony that settled in *New-England*, in the Year 1618 [1620]. Their Habitations, at their going on Shore, being empty *Hogs-heads*, which they whelm'd over their Heads to defend themselves from the cold Damps and falling Mischiefs of the Night. Each House having but one *Window*, and that's the *Bung-hole*, requiring a *Cooper* instead of a *Carpenter* to keep their Houses in repair. Their *Provision* (till better acquainted with the Country) being only *Pumkin*, which they Cook'd as many several ways, as you may Dress *Venison*: And is continued to this Day as a great dish amongst the *English*. *Pumpkin Porrage* being as much in esteem with *New-England* Saints, as *Jelly Broth* with *Old-England* Sinners.

Ten Years expired, before any other Colonies were Planted; since which time the Possessions of the *English* are so greatly improv'd, That in all their Colonies, they have above a Hundred and Twenty Towns, And is at this Time one of the most Flourishing Plantations belonging to the *English* Empire.

There is a large Mountain, of a Stupendious height, in an Uninhabitable part of the Country, which is call'd the *Shining Mountain*, from an amaizing Light appearing on the Top, visible at many Leages distance, but only in the Night.

The *English* have been very curious in examining the Reason of it; and have, in Bodies, with great Pains and Danger, attempted a rational Discovery of this Prodigy to no purpose: For they could not observe any thing upon it to occasion this unusual brightness. It is very terrible to the *Indians*, who are of a blind Opinion that it contains great Riches, and the Devil lives there; and do assert, That when any of them ascend this place, they are met by something in the figure of an Old *Indian*, that commands them to return, or if they proceed further they shall Die, which several have found true, by presuming to climb higher, heedless of the caution.

Of the Native English in General.

The Women (like the Men) are excessive *Smokers*; and have contracted so many ill habits from the *Indians*, that 'tis difficult to find a Woman cleanly enough for a *Cook* to a *Squemish Lady*, or a Man neat enough for a *Vallet* to Sir *Courtly Nice*. I am sure a *Covent-Garden Beau*, or a *Bell-fa* would appear to them much stranger *Monsters*, then ever yet were seen in *America*.

They *Smoke* in *Bed*, *Smoke* as they *Nead* their *Bread*, *Smoke* whilst they'r *Cooking* their *Victuals*, *Smoke* at *Prayers*, *Work*, and *Exoneration*, and their Mouths stink as bad as the *Bowl* of a Sailers *Pipe*, which he has funk'd in, without Burning, a whole Voyage to the *Indias*.

Eating, *Drinking*, *Smoking* and *Sleeping*, takes up four parts in five of their Time; and you may divide the remainder into *Religious Excercise*, *Day Labour*, and *Evacuation*. Four Meals a Day, and a good Knap after Dinner, being the Custom of the Country.

Rum, alias *Kill Devil*, is as much ador'd by the *American English*, as a dram of *Brandy* is by an old *Billingsgate*. Tis held as the *Comforter* of their *Souls*, the *Preserver* of their *Bodys*, the *Remover* of their *Cares*, and *Promoter* of their *Mirth*; and is a Soveraign Remedy against the *Grumbling* of the *Guts*, a *Kibe-heel*, or a *Wounded Conscience*, which are three Epidemical Distempers that afflict the Country.

Their *Industry*, as well as their *Honesty*, deserves equal Observation; for it is practicable amongst them, to go two miles to catch a Horse, and run three Hours after him, to Ride Half a Mile to *Work*, or a Quarter of a Mile to an *Ale-house*.

One husband-man in *England*, will do more Labour in a Day, then a *New-England* Planter will be at the pains to do in a Week: For to every Hour he spends in his *Grounds*, he will be two at an *Ordinary* [tavern].

They have wonderful *Appetites*, and will Eat like *Plough-men*; tho very *Lazy*, and *Plough* like *Gentlemen*: It being no rarity there, to see a Man *Eat* till he *Sweats*, and *Work* till he *Freezes*.

The Women are very *Fruitful*, which shows the Men are *Industrious* in *Bed*, tho' *Idle up*. *Children* and *Servants* are there very Plenty; but *Honest-men* and *Virgins* as scarce as in other places.

Provisions being Plenty, their Marriage-Feasts are very Sumptious. They are sure not to want Company to Celebrate their Nuptials; for its Customary in every Town, for all the Inhabitants to Dine at a Wedding without Invitation: For they value their *Pleasure* at such a rate, and bear such an affection to *Idleness*, that they would run the hazard of *Death* or *Ruin*, rather then let slip so Merry a *Holy-day*.

The *Women*, like Early *Fruits* are soon *Ripe* and soon *Rotten*. A *Girl* there at Thirteen, thinks herself as well Quallified for a *Husband*, as a forward *Miss* at a Boarding-School, does here at Fifteen for a *Gallant*.

He that Marrys a *New-England* Lass at Sixteen, if she prove a Snappish Gentlewoman, her Husband need not fear she will bite his Nose off; for its ten to one but she hath shed her Teeth, and has done Eating of Crust, before she arrives to that Maturity.

It is usual for the Men to be *Grey* at Thirty; and look as Shrivel'd in the *Face*, as an old *Parchment Indenture* pasted upon a *Barbers Block*. And are such lovers of *Idleness*, That they are desirous of being thought *Old*, to have a better pretence to be *Lazy*.

The Women have done bearing of Children by that time they are Four and Twenty: And she that lives un-Married till she's Twenty Five, may let all the Young Sports-men in the Town give her *Maidenhead* chase without the Danger of a *Timpany*.

Notwithstanding their *Sanctity*, they are very *Prophane* in their common *Dialect*. They can neither drive a *Bargain*, nor make a *Jest*, without a Text of Scripture at the end on 't.

An *English* Inhabitant having sold a Bottle of *Rum* to an *Indian* (contrary to the Laws of the Country) was detected in it; and order'd to be Lash'd. The Fellow brib'd the *Whipster* to use him tenderly; but the *Flog-master* resolving (being a Conscientious Man) to do his Duty Honestly, rather punish'd the Offender with the greater severity, who casting a sorrowful look over his Shoulder, Cry'd out, *the Scripture sayeth, Blessed is the Merciful Man*. The Scourgineer replying, *and it also says, Cursed is he that doeth the work of the Lord Negligently*: And for fear of coming under the *Anathema*, laid him on like an unmerciful *Dog*, till he had given him a thorough Fellow-feeling of his *Cat of Nine-tailes*.

Their Lecture-Days are call'd by some amongst them, *Whore Fair*, from the Levity and Wanton Frollicks of the Young People, who when their Devotion's over, have recourse to the *Ordinaries*, where they plentifully wash away the remembrance of their *Old Sins*, and drink down the fear of a *Fine*, or the dread of a *Whipping-post*. Then *Uptails-all* and the *Devils* as busie under the *Petticoat*, as a *Juggler* at a *Fair*, or a *Whore* at a *Carnival*.

Husking of *Indian-Corn*, is as good sport for the Amorous *Wagtailes* in *New-England*, as *Maying* amongst us is for our forward

Youths and Wenches. For 'tis observ'd, there are more *Bastards* got in that Season, than in all the Year beside; which Occasions some of the looser *Saints* to call it *Rutting Time*.

Many of the Leading *Puritans* may (without Injustice) be thus Characteris'd. They are *Saints* without *Religion*, *Traders* without *Honesty*, *Christians* without *Charity*, *Magistrates* without *Mercy*, *Subjects* without *Loyalty*, *Neighbours* without *Amity*, *Faithless Friends*, *Implacable Enemys*, and *Rich Men* without *Money*.

They all pretend to be driven over by *Persecution*, which their Teachers Roar out against in their Assemblies, with as much bitterness, as a double refin'd *Protestant* can belch forth against the *Whore* of *Babylon*: Yet have they us'd the *Quakers* with such severity, by *Whipping*, *Hanging*, and other Punishments, forcing them to put to Sea in Vessels without Provision, they flying with Gladness to the Merciless Ocean, as their only Refuge under Heaven, left to escape the *Savage Fury* of their *Unchristian Enemies*, till drove by *Providence* upon *Rhoad-Island* (so call'd from their accidental discovery of it in their Stroling Adventure) which they found full of *Fruits* and *Flowers*, a *Fertile Soil*, and extreamly Pleasant, being the Garden of *America*; where they happily Planted themselves, making great improvements: There Live and Flourish, as the *Righteous*, like a Bay-Tree under the Noses of their *Enemies*.

The *Clergy*, tho' they Live upon the Bounty of their Hearers, are as rediculously *Proud*, as their *Communicants* are shamefully *Ignorant*. For tho' they will not suffer their Unmannerly Flock to worship their Creator with that Reverence and Humility as they ought to do, but tell them 'tis *Popery* to uncover their Heads in the House and Presence of the *Deity*; yet they Oblige every Member to pay an humble respect to the *Parsons Box*, when they make their offerings every Sunday, and fling their *Mites* into their *Teachers Treasury*. So that the Haughty *Prelate* exacts more Homage, as due to his own Transcendency, than he will allow to be paid to Heaven or its place of Worship.

If you are not a Member in full Communion with one of their Assemblies, your Progeny is deny'd *Baptism*, for which Reason, there are Hundreds amongst them, at Mans Estate, that were never *Christened*.

All *Handicrafts-Men* may live here very well, except a *Pick-pocket*;

of all *Artificers* he would find the least Encouragement; for the scarcity of Money would baulk his Tallent.

An Eminent *Planter* came to me for an Ounce of *Venice-treacle*, which I would have sold him for a Shilling; he protested he had liv'd there Fifty Years, and never see in the whole Term, Ten Pounds in *Silver-Money* of his own; and yet was Rated at a Thousand Pounds, and thought the *Assessors* us'd him kindly: But gave me for my Medicine a Bushel of *Indian-Corn*, vallued at half a Crown, and Vow'd if a Shilling would save his Family from destruction, he knew not how to raise it.

They have a *Charter* for a *Fair* at *Salem*, but it Begins, like *Ingerstone* Market, half an Hour after Eleven a Clock, and Ends half an Hour before Twelve: For I never see any thing in it but by great Accident, and those were *Pumkins*, which were the chief Fruit that supported the *English* at their first settling in these parts. But now they enjoy plenty of good Provisions, *Fish*, *Flesh*, and *Fowl*, and are become as great *Epicures*, as ever Din'd at *Pontack's* Ordinary.

Lobsters and *Cod-fish* are held in such disdain, by reason of their Plenty, 'tis as Scandalous for a poor Man in *Boston* to carry one through the streets, as 'tis for an Alderman in the City of *London*, to be seen walking with a Groatsworth of *Fresh-Herrings*, from *Billings-gate* to his own House.

There were formerly amongst them (as they themselves Report) abundance of *Witches*, and indeed I know not, but there may be as many now, for the Men look still as if they were *Hag-ridden*; and every Stranger, that comes into the Country, shall find they will Deal by him to this Day, as if the *Devil* were in 'em.

Witchcraft they Punish'd with Death, till they had Hang'd the best People in the Country; and Convicted the *Culprit* upon a single Evidence: So that any prejudic'd person, who bore Malice against a Neighbour, had an easie method of removing their Adversary. But since, upon better consideration, they have Mitigated the severity of that unreasonable Law, there has not been one accused of *Witchcraft*, in the whole Country.

Many are the Bug-bear storys reported of these suppos'd *Negromancers*, but few Believ'd, tho' I presume none True, yet all Collected and already Printed, I shall therefore omit the relating of any.

They have one very wholesome Law, which would do mighty well to be in force in *Old-England*; which is a Peculiar method they have of Punishing *Scolds*. If any Turbulent Women be Troubled with an unruly Member, and uses it to the Defamation of any Body, or disquiet of her Neighbours, upon Complaint, she is order'd to be *Gag'd* and set at her own Door as many Hours as the Magistrates shall think fit, there to be gaiz'd at by all Passengers till the time's expired. Which, to me, seems the most Equitable Law imaginable to Punish more particularly that Member which committed the Offence.

Whipping is a Punishment so Practicable in this Country, upon every slight Offence, that at a Town upon the *Sound*, call'd *New-Haven*, the People do confess, that all the Inhabitants of that Place, above the Age of Fourteen, had been Whip'd for some Misdemeanour or other (except two) the *Minister* and the *Justice*.

IV. THE MELTING POT: NEW NETHERLANDS AND NEW YORK

From the arrival of the first settlers in 1624 to the surrender of the colony to the English in 1664, New Netherlands was wracked by one crisis after another. While New England had grown to over 50,000 persons, the Dutch colony, beset by poor Indian relations, inept governors, and unresponsive government by the Dutch West India Company, managed to garner a population of less than 8,000. What was the character of that population? What bound them together? What pulled them apart? What did they do for a living? How did their religious life compare with the New England Puritans'? What problems did their ministers face? What natural advantages did the colony possess? What disadvantages? How did the Directors and Governor of the Company impede the progress of the colony? What was the Dutch attitude toward the Indians? In what ways did the Indians help the Dutch establish their new colony? Did the Indians derive any benefit from the presence of the Dutch? Any disadvantage?

The Dutch ministers sent to New Netherlands cast as discerning an eye upon their Dutch brethren as they did upon the Indians. The Rev. Jonas Michaelius' observations on Fort Amsterdam's 270 persons are contained in his letter of 11 August 1628 to a colleague in Amsterdam. The following excerpts are taken from Ecclesiastical Records, State of New York *(Albany, 1901-1905), vol. 1, pp. 49-68.*

The favorable opportunity which now presents itself of writing to your Reverence I cannot let pass, without embracing it, according to my promise. And, first to unburden myself in this communication of a sorrowful circumstance, it pleased the Lord, seven weeks after we arrived in this country, to take from me my good partner, who had been to me, for more than sixteen years, a virtuous, faithful, and altogether amiable yokefellow; and I now find myself alone with three children, very much discommoded, without her society and assistance. But what have I to say? The Lord himself has done this, against whom no one can oppose himself. And why should I even wish to, knowing that all things must work together for good to them that love God? I hope therefore to bear my cross patiently, and by the grace and help of the Lord, not to let the courage fail me which in my duties here I so especially need.

The voyage was long, namely, from the 24th of January till the 7th of April, when we first set foot upon land here. Of storm and tempest which fell hard upon the good wife and children, though they bore it better as regards sea-sickness and fear than I had expected, we had no lack, particularly in the vicinity of the Bermudas and the rough coasts of this country. Our fare in the ship was very poor and scanty, so that my blessed wife and children, not eating with us in the cabin, on account of the little room in it, had a worse lot than the sailors themselves; and that by reason of a wicked cook who annoyed them in every way; but especially by reason of the captain himself, who, although I frequently complained of it in the most courteous manner, did not concern himself in the least about correcting the rascal; nor did he, even when they were all sick, give them anything which could do them any good, although there was enough in the ship: as he himself knew very well where to find it in order, out of meal times, to fill his own stomach. All the relief which he gave us, consisted merely in liberal promises, with a drunken head; upon which nothing followed when he was sober but a sour face; and he raged at the officers and kept himself constantly to the wine, both at sea and especially here while lying in the river; so that he daily walked the deck drunk and with an empty head, seldom coming ashore to the Council and never to Divine service. We bore all with silence on board the ship; but it grieves me, when I think of it, on account of my wife; the more, because she was so situated as she was—believing that she was with child—and the time so short which she had yet to live. On my first voyage I roamed about with him a great deal, even lodged in the same hut, but never knew that he was such a brute and drunkard. . . .

Our coming here was agreeable to all, and I hope, by the grace of the Lord, that my service will not be unfruitful. The people, for the most part, are rather rough and unrestrained, but I find in almost all of them both love and respect towards me; two things with which hitherto the Lord, has everywhere graciously blessed my labors, and which in our calling, as your Reverence well knows and finds, are especially desirable, in order to make our ministry fruitful.

From the beginning we established the form of a church; and as Brother Bastiaen Crol very seldom comes down from Fort Orange, because the directorship of that fort and the trade there is committed to him, it has been thought best to choose two elders for my assistance and for the proper consideration of all such ecclesiastical matters as might occur, intending the coming year, if the Lord permit, to let one of them retire, and to choose another in his place from a double number first lawfully proposed to the congregation. One of those whom we have now chosen is the Honorable Director [Peter Minuit] himself, and the other is the storekeeper of the Company, Jan Huygen, his brother-in-law, persons of very good character, as far as I have been able to learn, having both been formerly in office in the Church, the one as deacon, and the other as elder in the Dutch and French churches, respectively, at Wesel.

At the first administration of the Lord's Supper which was observed, not without great joy and comfort to many, we had fully fifty communicants—Walloons and Dutch; of whom, a portion made their first confession of faith before us, and others exhibited their church certificates. Others had forgotten to bring their certificates with them, not thinking that a church would be formed and established here; and some who brought them, had lost them unfortunately in a general conflagration, but they were admitted upon the satisfactory testimony of others to whom they were known, and also upon their daily good deportment, since one cannot observe strictly all the usual formalities in making a beginning under such circumstances.

We administer the Holy Supper of the Lord once in four months, provisionally, until a larger number of people shall otherwise require. The Walloons and French have no service on Sundays, otherwise than in the Dutch language, for those who understand no Dutch are very few. A portion of the Walloons are going back to the Fatherland, either because their years here are expired, or else because some are not very serviceable to the Company. Some of them live far away and could not well come in time of heavy rain and storm, so that they themselves cannot think it advisable to appoint any special service in. French for so small a number, and that upon an uncertainty. Nevertheless, the Lord's Supper is administered to them in the French language, and according to the French mode, with a sermon preceding, which I have before me in writing, so long as I can not trust myself extemporaneously. If in this and in other matters your Reverence and the Reverend Brethren of the Consistory, who have special superintendence over us here, deem it necessary to administer to us any correction, instruction or good advice, it will be agreeable to us and we shall thank your Reverence therefor; since we must all have no other object than the glory of God in the building up of his kingdom and the salvation of many souls. I keep myself as far as practicable within the pale of my calling, wherein I find myself sufficiently occupied. And although our small consistory embraces at the most —when Brother Crol is down here—not more than four persons, all of whom, myself alone excepted, have also public business to attend to, I still hope to separate carefully the ecclesiastical from the civil matters which occur, so that each one will be occupied with his own subject.

And though many things are *mixti generis* [of mixed origin], and political and ecclesiastical persons can greatly assist each other, nevertheless the matters and officers proceeding together must not be mixed but kept separate, in order to prevent all confusion and disorder. As the Council of this place consists of good people, who are, however, for the most part simple and have little experience in public affairs, I should have little objection to serve them in any difficult or dubious affair with good advice, provided I considered myself capable and my advice should be asked. . . .

In my opinion it would be well that the Honorable Directors should furnish this place with plainer and more precise instructions to the rulers, that they may distinctly know how to conduct themselves in all possible public difficulties and events; and also that I should some time have here all such *Acta Synodalia*, as have been adopted in the synods of Holland; both the special ones of our quarter [North Holland], and those which are provincial and national, in relation to ecclesiastical difficulties; or at least such of them as in the judgment of the Honorable Brethren at Amsterdam would be most likely to be of service to us here. . . .

As to what concerns myself and my household affairs: I find myself by the loss of my good and helpful partner very much hindered and distressed—for my two little daughters are yet small; maid servants are not here to be had, at least none whom they can advise me to take; and the Angola slave women are thievish, lazy, and useless trash. The young man whom I took with me, I discharged after Whitsuntide, for the reason that I could not employ him out-of-doors at any working of the land, and in-doors he was a burden to me instead of an assistance. He is now elsewhere at service among the farmers.

The promise which the Honorable Directors of the Company had made me of some morgens or acres of land for me to sustain myself, instead of a free table which otherwise belonged to me, is void and useless. For their Honors well knew that there are no horses, cows, or laborers to be obtained here for money. Every one is short in these particulars and wants more. I should not mind the expense if the opportunity only offered, for the sake of our own comfort, although there were no profit in it (the Honorable Directors nevertheless remaining indebted to me for as much as the value of a free table), for refreshment of butter, milk, etc., cannot be here obtained; though some is indeed sold at a very high price, for those who bring it in or bespeak it are jealous of each other. So I shall be compelled to pass through the winter without butter and other necessities, which the ships do not bring with them to be sold here. The rations, which are given out here, and charged for high enough, are all hard stale food, such as men are used to on board ship, and frequently not very good, and even so one cannot obtain as much as he desires. I began to get considerable strength, by the grace of the Lord, but in consequence of this hard fare of beans and gray peas, which are hard enough, barley, stockfish, etc., without much change, I cannot fully recuperate as I otherwise would. The summer yields something, but what is that for any one who does not feel well? The savages also bring some things, but one who has no wares, such as knives, beads, and the like, or *seewan* [wampum], cannot come to any terms with them. Though the people trade such things for proper wares, I know not whether it is permitted by the laws of the Company. I have now ordered from Holland almost all necessaries; and I hope to pass through the winter, with hard and scanty food.

The country yields many good things for the support of life, but they are all too unfit and wild to be gathered. Better regulations should be established, and people brought here who have the knowledge and implements for seeking out all kinds of things in their season and for securing and gathering them. No doubt this will gradually be done. In the meanwhile, I wish the Honorable Directors to be courteously enquired of, how I can best have the opportunity to possess a portion of land, and (even at my own expense) to support myself upon it. For as long as there is no more accommodation to be obtained here from the country people, and I shall be compelled to order everything from the Fatherland at great expense and with much risk and trouble, or else live here upon these poor and hard rations alone, it will badly suit me and my children. We want ten or twelve more farmers with horses, cows and laborers in proportion, to furnish us with bread, milk products, and suitable fruits. For there are convenient places which can be easily protected and are very suitable, which can be bought from the savages for trifling toys, or could be occupied without risk, because we have more than enough shares which have never been abandoned but have been always reserved for that purpose.

The business of furs is dull on account of the new war of the Maechibaeys [Mohawks] against the Mohicans at the upper end of this river. There have occurred cruel murders on both sides. The Mohicans have fled and their lands are unoccupied and are very fertile and pleasant. It grieves us that there are no people, and that there is no order from the Honorable Directors to occupy the same. Much timber is cut here to carry to the Fatherland, but the vessels are too few to take much of it. They are making a windmill to saw lumber and we also have a gristmill. They bake brick here, but it is very poor. There is good material for burning lime, namely, oyster shells, in large quantities. The burning of potash has not succeeded; the master and his laborers are all greatly disappointed.

We are busy now in building a fort of good quarry stone, which is to be found not far from here in abundance. May the Lord only build and watch over our walls. There is good opportunity for making salt, for there are convenient places, the water is salt enough, and there is no want of heat in summer. Besides, what the waters yield, both of the sea and rivers, in all kinds of fish; and what the land possesses in all kinds of birds, game, and woods, with vegetables, fruits, roots, herbs and plants, both for eating and medicinal purposes, and with which wonderful cures can be effected, it would take too long to tell, nor could I yet tell accurately. Your Reverence has already obtained some knowledge thereof and will be able to obtain from others further information. The country is good and pleasant, the climate is healthy, notwithstanding the sudden changes of cold and heat. The sun is very warm, the winter is fierce and severe and continues fully as long as in our country. The best remedy is not to spare the wood, of which there is enough, and to cover one's self with rough skins, which can also easily be obtained.

The harvest, God be praised, is in the barns, and is larger than ever before. There has been more work put on it than before. The ground is fertile enough to reward labor, but they must clear it well, and till it, just as our lands require. Until now there has been distress because many people were not very industrious, and also did not obtain proper sustenance for want of bread and other necessaries. But affairs are beginning to go better and to put on a different appearance, if only the Directors will send out good laborers and exercise all care that they be maintained as well as possible with what this country produces. . . .

David Pieterszoon de Vries was born in 1593-4 in Rochelle, France, to Dutch parents and spent his early life between France and Holland "in merchandising." In 1618 he began the first of many voyages to "the Four Quarters of the Globe"—the Mediterranean, Newfoundland, East India, and America. With several Dutch entrepreneurs, he founded the first settlement in Delaware in 1631, but it was soon destroyed by Indians. The following year he commanded a ship and a yacht sent to inspect the ruins of the village, warily traded with the Indians in the river, and in 1633 made his way to Manhattan. From 1638 to 1644 he was occupied with attempts to plant settlements on Staten Island and at Tappaan, both frustrated by the Indian war started by Governor Kieft. In 1655 he published his Short Historical and Journal-Notes of various Voyages performed in the Four Quarters of the Globe *(Alkmaar, Holland). The following excerpts come from the translation by Henry C. Murphy in the* Collections of the New York Historical Society, *2nd series, vol. 3 (1857), pp. 88-92, 107-111.*

The 10th February [1639], I have begun to make a plantation, a mile and a half, or two miles above the fort, as there was there a fine location, and full thirty-one morgens of maize-land, where there were no trees to remove; and hay-land lying all together, sufficient for two hundred cattle, which is a great article there. I went there to live, half on account of the pleasure of it, as it was all situated along the river. I leased out the plantation of Staten Island, as no people had been sent me from Holland, as was stipulated in the contract which I made with Frederick de Vries, a manager of the West India Company.

The 15th of April, I went with my sloop to Fort Orange, where I wanted to examine the land, which is on the river. Arrived at *Tapaen* in the evening, where a large valley of about two or three hundred morgens of clay-soil, lies under the mountain, three or four feet above the water. A creek, which comes from the highland, runs through it, on which fine water-mills could be erected. I bought this valley from the Indians, as it was only three miles above my plantation, and five miles from the fort. There was also much maize-land, but too stony to be ploughed.

The 25th, opposite Tapaen, lies a place called *Wickquaes-geck*, where there is much maize-land, but stony or sandy, and where many fir-trees grow. We generally haul fine masts from there. The land is also mountainous.

The 16th went further up the river. Passed the *Averstro*, where a kill runs out, formed from a large fall, the noise of which can be heard in the river. The land is also very high. At noon, passed the highlands, which are prodigiously high stony mountains, and it is about a mile going through them. Here the river, at its narrowest, is about five or six hundred paces wide, as well as I could guess. At night came by the *Dance-chamber*, where there was a party of Indians, who were very riotous, seeking only mischief, so that we were on our guard.

The 27th, we came to *Esoopes*, where a creek runs in, and there the Indians had some maize-land, but it was stony. Arrived at evening, as it blew hard, before the Cats-kill. Found the river up to this point, stony and mountainous, unfit for habitations. But there was some low-land here, and the Indians sowed maize along the Cats-kill.

The 28th, arrived at *Beeren* (Bears') Island, where were many Indians fishing. Here the land begins to be low along the margin of the river, and at the foot of the mountains it was good for cultivation. At evening, we reached Brand-pylen's Island, which lies a little below Fort Orange, and belongs to the patroons, Godyn, Ronselaer, Jan de Laet, and Bloemart, who had also there more farms, which they had made in good condition at the Company's cost, as the Company had sent the cattle from Fatherland at great expense; and these individuals, being the commissioners of New Netherland, had made a good distribution among themselves, and while the Company had nothing but an empty fort, they had the farms and trade around it, and every boor was a merchant.

The 30th of April. The land here is, in general, like it is in France. It is good, and very productive of every thing necessary for the life of man, except clothes, linens, woollens, shoes and stockings; but these they could have if the country were well populated; and there could be made good leather of the hides of animals, which multiply in great quantities. Good tan could be made of the bark of oak-trees. The land all along this river is very mountainous; some cliffs of stone are exceedingly high, upon which grow fine fir-trees, which may be discerned with the eye. There are, besides, in this country, oaks, alders, beeches, elms, and willows, both in the woods and along the water. The islands are covered with chestnut, plum, and hazel-nut trees, and large walnuts of different kinds, of as good flavour as they are in Fatherland, but hard of shell. The ground on the mountains is bedecked with shrubs of bilberries or blueberries, such as in Holland come from Veeluwes. The level land, or old maize-land, is covered with strawberries, which grow here so plentifully that they answer for food. There are also in the woods, as well as along the river, vines very abundant of two kinds, one bearing good blue grapes, which are pleasant when the vines are pruned, and of which good wine could be made. The other kind is like the grapes which grow in France on trellisses,—the large white ones which they make ver-juice of in France;—they are as large as the joints of the fingers, but require great labour, for these vines grow in this country on the trees, and the grapes are like the wild grapes which grow along the roads in France, on vines which are not pruned, and which are thick with wood, with little sap in it, for want of being attended to. There was this year, as they told me, a large quantity of deer at harvest and through the winter, very fat, having upon their ribs upwards of two fingers of tallow, so that they were nothing else than clear fat.

They also had this year, great numbers of turkeys. They could buy a deer for a loaf of bread, or for a knife, or even for a tobacco-pipe; at other times they give cloth, worth six or seven guilders. There are many partridges, heath-hens, and pigeons which fly together in thousands, and our people sometimes shoot thirty, forty, and fifty of them at a shot. Plenty of fowl, such as belong to the river, and all along the river are great numbers of them of different kinds; such as swans, geese, pigeons, teal, and wild geese, which go up the river in the spring by thousands, from the sea-coast, and fly back again in the fall.

Whilst I was at Fort Orange, the 30th of April, there was such a high flood at the island on which Brand-pylen lived,—who was my host at this time,—that we were compelled to leave the island, and go with boats into the house, where there were four feet of water. This flood continued three days, before we could use the dwelling again. The water ran into the fort, and we were compelled to repair to the woods, where we erected tents and kindled large fires. These woods are full of animals, bears, wolves, foxes, and especially of snakes, black snakes and rattlesnakes, which are very poisonous, and which have a rattle at the end of the tail, with many rattles, according to their age. As to what the land produces, the soil, which on the mountains is a red sand or cliffs of stone, but in the low plains, often clay-ground, is very fertile, as Brand-pylen told me that he had produced wheat on this island for twelve years successively without its lying fallow. . . .

Along this land runs an excellent river, which comes out of the Maquas [Mohawks] county, about four miles to the north of Fort Orange. I went there with some Indians, and passed by a farm upon which a boor lived, whom they called Brother Cornelis. This river runs between two high rocky banks, and falls over a rock as high as a church, with such a noise that it is frequently heard at the farm, and when I was there it made such a loud noise that we could hardly hear each other speak. The water flowed by with such force, that it was all the time as if it were raining, and the trees upon the hills, as high as the dunes at home, have their boughs constantly wet as if with rain. The water is as clear as crystal, and fresh as milk, and appears all the time as if a rainbow stood in it, but that arises from its clearness. There are a great many Indians here, whom they call Maquas, who catch many lampreys, otherwise called pricks. The river is about six hundred to seven hundred paces wide at this place, and contains large quantities of fine fish, such as pike, perch, eels, suckers, thickheads, sunfish, shad, striped bass, which is a fish which comes from the sea in the spring, and swims up the river into the fresh water as the salmon does. There are sturgeon, but our people will not eat them; also trout, slightly yellow inside, which I myself have caught, and which are considered in France the finest of fish. There are several islands in this river, of thirty, fifty, and seventy morgens of land in size. The soil is very good. The temperature is in extremes, in the summer excessively hot, and in winter exceedingly cold, so that in one night the ice will freeze hard enough to bear one. The summer continues to All Saints' day, and in December it will freeze so hard, that if there be a strong current, which loosens it, it will freeze in a night what has run over it in the day. The ice continues generally for three months, and although the latitude is forty-three, it is nevertheless always frozen for that period; for though sometimes it thaws, in pleasant days, it does not continue to do so, but it freezes again until March, when the river first begins to open, sometimes in February, though seldom. The severest cold comes from the north-west, as in Holland from the north-east. The reason of this cold is that the mountains to the north of it are covered with snow, and the north-west wind comes blowing over them, and drives all the cold down.

We will now speak of the Productions of the Country, and other things which serve for the support of the life of Man.

The productions are various. The principal one is maize, which is their [the Indians'] corn, and which is called by us Turkish wheat. . . . When they travel, they take a flat stone, and press it with another stone placed upon the first, and when it is pressed, they have little baskets, which they call *notassen*, and which are made of a kind of hemp, the same as fig-frails,—which they make to serve them as sieves,—and thus make their meal. They make flat cakes of the meal mixed with water, as large as a farthing cake in this country, and bake them in the ashes, first wrapping a vine-leaf or maize-leaf around them. When they are sufficiently baked in the ashes, they make good palatable bread. The Indians make use of French beans of different colours, which they plant among their maize. When the maize (which is sown three or four feet apart, in order to have room to weed it thoroughly) is grown one, two, or three feet high, they stick the beans in the ground alongside of the maize-stalks, which serve instead of the poles which we use in our Fatherland, for beans to grow on. In New Netherland, the beans are raised on the maize-stalks, which grow as high as a man can reach, and higher, according to the fertility of the soil. There are also pumpkins, water-melons, and melons. They (the Indians) dry the nuts of trees, and use them for food. There are also ground-nuts and white ground-nuts, which are poisonous to eat—a mason of the Company having died in consequence of eating one of them. There also grow here hazel-nuts, large nuts in great quantities, chestnuts, which they dry to eat, and wild grapes in great abundance. Our Netherlanders raise good wheat, rye, barley, oats, and peas, and can brew as good beer here as in our Fatherland, for good hops grow in the woods; and they can produce enough of those things which depend on labour, as everything can be grown which grows in Holland, England, or France, and they are in want of nothing but men to do the work. It is a pleasant and charming country, which should be well peopled by our nation only. Medlars grow wild and reversely from what they do in our country, as they grow in Holland open and broad above, but here they grow up sharp, the reverse of those in Holland. Mulberry trees there are too, so that silkworms could be raised, and good silk made; and good hemp, which they understand making up, much stronger than ours is, and for every necessary purpose, such as notassen, (which are their sacks, and in which they carry everything); they also make linen of it. They gather their maize and French beans the last of September and October, and when they have shelled the corn, they bury it in holes, which they have previously covered with mats, and so keep as much as they want for the winter and while hunting. They sow the maize in April and May.

Of the Animals and Cattle, and how they hunt and catch them.

There are great quantities of deer, which the Indians shoot with their bows and arrows, or make a general hunt of, a hundred more or less joining in the hunt. They stand a hundred paces more or less from each other, and holding flat thigh-bones in the hand, beat them with a stick, and so drive the creatures before them to the river. As they approach the river, they close nearer to each other, and whatever is between any two of them, is at the mercy of their bows and arrows, or must take to the river. When the animals swim into the river, the Indians lie in their canoes with snares, which they throw around their necks, and drag them to them, and force the deer down with the rump upwards, by which they cannot draw breath. At the north, they drive them into a *fuyk* [funnel-shaped net], which they make of palisades split out of trees, and eight or nine feet high, and set close to each other, for a distance of fourteen or fifteen hundred paces on both sides, coming together like a fuyk, . . . the opening is one or two thousand paces wide. When the animal is within the palisades, the Indians begin to come nearer to each other, and pursue it with great ardour, as they regard deer-hunting the noblest hunting. At the end of the fuyk it is so narrow that it is only five feet wide, like a large door, and it is there covered with the boughs of trees, into which the deer or animal runs, closely pursued by the Indians, who make a noise as if they were wolves, by which many deer are devoured, and of which they are in great fear. This causes them to run into the mouth of the fuyk with great force, whither the Indians pursue them furiously with bows and arrows, and from whence they cannot escape; they are then easily caught with snares. . . . There are elks, chiefly in the mountains; also hares, but they are not larger than the rabbits in Holland; foxes in abundance, multitudes of wolves, wild cats, squirrels,—black as pitch, and gray, also flying squirrels,—beavers in great numbers, minks, otters, polecats, bears, and many kinds of fur-bearing animals, which I cannot name or think of. The Indians understand the preparing of deer-skins, of which they make shoes and stockings, after their fashion, for the winter.

Of the Fowl which come in the River, and the Achter Col [Newark Bay]

There are great numbers of two kinds of geese, which stay here through the winter, by thousands, and which afford fine sport with the gun. One kind is the grey geese, which weigh fifteen or sixteen pounds each; the other they call white-heads, weighing six or seven pounds, very numerous, flying by thousands, and of good flavour. There are large quantities of ducks, which keep along the saltwater shore, and gulls, small star-birds, snipes, curlews, and many other shorebirds, which I cannot give the names of The geese and ducks come here in September and leave in April. Many of the Indians say that they go to the river of Canada, where they breed their young; for the fishermen who sail to Newfoundland, find them there in great numbers in the summer time, when they are fishing there. On the fresh water are many swans. Land birds are also very numerous, such as wild turkeys, which weigh from thirty to thirty-six and fifty pounds, and which fly wild, for they can fly one or two thousand paces, and then fall down, tired with flying, when they are taken by the Indians with their hands, who also shoot them with bows and arrows. Partridges are numerous, but they are small. There are meadow-hens, as large as a year-old hen, and with feathers like those of a partridge; and white and grey herons in great numbers. Nothing is wanted but good marksmen with powder and shot. Pigeons, at the time of year when they migrate, are so numerous, that the light can hardly be discerned where they fly. There are white and gray cranes, and a species of blackbird, as large as what is called in our country the starling or thrush, and which makes its appearance at harvest, when the corn named maize is ripe. These birds are called maize-thieves, because they fall upon the corn by thousands, and do great damage. I have seen one of our Netherlanders kill, in the commander's orchard at Fort Amsterdam, eighty-four of these birds at one shot. They are good-tasted, and similar to the thrushes in Fatherland. I have also seen, at different times, thirty to thirty-four pigeons killed at one shot, but they are not larger than turtle-doves, and their bodies are exactly like those of the turtle-doves in Fatherland, except they have longer tails.

Of the kinds of Fish which frequent the Sea and River as far up as the brackish and fresh water.

There are different kinds of fine fish on the seacoast for the wants of man, similar to those in Holland, as the codfish (in winter), haddock, plaice, flounders, herring, sole, and many more kinds of which I cannot give the names. There is a species of fish which by our people is called the *twelve* [striped bass], and which has scales like a salmon, and on each side six black streaks, which I suppose is the reason they call it twelve. It is the size of a codfish, very delicate, and good-tasted for eating; the head is the best, as it is full of brains like a lamb's head. The fish comes from the sea into the river in the spring, about the last of March and April, and continues until the last of May. It is caught in large quantities and dried by the Indians,—for at this time the squaws are engaged in sowing their maize, and cultivating the land, and the men go a-fishing in order to assist their wives a little by their draughts of fish. Sometimes they catch them with seines from seventy to eighty fathoms in length, which they braid themselves, and on which, in place of lead, they hang stones, and instead of the corks which we put on them to float them, they fasten small sticks of an ell in length, round and sharp at the end. Over the purse, they have a figure made of wood, resembling the devil, and when the fish swim into the net and come to the purse, so that the figure begins to move, they then begin to cry out and call upon the *mannetoe*, that is, the devil, to give them many fish. They catch great quantities of this fish; which they also catch in little set-nets, six or seven fathoms long, braided like a herring-net. They set them on sticks into the river, one, and one and a half fathoms deep. There is also another kind of fish on the seacoast, which is called *thirteen* [drumfish] by us, because it is larger than the twelve. The scales of the thirteen are yellow like those of the carp, to which it is not unlike in shape. It is of the size of a codfish. Herring also come into the river. There is a species of fish caught on the shore, called by us stone-bream, and by the English *schip-heet*, that is to say, *sheep's-head*, for the reason that its mouth is full of teeth, above and below, like a sheep's head. Sturgeon are numerous in the brackish water, and as high up in the fresh water as Fort Orange. There are many kinds of fish which we have not in our Fatherland, so that I cannot name them all. In the fresh waters, are pike, perch, roach, and trout. There are fine oysters, large and small, in great abundance. In the summer-time crabs come on the flat shores, very good tasted. Their claws are of the colour of the flag of our Prince of Orange, white and blue, so that the crabs show sufficiently that we ought, and that it belongs to us, to people the country.

Most of the visitors to New Netherlands came via the sea from Europe or the West Indies. Isaac Jogues, a scholarly French Jesuit priest, walked overland from Canada. In August 1642 he was captured by the Iroquois while canoeing up the St. Lawrence River to minister to the Hurons in Ontario. For the next year he was tortured and dragged from village to village before he escaped to the Dutch and made his way back to France and soon to Canada. His description of "New Belgium" in 1643 is taken from the translation by John Gilmary Shea in the Collections of the New York Historical Society, *2nd series, vol. 3 (1857), pp. 215-219.*

New Holland, which the Dutch call in Latin *Novum Belgium*—in their own language, *Nieuw Netherland*, that is to say, New Low Countries—is situated between Virginia and New England. The mouth of the river, which some people call Nassau, or the Great North River, to distinguish it from another which they call the South River, and from some maps that I have recently seen I think Maurice River, is at 40 deg. 30 min. The channel is deep, fit for the largest ships, which ascend to Manhatte's Island, which is seven leagues in circuit, and on which there is a fort to serve as the commencement of a town to be built here, and to be called New Amsterdam.

The fort, which is at the point of the island, about five or six leagues from the mouth, is called Fort Amsterdam; it has four regular bastions mounted, with several pieces of artillery. All these bastions and the curtains were, in 1643, but mounds, most of which had crumbled away, so that they entered the fort on all sides. There were no ditches. For the garrison of the said fort, and another which they had built still further up against the incursions of the savages, their enemies, there were sixty soldiers. They were beginning to face the gates and bastions with stone. Within the fort there was a pretty large stone church, the house of the Governor, whom they call Director General, quite neatly built of brick, the storehouses and barracks.

On the Island of Manhatte, and in its environs, there may well be four or five hundred men of different sects and nations: the Director General told me that there were men of eighteen different languages; they are scattered here and there on the river, above and below, as the beauty and convenience of the spot invited each to settle: some, mechanics, however, who ply their trade, are ranged under the fort; all the others were exposed to the incursions of the natives, who, in the year 1643, while I was there, actually killed some two score Hollanders, and burnt many houses and barns full of wheat.

The river, which is very straight, and runs due north and south, is at least a league broad before the fort. Ships lie at anchor in a bay which forms the other side of the island, and can be defended from the fort.

Shortly before I arrived there, three large ships of 300 tons each had come to load wheat; two found cargoes, the third could not be loaded, because the savages had burnt a part of their grain. These ships came from the West Indies, where the West India Company usually keeps up seventeen ships of war.

No religion is publicly exercised but the Calvinist, and orders are to admit none but Calvinists, but this is not observed; for there are in the Colony besides the Calvinists, Catholics, English Puritans, Lutherans, Anabaptists, here called Mnistes, &c., &c. When any one comes to settle in the country, they [the Company] lend him horses, cows, &c.; they give him provisions, all which he returns as soon as he is at ease; and as to the land, after ten years he pays to the West India Company the tenth of the produce which he reaps.

This country is bounded on the New England side by a river which they call the Fresche river, which serves as a boundary between them and the English. The English, however, come very near to them, choosing to hold lands under the Hollanders, who ask nothing, rather than depend on English Lords, who exact rents, and would fain be absolute. On the other side, southward, towards Virginia, its limits are the river which they call the South [Delaware] river, on which there is also a Dutch settlement, but the Swedes have one at its mouth extremely well supplied with cannons and men. It is believed that these Swedes are maintained by some Amsterdam merchants, who are not satisfied that the West India Company should alone enjoy all the commerce of these parts. It is near this river that a gold mine is reported to have been found. . . .

It is about forty years since the Hollanders came to these parts. The fort was begun in the year 1615; they began to settle about twenty years ago, and there is already some little commerce with Virginia and New England.

The first comers found lands fit for use, formerly cleared by the savages, who had fields here. Those who came later have cleared the woods, which are mostly oak. The soil is good. Deer hunting is abundant in the fall. There are some houses built of stone:—lime they make of oyster shells, great heaps of which are found here, made formerly by the savages, who subsist in part by that fishery.

The climate is very mild. Lying at 40-2/3° there are many European fruits, as apples, pears, cherries. I reached there in October, and found even then a considerable quantity of peaches.

Ascending the river to the 43d degree, you meet the second Dutch settlement, which the tide reaches but does not pass. Ships of a hundred and a hundred and twenty tons can come up to it.

There are two things in this settlement (which is called Renselaers-wick, as if to say, settlement of Renselaers, who is a rich Amsterdam merchant)—1st, a miserable little fort called Fort Orange, built of logs, with four or five pieces of Breteuil cannon, and as many swivels. This has been reserved, and is maintained by the West India Company. This fort was formerly on an island in the river; it is now on the mainland, towards the Hiroquois, a little above the said island. 2d, a colony sent here by this Renselaers, who is the patron.—This colony is composed of about a hundred persons, who reside in some twenty-five or thirty houses built along the river, as each found most convenient. In the principal house lives the patron's agent; the Minister has his apart, in which service is performed. There is also a kind of Bailiff here, whom they call the Seneschal, who administers justice. Their houses are merely of boards and thatched, with no mason work except the chimneys. The forest furnishing many large pines, they make boards by means of their mills, which they have here for the purpose.

They found some pieces of ground all ready, which the savages had formerly cleared, and in which they sow wheat and oats for beer, and for their horses, of which they have great numbers. There is little land fit for tillage, being hemmed in by hills, which are poor soil. This obliges them to separate, and they already occupy two or three leagues of country.

Trade is free to all; this gives the Indians all things cheap, each of the Hollanders outbidding his neighbor, and being satisfied provided he can gain some little profit.

This settlement is not more than twenty leagues from the Agniehronons [Mohawks], who can be reached by land or water, as the river on which the Iroquois lie, falls into that which passes by the Dutch, but there are many low rapids, and a fall of a short half league, where the canoe must be carried.

There are many [Indian] nations between the two Dutch settlements, which are about thirty German leagues apart, that is, about fifty or sixty French leagues. The Loups [Mohegans], whom the Iroquois call Agotsagenens, are the nearest to Renselaerswick and Fort Orange. War breaking out some years ago between the Iroquois and the Loups, the Dutch joined the latter against the former; but four men having been taken and burnt, they made peace. Since then some nations near the sea have killed some Hollanders of the most distant settlement; the Hollanders killed one hundred and fifty Indians, men, women and children. They having then, at intervals, killed forty Hollanders, burnt many houses, and committed ravages, estimated at the time that I was there at 200,000 liv. (two hundred thousand livres,) they raised troops in New England. Accordingly, in the beginning of winter, the grass being trampled down and some snow on the ground, they gave them chase with six hundred men, keeping two hundred always on the move and constantly relieving one another; so that the Indians, shut up in a large island, and unable to flee easily, on account of their women and children, were cut to pieces to the number of sixteen hundred, including women and children. This obliged the rest of the Indians to make peace, which still continues. This occurred in 1643 and 1644.

When Jaspar Dankers and Peter Sluyter came to America in 1679, they naturally focused their search for a religious haven on New Netherlands. The following descriptions of their tours around Long Island, Manhattan, and Staten Island is taken from Memoirs of the Long Island Historical Society, *vol. 1 (1867), pp. 118-127, 135-137, 140-148.*

[29 Sept. 1679]: As soon as we had dined we sent off our letters; and this being all accomplished, we started at two o'clock for Long Island. This island is called Long Island, not so much because it is longer than it is broad, but particularly because it is the longest island in this region, or even along the whole coast of New Netherland, Virginia and New England. It is one hundred and forty-four miles in length, and from twenty-four to twenty-eight miles wide, though there are several bays and points along it, and, consequently, it is much broader in some places than others. On the west is Staten island, from which it is separated about a mile, and the great bay over which you see the *Nevesincke*. With Staten island it makes the passage through which all vessels pass in sailing from or to the *Mahatans*, although they can go through the *Kil van Kol*, which is on the other side of Staten island. The ends of these islands opposite each other are quite high land, and they are, therefore, called the *Hoofden* (Headlands), from a comparison with the Hoofden of the channel between England and France, in Europe. On the north is the island of *Mahatans* and a part of the mainland. On the east is the sea, which shoots up to New England, and in which there are various islands. On the south is the great ocean. The outer shore of this island has before it several small islands and broken land, such as Coney island, a low sandy island of about three hours' circuit, its westerly point forming with Sandy Hook, on the other side, the entrance from the sea. It is oblong in shape, and is grown over with bushes. Nobody lives upon it, but it is used in winter for keeping cattle, horses, oxen, hogs and others, which are able to obtain there sufficient to eat the whole winter, and to shelter themselves from the cold in the thickets. This island is not so cold as Long Island or the *Mahatans*, or others, like some other islands on the coast, in consequence of their having more sea breeze, and of the saltness of the sea breaking upon the shoals, rocks and reefs, with which the coast is beset. There is also the Bear's island and others, separated from Long Island by creeks and marshes over-flown at high water. There are also on this sea coast various miry places, like the Vlaeck, and others, as well as some sand bays and hard and rocky shores. Long Island stretches into the sea for the most part east by south and east southeast. None of its land is very high, for you must be nearly opposite Sandy Hook before you can see it. There is a hill or ridge running lengthwise through the island, nearest the north side and west end of the island. The south side and east end are more flat. The water by which it is separated from the *Mahatans*, is improperly called the East river, for it is nothing else than an arm of the sea, beginning in the bay on the west and ending in the sea on the east. After forming in this passage several islands, this water is as broad before the city as the Y before Amsterdam, but the ebb and flood tides are stronger. There is a ferry for the purpose of crossing over it, which is farmed out by the year, and yields a good income, as it is a considerable thoroughfare, this island being one of the most populous places in this vicinity. A considerable number of Indians live upon it, who gain their subsistence by hunting

A View From Abroad in the 17th Century   147

and fishing, and they, as well as others, must carry their articles to market over this ferry, or boat them over, as it is free to every one to use his own boat, if he have one, or to borrow or hire one for the purpose. The fare over the ferry is three stuivers [three cents] in zeewan [wampum] for each person.

Here we three crossed over, my comrade, Gerrit, our guide, and myself, in a row-boat, as it happened, which, in good weather and tide, carries a sail. When we came over we found there Jan Teunissen, our fellow passenger, who had promised us so much good. He was going over to the city, to deliver his letters and transact other business. He told us he would return home in the evening, and we would find him there. We went on, up the hill, along open roads and a little woods, through the first village, called Breukelen [Brooklyn], which has a small and ugly little church standing in the middle of the road. Having passed through here, we struck off to the right, in order to go to *Gouanes*. We went upon several plantations where Gerrit was acquainted with most all of the people, who made us very welcome, sharing with us bountifully whatever they had, whether it was milk, cider, fruit or tobacco, and especially, and first and most of all, miserable rum or brandy which had been brought from Barbadoes and other islands, and which is called by the Dutch *kill-devil*. All these people are very fond of it, and most of them extravagantly so, although it is very dear and has a bad taste. It is impossible to tell how many peach trees we passed, all laden with fruit to breaking down, and many of them actually broken down. We came to a place surrounded with such trees from which so many had fallen off that the ground could not be discerned, and you could not put your foot down without trampling them; and, notwithstanding such large quantities had fallen off, the trees still were as full as they could bear. The hogs and other animals mostly feed on them. This place belongs to the oldest European woman in the country. We went immediately into her house, where she lived with her children. We found her sitting by the fire, smoking tobacco incessantly, one pipe after another. We enquired after her age, which the children told us was an hundred years. She was from Luyck (Liege), and still spoke good Waalsche (old French), with us. She could reason very well sometimes, and at other times she could not. She showed us several large apples, as good fruit of that country, and different from that of Europe. She had been about fifty years now in the country, and had above seventy children and grand-children. She saw the third generation after her. Her mother had attended women in child-bed in her one hundred and sixth year, and was one hundred and eleven or twelve years old when she died. We tasted here, for the first time, smoked *twaelft* (twelfth) [striped bass], a fish so called because it is caught in season next after the *elft* (eleventh) [shad]. It was salted a little and then smoked, and, although it was now a year old, it was still perfectly good, and in flavor not inferior to smoked salmon. We drank here, also, the first new cider, which was very fine.

We proceeded on to *Gouanes*, a place so called, where we arrived in the evening at one of the best friends of Gerrit, named Symon [Simon Aertsen De Hart]. He was very glad to see us, and so was his wife. He took us into the house, and entertained us exceedingly well. We found a good fire, half-way up the chimney, of clear oak and hickory, of which they made not the least scruple of burning profusely. We let it penetrate us thoroughly. There had been already thrown upon it, to be roasted, a pail-full of *Gouanes* oysters, which are the best in the country. They are fully as good as those of England, and better than those we eat at Falmouth. I had to try some of them raw. They are large and full, some of them not less than a foot long, and they grow sometimes ten, twelve and sixteen together, and are then like a piece of rock. Others are young and small. In consequence of the great quantities of them, everybody keeps the shells for the purpose of burning them into lime. They pickle the oysters in small casks, and send them to Barbadoes and the other islands. We had for supper a roasted haunch of venison, which he had bought of the Indians for three guilders and a half of *seewant* [wampum], that is, fifteen stuivers of Dutch money (fifteen cents), and which weighed thirty pounds. The meat was exceedingly tender and good, and also quite fat. It had a slight spicy flavor. We were also served with wild turkey, which was also fat and of a good flavor; and a wild goose, but that was rather dry. Every thing we had was the natural production of the country. We saw here, lying in a heap, a whole hill of watermelons, which were as large as pumpkins, and which Symon was going to take to the city to sell. They were very good, though there is a difference between them and those of the Caribly islands; but this may be owing to its being late in the season, and these were the last pulling. It was very late at night when we went to rest in

a Kermis bed, as it is called, in the corner of the hearth, along side
of a good fire.

[30 Sept. 1679]: Early this morning the husband and wife set off
for the city with their marketing; and we, having explored the land
in the vicinity, left after breakfast. We went a part of the way through
a woods and fine, new made land, and so along the shore to the west
end of the island called *Najack* [Fort Hamilton]. As we proceeded
along the shore, we found, among other curiosities, a highly marbled
stone, very hard, in which we saw Muscovy glass lying in layers
between the clefts, and how it was struck or cut out. We broke off
a small piece with some difficulty, and picked out a little glass in
the splits. Continuing onward from there, we came to the plantation
of the *Najack* Indians, which was planted with maize, or Turkish
wheat. We soon heard a noise of pounding, like thrashing, and went
to the place whence it proceeded, and found there an old Indian
woman busily employed beating Turkish beans out of the pods by
means of a stick, which she did with astonishing force and dexterity.
Gerrit inquired of her, in the Indian language, which he spoke perfectly well, how old she was, and she answered eighty years; at which
we were still more astonished that so old a woman should still have
so much strength and courage to work as she did. We went from
thence to her habitation, where we found the whole troop together,
consisting of seven or eight families, and twenty or twenty-two persons, I should think. Their house was low and long, about sixty feet
long and fourteen or fifteen feet wide. The bottom was earth, the sides
and roof were made of reed and the bark of chestnut trees; the posts,
or columns, were limbs of trees stuck in the ground, and all fastened
together. The top, or ridge of the roof was open about half a foot
wide, from one end to the other, in order to let the smoke escape,
in place of a chimney. On the sides, or walls, of the house, the roof
was so low that you could hardly stand under it. The entrances, or
doors, which were at both ends, were so small and low that they had
to stoop down and squeeze themselves to get through them. The doors
were made of reed or flat bark. In the whole building there was no
lime, stone, iron or lead. They build their fire in the middle of the
floor, according to the number of families which live in it, so that
from one end to the other each of them boils its own pot, and eats
when it likes, not only the families by themselves, but each Indian

alone, according as he is hungry, at all hours, morning, noon and night. By each fire are the cooking utensils, consisting of a pot, a bowl, or calabash, and a spoon also made of a calabash. These are all that relate to cooking. They lie upon mats with their feet towards the fire, on each side of it. They do not sit much upon any thing raised up, but, for the most part, sit on the ground or squat on their ankles. Their other household articles consists of a calabash of water, out of which they drink, a small basket in which to carry and keep their maize and small beans, and a knife. The implements are, for tillage, a small, sharp stone, and nothing more; for hunting, a gun and pouch for powder and lead; for fishing, a canoe without mast or sail, and without a nail in any part of it, though it is sometimes full forty feet in length, fish hooks and lines and scoops to paddle with in place of oars. I do not know whether there are not some others of a trifling nature. All who live in one house are generally of one stock or descent, as father and mother with their offspring. Their bread is maize, pounded in a block by a stone, but not fine. This is mixed with water, and made into a cake, which they bake under the hot ashes. They gave us a small piece when we entered, and although the grains were not ripe, and it was half baked and coarse grains, we nevertheless had to eat it, or, at least, not throw it away before them, which they would have regarded as a great sin, or a great affront. We chewed a little of it *with long teeth*, and managed to hide it so they did not see it. We had also to drink out of their calabashes the water which was their drink, and which was very good. We saw here the Indians who came on board the ship when we arrived. They were all very joyful at the visit of our Gerrit, who was an old acquaintance of theirs, and had heretofore long resided about there. We presented them with two jewsharpes, which much pleased them, and they immediately commenced to play upon them, which they could do tolerably well. Some of their *patroons* (chiefs), some of whom spoke good Dutch, and are also their medicine-men and surgeons as well as their teachers, were busy making shoes of deer leather, which they understand how to make soft by continually working it in their hands. They had dogs, fowls and hogs, which they learn by degrees from the Europeans how to manage better. They had, also, peach trees, which were well laden. Towards the last, we asked them for some peaches, and they answered: "Go and pick them," which showed their politeness. However, in order not to offend them, we went off and pulled some. Although they are such a poor, miserable people, they are, nevertheless, licentious and proud, and given to knavery and scoffing. Seeing a very old woman among them, we inquired how old she was, when some young fellows, laughing and jeering, answered twenty years, while it was evident to us she was not less than an hundred. We observed here the manner in which they travel with their children, a woman having one which she carried on her back. The little thing clung tight around her neck like a cat, where it was kept secure by means of a piece of daffels, their usual garment. Its head, back and buttocks were entirely flat. . . .

These Indians live on the land of Jaques (Cortelyou), brother-in-law of Gerrit. He bought the land from them in the first instance, and then let them have a small corner, for which they pay him twenty bushels of maize yearly, that is, ten bags. Jaques had first bought the whole of *Najack* from these Indians, who were the lords thereof, and lived upon the land, which is a large place, and afterwards bought it *again*, in parcels. He was unwilling to drive the Indians from the land, and has therefore left them a corner of it, keeping the best of it himself. We arrived then upon this land, which is all good, and yields large crops of wheat and other grain. It is of a blackish color, but not clayey, and almost like the garden mould I have seen in Holland. . . .

[6 Oct. 1679]: We remained in the house during the forenoon, but after having dined we went out about two o'clock to explore the island of *Manathans*. This island runs east and west, or somewhat more northerly. On the north side of it is the North river, by which it is separated from the main land on the north; on the east end it is separated from the main land by a creek, or rather a branch of the North river, emptying itself into the East river. They can go over this creek at dead low water, upon rocks and reefs, at the place called *Spyt den duyvel*. This creek coming into the East river forms with it the two *Barents islands*. At the west end of these two running waters, that is, where they come together to the east of these islands, they make, with the rocks and reefs, such a frightful eddy and whirl-pool that it is exceedingly dangerous to pass through them, especially with small boats, of which there are some lost every now and then, and the persons in them drowned; but experience has taught men the way of passing through them with less danger. Large vessels have always less danger because they are not capable of being carried along so quickly. There are two places where such whirling of the stream occurs, which are on account of the danger and frightfulness called the Great and Little Hellgate. After these two streams are united, the island of *Manathans* is separated on the south from Long Island by the East river, which, beginning at the bay before New York, runs eastwardly, after forming several islands, again into the sea. This island is about seven hours' distance in length, but it is not a full hour broad. The sides are indented with bays, coves and creeks. It is almost entirely taken up, that is, the land is held by private owners, but not half of it is cultivated. Much of it is good wood land. The west end on which the city lies, is entirely cleared for more than an hour's distance, though that is the poorest ground; the best being on the east and north side. There are many brooks of fresh water running through it, pleasant and proper for man and beast to drink, as well as agreeable to behold, affording cool and pleasant resting places, but especially suitable places for the construction of mills, for although there is no overflow of water, yet it can be shut off and so used. A little eastward of *Nieu Haerlem* [New Harlem] there are two ridges of very high rocks, with a considerable space between them, display-ing themselves very majestically, and inviting all men to acknowledge in them the majesty, grandeur, power and glory of their creator, who has impressed such marks upon them. Between them runs the road to *Spyt den duyvel*. The one to the north is most apparent; the south ridge is covered with earth on its north side, but it can be seen from the water or from the main land beyond to the south. The soil between these ridges is very good, though a little hilly and stony, and would be very suitable in my opinion for planting vineyards, in consequence of its being shut off on both sides from the winds which would most injure them, and is very warm. We found blue grapes along the road which were very good and sweet, and as good as any I have tasted in the Fatherland.

We went from the city, following the Broadway, over the *valey*, or the fresh water. Upon both sides of this way were many habitations of negroes, mulattoes and whites. These negroes were formerly the proper slaves of the (West India) company, but, in consequence of the frequent changes and conquests of the country, they have obtained their freedom and settled themselves down where they have thought proper, and thus on this road, where they have ground enough to live on with their families. We left the village, called the *Bouwerij* [Bowery], lying on the right hand, and went through the woods to New Harlem, a tolerably large village situated on the south side of the island, directly opposite the place where the northeast creek and the East river come together, situated about three hours journey from New Amsterdam, like as old Harlem, in Europe, is situated about three hours distance from old Amsterdam. As our guide, Gerrit, had some business here, and found many acquaintances, we remained over night at the house of one *Geresolveert*, scout (sheriff or constable), of the place, who had formerly lived in Brazil, and whose heart was still full of it. This house was constantly filled with people, all the time drinking, for the most part, that execrable rum. He had also the best cider we have tasted.

[10 Oct. 1679]: Finding no opportunity of going to Staten island, we asked our old friend Symon, who had come over from *Gouanes*, what was the best way for us to get there, when he offered us his services to take us over in his skiff, which we accepted; and at dusk accompanied him in his boat to *Gouanes*, where we arrived about eight o'clock, and where he welcomed us and entertained us well.

[11 Oct. 1679]: We embarked early this morning in his boat and rowed over to Staten island, where we arrived about eight o'clock. He left us there, and we went on our way. This island is about thirty-two miles long and four broad. Its sides are very irregular, with projecting points and indented bays, and creeks running deep into the country. It lies for the most part east and west, and is somewhat triangular. The most prominent point is to the west. On the east side is the narrow passage which they call the channel, by which it is separated from the high point of Long Island. On the south is the great bay which is inclosed by *Nayaq, t' Conijnen* island, *Rentselaer's* Hook, *Nevesinck*, &c. On the west is the *Raritans*. On the north or northwest is New Jersey, from which it is separated by a large creek or arm of the river, called *Kil van kol*. The eastern part is high and steep, and has few inhabitants. It is the usual place where ships, ready for sea, stop to take in water, while the captain and passengers are engaged in making their own arrangements and writing letters previous to their departure. The whole south side is a large plain, with much salt meadow or marsh, and several creeks. The west point is flat, and on or around it is a large creek with much marsh; but to the north of this creek it is high and hilly, and beyond that it begins to be more level, but not so low as on the other side, and is well populated. On the northwest it is well provided with creeks and marshes, and the land is generally better than on the south side, although there is a good parcel of land in the middle of the latter. As regards the middle or most hilly part of the island, it is uninhabited, although the soil is better than the land around it; but, in consequence of its being away from the water, and lying so high, no one will live there, the creeks and rivers being so serviceable to them in enabling them to go to the city, and for fishing and catching oysters, and for being near the salt meadows. The woods are used for pasturing horses and cattle, for being an island, none of them can get off. Each person has marks upon his own by which he can find them when he wants them. When the population of the country shall increase, these places will be taken up. Game of all kinds is plenty, and twenty-five and thirty deer are sometimes seen in a herd. A boy who came in a house where we were, told us he had shot ten the last winter himself, and more than forty in his life, and in the same manner other game. We tasted here the best grapes. There are now about a hundred families on the island, of which the English constitute the least portion, and the Dutch and French divide between them about equally the greater portion. They have neither church nor minister, and live rather far from each other, and inconveniently to meet together. The English are less disposed to religion, and inquire little after it, but in case there were a minister, would contribute to his support. The French and Dutch are very desirous and eager for one, for they spoke of it wherever we went, and said, in the event of not obtaining Domine Tessemaker, they would send, or had sent, to France for another. The French are good Reformed churchmen, and some of them are Walloons. The Dutch are also from different quarters.

We reached the island, as I have said, about nine o'clock, directly opposite *Gouanes*, not far from the watering place. We proceeded southwardly along the shore of the high land on the east end, where it was sometimes stony and rocky, and sometimes sandy, supplied with fine constantly-flowing springs with which at times we quenched our thirst. We had now come nearly to the furthest point on the southeast, behind which I had observed several houses when we came in with the ship. We had also made inquiry as to the villages through which we would have to pass, and they had told us the *Oude Dorp*

would be the first one we would come to; but my comrade finding
the point very rocky and difficult, and believing the village was
inland, and as we discovered no path to follow, we determined to
clamber to the top of this steep bluff, through the bushes and thickets,
which we accomplished with great difficulty and in a perspiration.
We found as little of a road above as below, and nothing but woods,
through which one could not see. There appeared to be a little footpath along the edge which I followed a short distance to the side of
the point, but my comrade calling me and saying that he certainly
thought we had passed by the road to the *Oude Dorp*, and observing
myself that the little path led down to the point, I returned again,
and we followed it the other way, which led us back to the place
from where we started. We supposed we ought to go from the shore
in order to find the road to the *Oude Dorp*, and seeing here these
slight tracks into the woods, we followed them as far as we could,
till at last they ran to nothing else than dry leaves. Having wandered
an hour or more in the woods, now in a hollow and then over a hill,
at one time through a swamp, at another across a brook, without finding any road or path, we entirely lost the way. We could see nothing
except a little of the sky through the thick branches of the trees above
our heads, and we thought it best to break out of the woods entirely
and regain the shore. I had taken an observation of the shore and
point, having been able to look at the sun, which shone extraordinarily
hot in the thick woods, without the least breath of air stirring. We
made our way at last as well as we could out of the woods, and struck
the shore a quarter of an hour's distance from where we began to
climb up. We were rejoiced, as there was a house not far from the
place where we came out. We went to it to see if we could find any
one who would show us the way a little. There was no master in
it, but an Englishwoman with negroes and servants. We first asked
her as to the road, and then for something to drink, and also for some
one to show us the road; but she refused the last, although we were
willing to pay for it. She was a cross woman. She said she had never
been in the village, and her folks must work, and we would certainly
have to go away as wise as we came. She said, however, we must
follow the shore, as we did. We went now over the rocky point, which
we were no sooner over than we saw a pretty little sand bay, and
a small creek, and not far from there, cattle and houses. We also

saw the point to which the little path led from the hill above, where
I was when my comrade called me. We would not have had more
than three hundred steps to go to have been where we now were.
It was very hot, and we perspired a great deal. We went on to the
little creek to sit down and rest ourselves there, and to cool our feet,
and then proceeded to the houses which constituted the *Oude Dorp*.
It was now about two o'clock. There were seven houses, but only
three in which any body lived. The others were abandoned, and their
owners had gone to live on better places on the island, because the
ground around this village was worn out and barren, and also too
limited for their use. We went into the first house which was inhabited
by English, and there rested ourselves and eat, and inquired further
after the road. The woman was cross, and her husband not much better. We had to pay here for what we eat which we had not done
before. We paid three guilders in zeewan, although we only drank
water. We proceeded by a tolerably good road to the *Nieuwe Dorp*,
but as the road ran continually in the woods, we got astray again
in them. It was dark, and we were compelled to break our way out
through the woods and thickets, and we went a great distance before
we succeeded, when it was almost entirely dark. We saw a house
at a distance to which we directed ourselves across the bushes. It was
the first house of the *Nieuwe Dorp*. We found there an Englishman
who could speak Dutch, and who received us very cordially into his
house, where we had as good as he and his wife had. She was a
Dutch woman from the *Manhatans*, who was glad to have us in her
house.

[12 Oct. 1679]: Although we had not slept well, we had to resume
our journey with the day. The man where we slept set us on the road.
We had now no more villages to go to, but went from one plantation
to another, for the most part belonging to French, who showed us
every kindness because we conversed with them in French, and spoke
of the ways of the Lord according to their condition. About one-third
part of the distance from the south side of the west end is still all
woods, and is very little visited. We had to go along the shore, finding
sometimes fine creeks well provided with wild turkeys, geese, snipes
and wood hens. Lying rotting upon the shore were thousands of fish
called *marsbancken*, which are about the size of a common carp.
These fish swim close together in large schools, and are pursued so

by other fish that they are forced upon the shore in order to avoid the mouths of their enemies, and when the water falls they are left there to die, food for the eagles and other birds of prey. Proceeding thus along we came to the West point where an Englishman lived alone some distance from the road. We eat something here, and he gave us the consolation that we would have a very bad road for two or three hours ahead, which indeed we experienced, for there was neither path nor road. He showed us as well as he could. There was a large creek to cross which ran very far into the land, and when we should get on the other side of it, we must, he said, go outward again along (the shore). After we had gone a piece of the way through the woods, we came to a valley with a brook running through it, which we took to be the creek or the end of it. We turned round it as short as we could, in order to go back again to the shore, which we reached after wandering a long time over hill and dale, when we saw the creek, which we supposed we had crossed, now just before us. We followed the side of it deep into the woods, and when we arrived at the end of it saw no path along the other side to get outwards again, but the road ran into the woods in order to cut off a point of the hills and land. We pursued this road for some time, but saw no mode of getting out, and that it led further and further from the creek. We, therefore, left the road and went across through the bushes, so as to reach the shore by the nearest route according to our calculation. After continuing this course about an hour, we saw at a distance a miserably constructed tabernacle of pieces of wood covered with brush, all open in front, and where we thought there were Indians; but on coming up to it we found in it an Englishman sick, and his wife and child lying upon some bushes by a little fire. We asked him if he were sick. "Do you ask me whether I am sick? I have been sick here over two months," he replied. It made my heart sore indeed, for I had never in all my life seen such poverty, and that, too, in the middle of a woods and a wilderness. After we obtained some information as to the way, we went on, and had not gone far before we came to another house, and thus from one farm to another, French, Dutch and a few English, so that we had not wandered very far out of the way. We inquired at each house the way to the next one. Shortly before evening we arrived at the plantation of a Frenchman, whom they called *Le Chaudronnier* (the coppersmith), who was formerly a soldier under the Prince of Orange, and had served in Brazil. He was so delighted, and held on to us so hard, that we remained and spent the night with him.

[13 Oct. 1679]: We pursued our journey this morning from plantation to plantation, the same as yesterday, until we came to that of *Pierre le Gardinier*, who had been a gardener of the Prince of Orange, and had known him well. He had a large family of children and grandchildren. He was about seventy years of age, and was still as fresh and active as a young person. He was so glad to see strangers who conversed with him and his in the French language about the good, that he leaped for joy. After we had breakfasted here they told us that we had another large creek to pass called the Fresh kil, and there we could perhaps be set across the *Kil van Kol* to the point of Mill creek, where we might wait for a boat to convey us to the *Manhatans*. The road was long and difficult, and we asked for a guide, but he had no one, in consequence of several of his children being sick. At last he determined to go himself, and accordingly carried us in his canoe over to the point of Mill creek in New Jersey behind Kol (*achter Kol*). We learned immediately that there was a boat up this creek loading with brick, and would leave that night for the city. After we had thanked and parted with Pierre le Gardinier, we determined to walk to Elizabethtown, a good half hour's distance inland, where the boat was. From the point to this village there is a fine wagon road, but nowhere in the country had we been so pestered with mosquitos (*muggen*) as we were on this road. The land about here is very poor, and is not well peopled. We found the boat, and spoke to the captain who left about two hours afterwards; but as the wind was against going out of the creek, he lay by and waited for the tide. We returned by evening to the point where we were to stay until morning. There was a tavern on it, kept by French papists, who at once took us to be priests, and so conducted themselves towards us in every respect accordingly, although we told them and protested otherwise. As there was nothing to be said further we remained so in their imaginations to the last, as shown both in their words and actions, the more certainly because we spoke French, and they were French people. We slept there this night, and at three o'clock in the morning we set sail.

[14 Oct. 1679]: Being under sail, as I have said, it was so entirely calm that we could only float with the stream until we came to the *Schutters* island, where we obtained the tide again. It was now about four o'clock. In order to protect ourselves from the air which was very cold and piercing, we crept under the sail which was very old and full of holes. The tide having run out by daylight, we came under sail again, with a good wind which brought us to the city at about eight o'clock, for which we were glad, and returning thanks to God, betook ourselves to rest.

V. THE HEARTLAND: NEW SWEDEN AND PENNSYLVANIA

When William Penn received title to the huge domain of Pennsylvania from King Charles II in settlement of a £16,000 debt that Penn's father held against the crown, he acquired a region rich in resources and favored by geography. Consequently, it was also a region with a history that reached back into the 17th century. What kinds of problems did the early explorers of the region face? Did the Swedes treat the Indians better than the English and Dutch treated them? How was land acquired from the Indians for settlement? Did the Indians realize that they were alienating the ownership and use of the land permanently? Was the pattern of Swedish settlement different from that of their Dutch neighbors? How were they supplied in the early years? In what ways did they adapt themselves to their new situation? Did the Indians and the Swedes understand each other's religion? Were the Indians politically astute in their dealings with the white men? Was overpopulation a problem for the early settlers of Pennsylvania? Why would an English worker benefit from moving to Pennsylvania? What difficulties would he encounter? Why did Pennsylvania's population grow so rapidly?

In the 17th century the principal route into the lands that became Pennsylvania in 1681 was the Delaware River. But at least one sailor thought it was the Northwest Passage to the Pacific Ocean and the treasures of the Orient. In July 1634 Captain Thomas Yong, a 54-year-old English gentleman, sailed from a temporary stop at Jamestown in Virginia up the Delaware to explore the unknown and secure the glory of discovering the illusive Passage. In October he sent to King Charles—for whom he renamed the river the Charles—the following report of his cruise. It is taken from the Collections of the Massachusetts Historical Society, *4th series, vol. 9 (1871), pp. 117-131; the original manuscript is in the Virginia State Library at Richmond.*

A breife Relation of a voyage lately made by me Captayne Thomas Yong, since my departure from Virginia, upon a discovery, which I humbly present to the Right Hoble Sir Francis Windebanke, knight, Principall Secretary of State to his Matie.

The particulars of all occurrents, that happened unto mee, from my departure out of England till my arrivall in Virginia; and likewise, what passed while I was there; I sent in a Relation to Sr Tobie Matthew, entreating him to present it to yor Honor; wch I presume, is already come to yor handes; And therefore I omitt to trouble yor honor, wth a second repetition thereof, and now only intend humbly to give yor honor account of such thinges, as since that time have passed in my voyage.

As soon as I had stopped the leakes of my ship, and finished [building] my shallopp, I sett sayle from Virginia, the 20th of July, coasting along the Coast from Virginia to the Northward, faire by the shoare, and the 24th of the same month, I made that great [Delaware] Bay, wherein I purposed at my departure from England, to make triall for the Passage. I came to an Anchor that night in the mouth of the Bay and the next morning, I entered the same. This Bay is in the mouth thereof 6 leagues broad, and hath in the entrance thereof 12 fathome water. When I was gott into the Bay, I came to an anchor, and sent my Leiuitennant in my shallop ashore, on the Southwest part of the Bay, to see if he could speake with any of the Natives, and to learne what he could of them, concerning this Bay, and the course thereof, who after he had spent most part of the day in searching up and downe, for the Natives, returned towards night, without speaking wth any of them. The next morning, being the 26, I sayled some tenne leagues higher up into the Bay, and then came to an Anchor, and agayne sent out my shallopp, to see if I could meet wth any of those natives; but they returned as they did the day before, without speaking with any of them. The 27 in the morning I weighed to proceed yet further into the Bay and after I had passed some 7 leagues up the Bay, my shallop being then on head of me, espied certayne Indians on the West side of the Bay, to whome they made presently, but the Indians made away from them, as soon as they came neere the shoare; soe I sayled along in the middest of the Bay, and they coasted along by the shoare, till about two in the afternoone; and then there came an Indian running along the shoare, and called to my shallop; The shallop presently made towards him, who stayed till theire arrivall, but would not come aboard, wherefore they landed, and went to him, to whome presently also came three or foure more. At last they perswaded one of them to goe aboard my ship, and so they brought him to mee. I entertained him curteously, and gave him buiscuit to eat, and strong water to drinke, but the water he seemed not to rellish well. I also gave him some trifles, as knives and beades and a hatchett, of which he was wonderfull glad. Then I began to enquire of him, (by my Interpreter, who understood that language) how farr the sea ran, who answered me that not farre above that place I should meet with fresh water, and that the River ranne up very farre into the land, but that he had never bene at the head thereof. He told me further that the people of that River were at warre with a certaine Nation called the Minquaos [Susquehannocks], who had killed many of them, destroyed their corne, and burned their houses; insomuch as that the Inhabitants had wholy left that side of the River, which was next to their enimies, and had retired themselves on the other side farre up into the woods, the better to secure themselves from their enimies. He also told me that not long since there had bene a ship there, and described the people to me, and by his description, I found they were Hollanders, who had bene there trading for furrs; Towards night he desired to be sett on shoare, which accordingly I commanded to be done. The next day being the 28, there came aboard of my ship an Indian, with a Canoa with store of Eeles, whereof I bought some for a knife and a hatchett, and whilest I was discoursing with him concerning the River, for now I was entered into the mouth thereof, on a suddayne he fell into a great passion of feare and trembling; I wondered what the matter was, and comforted him, and bad him feare nothing, he then shewed me a Canoa, a good way of, making towards the ship, in which, he said, were some of the Minquaos and that they were enimies to him, and to his Nation, and had already killed many

of them, and that they would kill him also, if they saw him, and
therefore he desired me to hide him from them; I told him, I would
defend him, and that they should not hurt him, and that if they should
dare to offer him any violence, I then would kill them, he seemed
very glad to heare me say so, and gave me thankes, but yet was very
earnest to be hid from them, saying, that if they saw him, they would
watch for him ashore, and there murther him, then I caused him to
be putt into a cabbin, betweene deckes, where he could not be seene.
The Minquaos rowed directly to my ship, and as soone as they gott
neere her, they made signes for a Rope, which was cast out to them,
with which they made fast their Canoa, and presently came aboard
without any difficultie. Our Interpreter understood but only some few
words of their language, so as wee were forced for the most part to
gather their meaning by signes the best wee could. They told us, they
were Minquaos, and that one of them was a king, (for soe all the
Indians call them, who are most eminent among themselves, and they
are in nature of Captaynes or Governors of the rest, and have power
of life and death, of warre and peace, over their subjects, Some have
1000, some 500, some more, some lesse) and made signes to us, that
they were lately come from warre with the other Indians, whome they
had overcome, and slayne some of them, and cutt downe their corne,
(which is of the same kind with the corne of Virginia which they
commonly call Maiz). They brought a good quantitie of greene eares
thereof with them, and some they presented to mee, and others they
roasted and eate themselves. I used them curteously, and gave them
each of them a hatchett, a pipe, a knife, and a paire of sizers, for
which they were very thankfull to mee, and then desired to see my
trucke [Trade items], whereof I shewed them samples. The King
desired some of my cloath, but having nothing to give me in exchange
thereof, I gave him two small peices, one of redd and the other of
blew. They made signes to us, that about 10 dayes (as wee thought,
but wee were mistaken for they meent weekes, as wee perceaved afterwards), they would come to us agayne, and bring with them great
store of trucke of beavers and ottors, and therefore they desired to
know where wee would bee; soe I told them that about that time I
would send my shallop to meet them there, soe they departed, and
as soone as they were gone, I called for the Indian who all this time
lay hid in my cabbin, who stayed aboard of me till night, and then
departed a contrary way to that which the Minquaos went, promising

to be with me the next day. Some two days after I being then gotten some tenne leagues up the River there came to the shoare side 5 or 6 Indians, and haled us. I sent my boate for them; when they were arrived, they told me they came to see me from a king, who lived not farre of[f], and that if I pleased to morrow he would come and visitt mee. I answered them, he should be welcome, and so after they had stayed awhile, and refreshed themselves aboard my shippe, they departed. The next day wee expected him but he came not, soe wee departed up a little higher up the River, and on the second of August this king came aboard us about noone, accompanied with 40 or 60 Indians. After he had sate still awhile, which they are wont to doe upon the ground, he then told mee I was welcome into the Countrey, and that he came to see me with desire to make peace with me, in regard he understood by an Indian that I was a good man, and that I had preserved him from the Minquaos, who would otherwise have slayne him, and withall asked, if wee had any trucke. He also presented mee with two Otters skinnes, and some greene eares of corne, excusing himself that he had no better present for me, in regard the Minquaos had lately harrowed his countrey, and carried much beaver from him and his subjects, and that the rest they had trucked away to the Hollanders, who had lately bene there. I told him that I was sent thither by a great king in Europe, namely the king of England, and that I came thither to discover that Countrey and to make peace with them, if they desired to imbrace it and that if they would soe do, I would defend them from their enimies, he was very joyfull to hear this, and desired me to tarry two dayes there, for he would bring thither another king, who was his father in law, to make peace with mee, and another king also who was his neighbour, and the proprietor of that part of the River, wherein I then rode. I condiscended [agreed] with him to stay two dayes. In the meane time, I tooke possession of the countrey, for his Majestie, and there sett up his Majesties armes upon a tree, which was performed with solemnities usuall in that kind. I enquired of this king how farre this River ranne up into the Countrey, and whither it were navigable or no, he told me it ranne a great way up, and that I might goe with my shippe, till I came to a certaine place, where the rockes ranne cleane crosse the River [Trenton, N.J.], and that there he thought I could not goe over with my great Canoas, (for soe they call all vessells that swimme upon the water). I then desired him to lend me a pilott to goe up to that place, which he most willingly granted. I presented him with a Coate, a hatchett, and a knife, wherewith he was very well contented, and so after he had stayd some 4 or 5 houres he tooke his leave. About some 3 or foure dayes after, this king returned to me, and in company with him two other kings, whome I mentioned before, with whome I also made peace. Of the old king I enquired if he had ever bene at the head of the River, he answered me no, but that he had heard that the River ranne farre up into the land, and that some few dayes journey beyond the rockes of which I spake before there was a mountainous countrey where there were great store of Elkes and that before the warr with the Minquaos, they were wont to goe thither to hunt them, but he said that neither he himself nor any of his people had ever bene further then those mountaines. These kings prayed me that I would do them the curtesie to stay foure or five dayes with them, because they were certainly informed, that the Minquaos would within that time passe over the River to assault them, wherefore they desired me not to suffer them to passe over. I told them I would at their request stay five dayes, and that I would labour to procure them peace, and that if their enimies refused the same that then I would joyne with them against them, and I would lend them souldiers to goe to warre in company with them, and that I would also, if occasion were, invade the Minquaos within their owne countrey, upon this condition, that they shall renounce all trade or alliance with all other persons, save only his Majesties Ministers and subjects, and that they shall be wholy dependant on him, of which they were very joyfull and accepted the conditions and soe wee made a solemne peace, they not long after departed, and it was spread all over the River, that I had made peace with them, and that I was a just man, and would defend them against their enimies the Minquaos. Upon the report heer of some three dayes after, there came to me messengers with a present from two other kings, who lived in a lesser River [the Schuylkill], which falleth into this great River, somewhat neerer the rockes. They told me that their kings desired to make peace with me, according as the other kings their neighbours had done, and that they had some Beaver and Otter skinnes, which they would trucke with me for such commodities as I had. I sent them word that some three days after I would come up to the mouth of that River, where I would desire them to meet mee, and that I would entreat one of those messengers to stay with me, till I were ready to goe, whome I would send to them as soon as I was arrived, and one of them presently offered himself to stay with mee. When the five dayes were expired I sent to the former kings, to let them understand that now I had tarried five days expecting the Minquaos and that seeing they came not, I had sent my shallop to seeke them out, but it was returned without any notice of them, and therefore that I thought they were not in the River, wherefore now I would goe up higher into the River to meet with the other kings, whither if they had occasion they should send to mee, and I would send to assist them, desiring them withall to send me a pilot to carrie me to the Rockes. They sent me word they were sorry I was departing from them, neverthelesse they hoped I would shortly returne thither againe, and that if they had occasion they would send to mee, and moreover one of them sent me his Brother in company of my messenger, and commanded him to goe up along with me, and to attend mee, and remayne with me till my returne thither againe, which he did accordingly. As soone as my messengers were come backe, I sett forward and arrived at the mouth of the said River, and not long after I was come to an anchor, about 8 of the clocke in the evening, came the two kings aboard of mee, attended only with some foure or 5 of their principall men, for the rest of their company in regard it was night, I desired them to leave on shoare, till the morning. I entertained them aboard all night, and in the morning early being the 23 of August, the rest of their company came aboard. I gave each of them a present, as I had done to the other kings, which when they had receaved, first the ancient king, and afterward the yonger, called together all their people, and made to them a long oration to this purpose. That wee were a good people. That wee were just. That wee were ready to defend the oppressed from the crueltie of their neighbours. That wee were loving people, as a testimony whereof they shewed the presents I had given them. That wee had brought thither such things as they stood in need of, for which wee desired only Beaver and Otter skinnes, whereof they had to spare. That therefore they comanded them to trade lovingly and freely with our people, that they should be carefull that no injuries were either privately or publikely done to them. That they should use them as friends and Brothers, and that for me in particular they should honor and esteeme of me as a Brother of their kings, and that they should be carefull to carrie themselves dutifully towards mee, with a great deale more complement, then I expresse. This being done my company and the

Indians fell a trucking [trading], while these two kings entered into the same league with me, which the former had done, and then towards evening the elder king went ashore, the yonger remayning aboard with mee. Thither also came two other neighboring kinges, with whom also I made peace. Heere also was the first place, where some of their weomen came aboard our shippes, and heere during the space of five dayes that wee tarried we had continually store of Indians aboard us. One night about one of the clock in the night, there rose an alarme amongst the Indians that lay ashore, that the Minquaos were come upon them; the yonger king was then aboard my ship, who desired me to receave his people aboard till the morning, which I did, setting a good guard upon them and disarming them. In the morning I found this to proceed of nothing else but their pollicie to trie whether, if occasion were, I would really assist them or no. But howsoever the king gave me great thankes for my love to him and his people. After I had stayed there some five dayes, I departed towards the head of the River, and many Indians as I passed along came aboard my shippe, with such commodities as they had, some with furrs, some with victualls. On the 29 of August I had gotten up with my shippe as far as I could goe with her for now the water beganne to be shoaly, so I came to an anchor, neere to the dwelling of one of the principall kings of this Countrey, who that same night hearing that I was come to his Countrey, came aboard of me to visitt me, with whome also I made peace as with the former. This king and his Brother are the greatest Travaylors that I mett among all the Indians, in the River, for they have bene by land at the lower fort of Hudsons River [Fort Amsterdam], and likewise very farre up the River, beyond the rockes, I spake of. On the first of September I sent my leiuetennant in my shallop up to the Rockes, both to sound the water as he went, and likewise to trie whether my boates would passe those rockes or no. The Hollanders of Hudsons River having gotten some intelligence of our being heere by the Indians, who in some places live not above a dayes journey from them, overtooke me heere within six houres after I had sent away my leiuetennant to the rockes. They came to an Anchor close by me. I sent my boate presently aboard them to know what they were, and from whence they came, and to bring the master to mee, who soone after came together with his Marchant in their owne boate. When they were come aboard of me, I sent for them into my cabbin, and asked them what they

made heere, they answered mee they came to trade as formerly they
had done. I asked them if they had any commission from his Majestie
to trade in the River or no, they answered they had none from the
King of England, but from the Governor of new Netherlands they
had, to which I replyed that I knew no such Governor, nor no such
place as new Netherlands. I told them that this Country did belong
to the crowne of England, as well by ancient discovery as likewise
by possession lawfully taken, and that his Majestie was now pleased
to make more ample discovery of this River, and of other places also,
where he would erect Collonies, and that I was therefore sent hither
with a Royall Commission under the great Seale to take possession
heereof. I perceaved by their countenance that this newes strooke them
could at heart, and after a little pawse they answered me, that they
had traded in this River heeretofore. I then replyed that therein they
had done his Majestie and his subjects the greater injurie, for supposing, as some of the Dutch pretended, that they had by his Majesties
leave traded and planted in Hudsons River, yet ought they not to
usurpe upon other trades and Countreyes of his Majesties without his
leave, and since that he is now pleased to make use of this River,
either for himself, or his subjects, it would be good manners in them
to desist. Then they desired to see my Commission, which I shewed
them, and after they had read it, and considered well thereof,
apprehending the power I had, if they should trade without licence,
to make them prize, they desired me to give them a Copie thereof.
I answered them that it was not the custome of England for his
Majesties Ministers to give Copies of their Commissions, they then
desired to know how I would proceed with them, which they hoped
would be the better in regard they knew not of my commission, I
told them I would let them know that heereafter, when my leiuetennant
was returned which perhaps would be the next morning.

The next day my leiuetennant being returned, I sent for the Hollanders to dine with me, and this day I spent in making them wellcome,
and after dinner one of their company dranke to me saying, Heere
Governor of the South River, (for soe they call this) I drinke to you
and indeed confesse your Commission is much better then ours, how
say you Copeman [Koopman] (who is the head marchant) said he is
it not. To whome the Copeman answered yes indeede, I have not
seene a larger Commission. The next day about 8 of the clocke I
sent for them to give them an answerre which was this. That in regard

they were subjects to so ancient allies of my Prince, and that they were neighbours heere, and since they had carried themselves civilly, I had used them with all curtesy, that I might lawfully use. That since I had also shewed them my commission, I made no question but that they knew sufficiently well what they had to doe, neverthelesse, I was willing they might stay at Anchor two dayes longer, to provide themselves of whatsoever they should need, and that I would not suffer any thing to be taken from them during their stay. They then asked me if I would command them to be gone, I answered I command you not to be gone, but you may looke into my Commission, and there you may see whether it be lawfull for you to vizitt or trade into any places I shall possesse, where upon they read over the second time that part of the Commission, and then they answered they would be gone, but they desired a note under my hand for their discharge, unto their Governor, to shew the cause why they returned without trading. I answered it was not the custome of England and that they had no need of any such note, since they had seene the Commission under the great Seale, and that I could not beleeve but that their Governor would both creditt and be satisfied with their Relation. Soe they parted civilly though very sadly from mee. Before the time of two dayes was expired, they weighed Anchor and went downe the River, I sent my Leiuetennant in my pinnace to see them cleare of the River, and to watch them least they should doe me ill offices with the Indians, in their way homewards. In their going downe they sometimes went aboard of one another after the manner of the Sea, and the Merchant of the Ship upon some discourse said, that if they had bene in possession at my arrivall they would not have removed, for all my Commission, and not long after he said I would we were in possession of it agayne, yet if the [Dutch] West India Company had been ruled by me, they had planted this River, rather than Hudsons River, and whilest my Leiuetennant commended Hudsons River, for a good place, he replyed, yea so it is, but this is better, and further said were I sure we should loose this River, I would tell you something that would please you. I gave my leiuetennant order that after he had watched these Hollanders out of the Bay he should then goe, and discover all along the Coast, as farre as Hudson's River and so on towards Cape Cod, to see if there were any probability of a [northwest] passage through. Hee accordingly discovered along the coast as farre as Hudsons River, where he was overtaken with foule weather, and contrary windes, where he endured the stormes till he was forced by the incommodiousnes of his vessell, and want of victualls to returne. In this voyage he lost two men who were killed by the Indians, but found nothing worthy of particular Relations.

As soone as he was returned I sent him presently up once more to the falls to trie whether he could passe those rockes at a spring tide, which before he could not doe in a neap tide, but it was then also impassable with any great boate, wherefore he returned backe to mee agayne. When he saw he could not passe over the rockes, he went up the River side some five miles above the rockes, to see whither the River were passable or no, who informeth me [it] is deepe and likely to runne very farre up into the Countrey. Heere also is the Brother of the king of Mohigon, who is the uppermost king that wee have mett with who relateth that he hath bene in a Canoa 20 dayes journey up the River, above the rockes which [the river] he describeth to runne northwest and westnorthwest, that he was sent thither by his brother to a king of his Alliance, and that there he heard that this River some five dayes journey higher issueth from a great Lake, he saith further that four days journey from this River, over certayne mountaines there is a great mediterranean [inland] sea and he offereth to goe him self along in person the next sommer with myself or my leiuetennant to shew us the same, he saith further that about two dayes journey above the falls or rocks, the River divides itself into two branches, the one whereof is this wherein wee are, and the other trendeth towards Hudsons River, and that the farther you goe up the River the broader.

I beseech yr honor give me leave by the way to give you a short relation of the commodities [advantages] and scituation of this River. This River dischargeth itself into a great Bay in the North part of Virginia, in 39 and almost a half of latitude. The river is broad and deepe, and is not inferior to any in the North of America, and a ship of 300 Tonnes may saile up within three leagues of the rockes. The River aboundeth with beavers, otters, and other meaner furrs, which are not only taken upon the bankes of the mayne River, but likewise in other lesser rivers which discharge themselves into the greater, whereof I thinke few Rivers of America have more or more pleasant. The people are for the most part very well proportioned, well featured, gentle, tractable and docible. The land is very good and fruitfull and withall very healthfull. The soyle is sandy and produceth divers sorts of fruites, especially grapes, which grow wild in great quantity, of which I have eaten sixe severall sorts, some of them as good as they are ordinarily in Italy, or Spaine; and were they replanted I thinke they whould be farre better. Heere also growes the fruite which in Italy they call lazarroli [medlar], plumms, divers sorts of berries and divers other fruites not knowne in Europe. The climate is much like that of Italy and all sorts of fruites of that Countrey will thrive heere exceedingly. The earth being fruitefull is covered over with woods and stately timber, except only in those places, where the Indians had planted their corne. The Countrey is very well replenished, with deere and in some places store of Elkes. The low grounds of which there is great quantitie excellent for meadowes and full of Beaver and Otter. The quantity of fowle is so great as can hardly be beleeved, wee tooke at one time 48 partriches together, as they crossed the river, chased by wild hawkes. I myselfe sprang in two houres 5 or 6 covies in walking of a mile. There are infinit number of wild pidgeons, black birds, Turkeyes, Swans, wild geese, ducks, Teales, widgins, brants, herons, cranes etc. of which there is so great aboundance, as that the Rivers and creekes are covered with them in winter. Of fish heere is plentie, but especially sturgeon all the sommer time, which are in such aboundance in the upper parts of the River, as that great benefitt might be raysed by setting up a fishing for them, for in the spring and beginning of summer the weather is so temperate, that they will keepe very well. Heere are also great store of wild hops yet exellent good and as faire as those in England, heere are also divers other things which with industrie will prove exellent good commodities, and for my part I am confident that this River is the most healthfull, fruitefull and commodious River in all the North of America, to be planted.

Hither also very lately came the Hollanders a second time, sent hither by the Governor of the Dutch plantation, with a Commission to plant and trade heere, but after much discourse to and fro, they have publikely declared, that if the king of England please to owne this River, they will obey, and they humbly desire that he will declare to them their limitts in these parts of America, which they will also observe.

Holland and England were not the only European powers interested in the Delaware region. In 1638 Sweden, represented by Peter Minuit, the former governor of New Netherland and now serving the Swedish West India Company, established the first permanent white settlement on the Delaware River at Fort Christina (Wilmington, Delaware). From then until 1655, when the Dutch forced them to capitulate, the Swedish enjoyed a modest prosperity from the Indian fur trade, though their settlements were little more than trading posts and their numbers seldom reached two hundred. The best accounts of these few early years of Swedish activity were written by two 18th-century Swedish visitors, who effectively used the oral testimony of old settlers and several original records that have since been lost.

The first, the Rev. Israel Acrelius, was a Swedish-born and educated Lutheran clergyman sent in 1749 to minister to the Swedish congregations on the Delaware. After seven years as pastor of the Old Swedes' Church at Christina (Wilmington), he returned to Sweden and retirement. His Description of the Former and Present State of the Swedish Churches, *in the so-called New Sweden (Stockholm, 1759) was translated by the Rev. William M. Reynolds for the* Memoirs of the Historical Society of Pennsylvania, *vol. 9 (1874). The following excerpts are taken from pp. 47-55 of that translation.*

To what Land the Swedes had a Right, partly by Purchase and partly by Agreement.

The land on the west side of the river, which the Swedes had purchased of the heathen, already in Menewe's [Peter Minuit's] time, and afterwards under Governor [Johan] Printz, or had acquired a right to by agreement, stretched from Cape Hinlopen to the Falls of the Delaware, and thence westward to the Great Fall in the river Susquehanna, near the mouth of the Conewaga Creek. These Indians were called, by Europeans in general, Delawares, but within a circle of eighteen miles [118 English miles] around the Swedes, there were ten or eleven separate tribes, each having its own *Sackheman*, or king. Among these were especially the Minesinkos, the Mynkusses, or Minequesses, upon the so-called Maniquas, or Minqua's Kihl (Christina), with whom the Swedes formed a special friendship. These extended twelve Swedish miles [78 English miles] into the interior of the country, on to the Conestoga and the Susquehanna, where they had a fort which was a square surrounded by palisades, with some iron pieces on a hill, and some houses within it. But some of them were with the Swedes every day, who also, once or twice in a year, made a journey up into the country among the Minequesses, with their wares for sale. The road was very difficult, over sharp gray stones, morasses, hills, and streams, which can still be very well seen by those who travel between Christina and Lancaster.

Proof of this.

The old Indians still remember the treaties which their forefathers made with the Swedes, as also how far they were disposed to open their land to them. Of this it may serve as evidence to introduce the following extract from the minutes of the treaty made in Lancaster:

THE COURT-HOUSE IN LANCASTER,
June 26, 1744, P.M.

Present.—Hon. George Thomas, Esq., Lieutenant-Governor of Pennsylvania, etc.; the Hon. Commissioners of Virginia; the Hon. Commissioners of Maryland; the Deputies of the Six Nations of Indians. Conrad Weiser, Interpreter.

Canasatego, the Indians' spokesman, spoke as follows:

Brother, the Governor of Maryland: When you spoke of the condition of the country yesterday, you went back to old times, and told us you had been in possession of the province of Maryland above one hundred years. But what is one hundred years in comparison to the length of time since our claim began?—since we came up out of this ground? For we must tell you that, long before one hundred years, our ancestors came out of this ground, and their children have remained here ever since. You came out of the ground in a country which lies on the other side of the big lake; there you have claim, but here you must allow us to be your elder brethren, and the lands to belong to us long before you knew anything of them. It is true that, about one hundred years ago, a German [Dutch] ship came hither and brought with them various articles, such as awls, knives, hatchets, guns, and many other things, which they gave us. And when they had taught us to use these things, and we saw what kind of a people they were, we were so well pleased with them that we tied their ships to the bushes on the shore. And afterwards, liking them still better, and the more the longer they stayed with us, thinking that the bushes were too weak, we changed the place of the rope, and fastened it to the trees. And as the trees might be overthrown by a storm, or fall down of themselves, (for the friendship we had for them) we again changed the place of the rope, and bound it to a very strong cliff. Here the Interpreter said, They mean the land of Onondago. There we fastened it very securely, and rolled wampum around it. For still greater security, we stood upon the wampum, and sat upon it to guard it, and to prevent all injury, and we took the greatest care to keep it uninjured for all time. As long as that stood, the newly-arrived Germans [Dutch] recognized our right to the country, and from time to time urged us to give them portions of our land, and that they might enter into a union and treaty with us, and become one people with us.

That this is more correctly said of the Swedes than of the Hollanders can be inferred from this, that the Hollanders never made such a purchase from them as to include their whole country, which the Swedes did; yet the English are rather disposed to explain this in favor of the Hollanders. The savages regarded both the Swedes and Hollanders, being Europeans, as one people, and looked upon their quarrels as disagreements between private families.

How Purchases of Land were made from the Heathen.

Purchases of land from the savages were made in this way: Both parties set their names and marks under the purchase-contract. Two witnesses were also taken from among the Christians. When these made their oath that they wre present at the transaction, and had seen the payment made, then the purchase was valid. If the kings or chiefs of the Indians signed such an agreement in the presence of a number of their people, then it was legitimate on their side. In former times they were quite faithful, although oaths were not customary among them. But it was not so in later times, after they had had more intercourse with Christians. Payments were made in awls, needles, scissors, knives, axes, guns, powder and balls, together with blankets of frieze or felt, which they wrap around themselves. One blanket suffices for their dress. The same wares they purchased for themselves, for their skins of beavers, raccoons, sables, gray foxes, wildcats, lynxes, bears, and deer.

The Indians a Dissatisfied People.

It is true the savages sold their lands at a low rate, but they were a discontented people, who, at no great intervals, must have new gifts of encouragement, if their friendship was to remain firm. Such they always have been, and still are. As they regarded the Swedes and the Hollanders as one people, it was all the same to them which of them had their land, provided only that they frequently got bribes. Three years after Governor Printz's arrival, as gifts were withheld, and Swedish ships came but seldom, the Indians murmured that they did not receive more, and that the Swedes had no more goods for their traffic. Then there came out a rumor that the savages had a mind to fall upon and exterminate them. This went so far that in the year 1654 their *sackkeman* sent out his son, called his elders together, and had a consultation as to what was to be done. But as they regarded the Swedes as a warlike people, who had better not be irritated, as also that they had dealt justly with them, and were shortly expecting other ships with costly wares, they therefore laid aside all hostile thoughts, and confirmed anew their former friendship.

They frequently visited the Swedes.

After the Christians came in, and the savages gave over their country to them, the latter withdrew farther into the forests in the interior of the country. But it was their habit and custom, at certain times of the year, to come forth in great numbers to visit the Swedes, and trade with them. That was done for the most part after they had planted their maize, namely, in the month of June, and so they remained for some time of the summer, when they gathered wild pease, which grew along the river, and dried them. These pease, in their language, were called *Tachy*. The Indians were not troublesome, as in the meantime they supported themselves by fishing and hunting, which custom they kept until within fifty years since. These tribes were the Delawares and Mynquesses, or Minnesinks, who called the Swedes their brothers. Sometimes there came with them some of that race which the Swedes called Flatheads, for their heads were flat on the crown. These were dangerous, and murdered people, when they found anyone alone in the woods. They first struck the person on the head, so that he either died or swooned, after which they took off the skin of the head, after which some persons might revive again. That is called scalping, and is still in use among all the American Indians, and the skin of the head is called a scalp, which is their usual token of victory. An old Swedish woman, called the mother of Lars Buré, living at Chinsessing, had the misfortune to be scalped in this manner, yet lived many years thereafter, and became the mother of several children. No hair grew on her head again, except short down. On their account the people were compelled to live close together, as also to have stories on their houses provided with loopholes. By their intercourse with the savages the Swedes became well acquainted with the Indian language, and there are still a few of the older ones who express themselves quite well in it. The savages stayed much with Olof Stille at Techoheraffi, and were very fond of the old man; but they made a monster of his thick black beard, from which also they gave him a special name.

The second Swedish visitor, Pehr Kalm, was a noted Swedish scientist and clergyman sent by the Swedish Academy of Sciences in 1748 to expand the number of useful plants and trees in Sweden by locating adaptable species in the comparable environment of North America. This perceptive student of Carl von Linné, the famous Linnaeus, spent several months travelling and studying the Middle Atlantic states, where he talked with several descendants of the early Swedish colonists. His account is taken from The America of 1750. Peter Kalm's Travels in North America. The English Version of 1770, *revised and edited by Adolph B. Benson (New York: Wilson-Erickson, 1937), vol. 1, pp. 265-273.*

MARCH THE 27TH [1749]

New Sweden. In the morning I went to speak with the old Swede, Nils Gustafson, who was ninety-one years of age. I intended to get some account of the former state of New Sweden. The country which I now passed through was the same as that which I had found in those parts of North America I had already seen. It was diversified with a variety of little hills and valleys: the former consisted of a very pale brick-colored earth, composed, for the greatest part, of a fine sand, mixed with some mould. I saw no mountains and no stones, except some little ones not above the size of a pigeon's or hen's egg lying on the hills and commonly consisting of white quartz, which was generally smooth and polished on the outside. At the bottom, along the valleys, ran sometimes creeks of crystalline water, the bottom of which were covered with white pebbles. Now and then I came upon swamps in the valleys. Sometimes there appeared, though at considerable distances from each other, some farms, frequently surrounded on all sides by grain fields. Almost on every field there yet remained the stumps of trees, which had been cut down, a proof that this country had not been long cultivated, having been overgrown with trees forty or fifty years ago. The farms did not lie together in villages, or so that several of them were near each other in one place, but were all unconnected. Each countryman lived by himself, and had his own ground about the house separated from the property of his neighbor. The greatest part of the land, between these farms so far apart, was overgrown with woods, consisting of tall trees. However, there was a fine space between the trees, so that one could ride on horseback without inconvenience in the woods, and even with a cart in most places; and the ground was very flat and uniform at the same time. Here and there appeared some fallen trees, thrown down by the wind; some were torn up by the roots; others broken straight across the trunk. In some parts of the country the trees were thick and tall, but in others I found large tracts covered with young trees, only twenty, thirty, or forty years old. On these tracts, I am told, the Indians formerly had their little plantations. I did not yet see any marks of the leaves coming out, and I did not meet with a flower in the woods, for the cold winds, which had blown for several days successively, had hindered this. The woods consisted chiefly of several species of oak, and of hickory. The swamps were filled with red maple which was now all in flower and made these places look real red at a distance.

A Nonagenarian. The old Swede, whom I came to visit, seemed to be still pretty healthy and could walk by the help of a cane, but he complained of having felt in these later years some pains in his back and limbs, and confessed that he now could keep his feet warm in winter only by sitting near the fire. He said he could very well remember the state of this country at the time when the Dutch possessed it, and in what circumstances it was in before the arrival of the English. [He was born in 1658.] He added, that he had brought a great deal of timber to Philadelphia at the time that it was built. He still remembered to have seen a great forest on the spot where Philadelphia now stands. The father of this old man had been one of the Swedes who were sent over from Sweden in order to cultivate and inhabit this country. He gave me the following answers to the questions I asked him.

The Swedish Settlers. Query, Whence did the Swedes, who first came hither, get their cattle? The old man answered, that when he was a boy, his father and other people had told him that the Swedes brought their horses, cows and oxen, sheep, hogs, geese, and ducks, over with them. There were but few of a kind at first, but they multiplied greatly here afterwards. He said that Maryland, New York, New England, and Virginia, had been earlier inhabited by Europeans than this part of the country; but he did not know whether the Swedes ever got cattle of any kind from any of these provinces, except from New York. While he was yet very young, the Swedes, as far as he could remember, had already a sufficient stock of all these animals. The hogs had propagated so much at that time, there being so great a plenty of food for them, that they ran about wild in the woods, and that the people were obliged to shoot them when they wanted them. The old man likewise recollected, that horses ran wild in the woods, in some places; but he could not tell whether any other kind of cattle turned wild. He thought that the cattle grew as big at present as they did when he was a boy, provided they received as much food as they needed. For in his younger years food for all kinds of cattle was so plentiful and abundant that the cattle were extremely fat. A cow at that time gave more milk than three or four do at present; but she got more and better food at that time than three or four get now; and, as the old man said, the scanty allowance of grass which the cattle get in summer is really very pitiful. . . .

Query, Whence did the English in Pennsylvania and New Jersey get their cattle? They bought them chiefly from the Swedes and Dutch who lived here, and a small number were brought over from Old England. The physical form of the cattle and the unanimous accounts of the English here confirmed what the old man had said.

Query, Whence did the Swedes here settled get their several sorts of grain and likewise their fruit trees and kitchen herbs? The old man told me that he had frequently heard when he was young, that the Swedes had brought all kinds of grain and fruits and herbs or seeds of them with them. For as far as he could recollect, the Swedes here were plentifully provided with wheat, rye, barley and oats. The Swedes, at that time, brewed all their beer of malt made of barley, and likewise made good strong beer. They had already got distilling apparatus, and when they intended to distil they lent their apparatus to one another. At first they were forced to buy corn of the Indians, both for sowing and eating. But after continuing for some years in this country, they extended their corn plantations so much that the Indians were obliged some time after to buy corn of the Swedes. The old man likewise assured me that the Indians formerly, and about the time of the first settling of the Swedes, were more industrious, but that now they had become very lazy in comparison. While he was young the Swedes had a great quantity of very good white cabbage. Winter cabbage, or kale, which was left on the ground during winter, was also abundant. They were likewise well provided with turnips. In winter they kept them in holes under ground. But the old man did not like that method, for when they had lain too long in these holes in winter they became spongy. He preferred that method of keeping them which is now commonly adopted, and which consists in the following particulars. After the turnips have been taken out of the ground in autumn, and exposed to the air for a while, they are put in a heap upon the field, covered with straw at the top, and on the sides, and with earth over the straw. By this means they stand the winter very well here, and do not become spongy. The Indians were very fond of turnips, and called them sometimes *hopniss*, sometimes *katniss*. Nobody around here had ever heard of *rutabagas* or Swedish turnips. The Swedes likewise cultivated carrots, in the old man's younger years. Among the fruit trees were apple trees. They were not numerous, and only some of the Swedes had little orchards of them, while others had not a single tree. None of the Swedes made cider, for it had come into use but lately. The Swedes brewed beer and that was their common drink. But at present there are very few who brew beer, for they commonly make cider. Cherry trees were abundant when Nils Gustafson was a boy. Peach trees were at that time more numerous than at present and the Swedes brewed beer of the fruit. The old man could not tell from whence the Swedes first of all got the peach trees.

Indians. During the younger years of this old man, the Indians were everywhere in the country. They lived among the Swedes. The old man mentioned Swedes who had been killed by the Indians, and he mentioned two of his countrymen who had been scalped by them. They stole children from the Swedes, and carried them off, and they were never heard of again. Once they came and killed some of them and took their scalps; on that occasion they scalped a little girl, and would have killed her, if they had not perceived a boat full of Swedes, making towards them, which obliged them to flee. The girl's scalp afterwards healed, but no hair grew on it; she was married, had many children, and lived to a great age. At another time the Indians attempted to kill the mother of this old man, but he vigorously resisted them until a number of Swedes came up, who frightened the Indians and made them run away. Nobody could ever find out to what nation these savages belonged; for in general they lived very peaceably with the Swedes.

The *Indians* had their little plantations of corn in many places. Before the Swedes came into this country, the Red Men had no other hatchets than those made of stone; in order to make corn plantations they cut out the trees and prepared the ground in the manner I have mentioned before. They planted but little corn, for they lived chiefly by hunting, and throughout the greatest part of the summer *hopniss, katniss, taw-ho,* and whortleberries were their chief food. They had no horses or other cattle which could be employed in their agriculture, and therefore did all the work with their own hands. After they had reaped the corn, they kept it in holes under ground during winter; they seldom dug these holes deeper than a fathom, and often not so deep; at the bottom and on the sides they put broad pieces of bark. If bark could not be had, the *Andropogon bicorne*, a grass which grows in great plenty here, and which the English call Indian grass and the Swedes wildgrass, supplied the want of the former. The ears of corn were then thrown into the hole and covered to a considerable thickness with this grass, and the whole again covered by a sufficient quantity of earth. Corn was kept extremely well in those holes, and each Indian had several such subterraneous stores, where his corn lay safe, though he travelled far from it. After the Swedes had settled here and planted apple trees and peach trees, the Indians, and especially their women, sometimes stole the fruit in great quantity; but when the Swedes caught them, they gave them a severe drubbing, took the fruit from them, and often their clothes too. In the same manner it happened sometimes that as the Swedes had a great increase of hogs, and they ran about in the woods, the Indians killed some of them privately and ate them: but there were likewise some Indians who bought hogs of the Swedes and raised them. They taught them to follow them like dogs, and whenever they moved from one place to another their pigs always went with them. Some of those savages got such numbers of these animals, that they afterwards gave them to the Swedes for a trifle. When the Swedes arrived in America the Indians had no domestic animals, except a species of little dog. The Indians were extremely fond of milk and drank it with pleasure when the Swedes gave it to them. They likewise prepared a kind of liquor like milk by gathering a great number of hickory and black walnuts, dried and crushed them. Then they took out the kernels, pounded them as fine as flour, and mixed this with water so that it looked like milk and was almost as sweet. They had tobacco pipes of clay, manufactured by themselves, at the time that the Swedes arrived here; they did not always smoke true tobacco, but made use of another plant instead of it, which was unknown to the old Swedes. It was not the common mullein, or *Verbascum thapsus*, which is generally called Indian tobacco here.

Religion among the Indians. As to their religion the old man thought it very trifling, and even believed that they had none at all. When they heard loud claps of thunder they said that the evil spirit was angry. Some of them said that they believed in a god, who lives in heaven. The old Swede once walked with an Indian, and they encountered a red-spotted snake on the road: the old man therefore went to seek a stick in order to kill it, but the Indian begged him not to touch it, because it was sacred to him. Perhaps the Swede would not have killed it, but on hearing that it was the Indian's deity, he took a stick and killed it, in the presence of the Indian, saying: "Because thou believest in it, I think myself obliged to kill it." Sometimes the Indians came into the Swedish churches, looked around, listened and went away again. One day as this old Swede was at church and did not sing, because he had no psalmbook, one of the Indians, who was well acquainted with him, tapped him on the shoulder, and said: "Why dost thou not sing with the others, Tantánta! Tantánta! Tantánta?" On another occasion, as a sermon was preached in the Swedish church at Raccoon, an Indian came in, looked about him, and after listening awhile to the preacher, he said: "Ugh! A lot of prattle and nonsense, but neither brandy nor cider!" and went out again. For it is to be observed that when an Indian makes a speech to his companions, in order to encourage them to war, or to anything else, they all drink immoderately on those occasions.

At the time when the Swedes arrived, they bought land at a very small price. For a piece of baize, or a pot full of brandy or the like, they could get a piece of ground, which at present would be worth more than four hundred pounds, Pennsylvania currency. When they sold a piece of land, they commonly signed an agreement; and though they could neither read nor write, they scribbled their marks, or signatures, at the bottom of it. The father of old Nils Gustafson bought a piece of ground from the Indians in New Jersey. As soon as the agreement was drawn up, and the Indians were about to sign it, one of them, whose name signified a beaver, drew a beaver; another of them drew a bow and arrow; and a third a mountain, instead of his name. Their canoes were made of thick trees, which they hollowed out by fire, and made them smooth again with their hatchets, as has been mentioned before.

Weather. The following account the old man gave me in answer to my questions with regard to the weather and its changes. It was his opinion that the weather had always been pretty uniform ever since his childhood; that there happened as great storms at present as formerly; that the summers now were sometimes hotter and sometimes colder than they were at that time; that the winters were often as cold and as long as formerly; and that there still often falls as great a quantity of snow as in former times. However, he thought that no cold winter came up to that which reigned after the summer when the Swedish clergymen Rudman and Björk came here, in the year 1697, which is often mentioned in the almanacks of this country; . . . For in that winter the river Delaware was so thickly covered with ice that the old man brought many wagons full of hay over it near Christina; and that it was passable on sledges even lower down. No cattle, as far as he could recollect, were frozen to death during the cold winters, except, in later years, such cattle as were lean, and had no stable in which to seek protection. It commonly rains in summer as it did formerly, excepting that, during the last years the summers have been drier. Nor could the old Swede find a diminution of water in the brooks, rivers and swamps. He allowed, as a very common and certain fact, that wherever you dug wells you would strike oyster shells in the ground.

Old Gustafson was of the opinion, that intermitting fevers were as frequent and violent formerly as they are now; but believed that they seemed more uncommon, because there were fewer people at that time here. When he got this fever, he was not yet full grown. He got it in summer, and had it till the ensuing spring, which is almost a year; but it did not hinder him from doing his work, either within or out of doors. Pleurisy likewise attacked one or two of the Swedes formerly; but it was not nearly so common as it is now. The people in general were very healthy at that time.

Some years ago the old Swede's eyes were so much weakened that he was forced to make use of a pair of spectacles. He then got a fever, which was so violent that it was feared he would not recover. However, he became quite well again, and at the same time got new strength in his eyes, so that he has been able to read without spectacles ever since.

Houses in New Sweden. The houses which the Swedes built when they first settled here were very poor. The whole house consisted of one little room, the door of which was so low, that one was obliged to stoop in order to get in. As they had brought no glass with them, they were obliged to be content with little holes, before which a moveable board was fastened. They found no moss, or at least none which could have been serviceable in stopping up holes or cracks in the walls. They were therefore forced to close them, using clay, both inside and out. The chimneys were masoned in a corner, either of gray stone, or (in places where there were no stone) of mere clay, which they laid very thick in one corner of the house. The ovens for baking were likewise inside. So far as we know the Swedes never used any dampers, perhaps because they had none of iron and did not feel that the winters here were either cold or long enough [to need them], and also because in the beginning they had an abundance of fuel.

Dress in New Sweden. Before the English came to settle here, the Swedes could not get as many clothes as they needed, and were therefore obliged to get along as well as they could. The men wore waist-coats and breeches of skins. Hats were not in fashion, and they made little caps, provided with flaps; some made fur caps. They had worsted stockings. Their shoes were of their own making. Some of them had learned to prepare leather, and to make common shoes, with heels; but those who were not shoemakers by profession took the length of their feet and sewed the leather together accordingly, taking a piece for the sole, one for the hind-quarters, and another one for the uppers. These shoes were called *kippaka*. At that time, they likewise sowed flax here, and wove linen cloth. Hemp was not to be had; and they made use of linen and wild hemp for fishing tackle. The women were dressed in jackets and petticoats of skins. Their beds, excepting the sheets, were skins of various animals; such as bears, wolves, etc.

Tea, coffee, and chocolate, which are at present universally in use here, were then wholly unknown. Bread and butter, and other substantial food, was what they breakfasted upon; and the above-mentioned superfluities have only been lately introduced, according to the account of the old Swede. Sugar and molasses they had in abundance, so far back as he could remember. Rum could formerly be had for a more moderate price than at present.

English Customs Replace the Swedish. From the accounts of this old man I concluded, that before the English settled here they followed wholly the customs of Old Sweden; but after the English had been in the country for some time, the Swedes began gradually to follow theirs. When this Swede was but a boy, there were two Swedish smiths here, who made hatchets, knives, and scythes, exactly like the Swedish ones, and made them sharper than they can be gotten now. The hatchets now in use are often the English style, with a broad edge, and their handles are very narrow. They had no jack-knives. Almost all the Swedes had bath-houses and they commonly bathed every Saturday, but now these bath-houses are done away with. They celebrated Christmas with several sorts of games, and with various special dishes, as is usual in Sweden; all of which is now, for the greatest part, given up. In the younger years of this Swede, they made a strange kind of cart here. They sawed off round cross sections of thick liquidambar logs, and used two of them for the front wheels and two more for the back wheels. With those carts they brought home their wood. Their sledges were at that time made almost as they are now, being about twice as broad as the true Swedish ones. Timber and great beams of wood were carried upon a dray. They baked great loaves, such as they do now. They never had any hard, crackerhole-bread or *knäckebröd* [now called "health bread" in the United States], though the clergymen who came from Sweden commonly had some baked.

The English on their arrival here bought large tracts of land of the Swedes for almost nothing. The father of the old Swede sold an estate to the English, which at this time would be reckoned worth three hundred pounds, for which he got a cow, a sow, and a hundred pump-kins.

More than anything new colonies needed colonists, so the ancient art of advertising was turned to that end many times in the 17th century. One of the most effective advertisements for the new colony of Pennsylvania was Gabriel Thomas's Historical and Geographical Account of Pensilvania and West-New-Jersey *(London, 1698), which, he later boasted, "proved to the province's great advancement by causing great numbers of people to goe over to those parts." Thomas, a Welsh-born yeoman farmer and birthright Quaker, sailed to Pennsylvania in 1681 on the first ship of emigrants at the age of twenty. He spent the next sixteen years in Philadelphia before sailing to England in 1697 to see his book through the press. After almost ten years in England, he returned to America to farm a thousand acres in Delaware and eventually to die in his beloved Philadelphia. His description of the colony's advantages is found on pp. 23-45 of the first edition.*

And now for their Lots and Lands in City and Countrey, in their great Advancement since they were first laid out, which was within the compass of about Twelve Years, that which might have been bought for Fifteen or Eighteen Shillings, is now sold for Fourscore Pounds in ready Silver; and some other Lots, that might have been then Purchased for Three Pounds, within the space of Two Years, were sold for a Hundred Pounds a piece, and likewise some Land that lies near the City, that Sixteen Years ago might have been Purchas'd for Six or Eight Pounds the Hundred Acres, cannot now be bought under One Hundred and Fifty, or Two Hundred Pounds.

Now the true Reason why this Fruitful Countrey and Florishing City advance so considerably in the Purchase of Lands both in the one and the other, is their great and extended Traffique and Commerce both by Sea and Land, viz. to New-York, New-England, Virginia, Mary-Land, Carolina, Jamaica, Barbadoes, Nevis, Monserat, Antego, St. Cristophers, Barmudoes, New-Found-Land, Maderas, Saltetudeous, and Old-England; besides several other places. Their Merchandize chiefly consists in Horses, Pipe-Staves, Pork and Beef Salted and Barrelled up, Bread, and Flower, all sorts of Grain, Pease, Beans, Skins, Furs, Tobacco, or Pot-Ashes, Wax, etc., which are Barter'd for Rumm, Sugar, Molasses, Silver, Negroes, Salt, Wine, Linen, Houshold-Goods, etc.

However there still remain Lots of Land both in the aforesaid City and Country, that any may Purchase almost as cheap as they could at the first Laying out or Parcelling of either City or Country; which is, (in the Judgment of most People) the likeliest to turn to account to those that lay their Money out upon it, and in a shorter time than the aforementioned Lots and Lands that are already improved, and for several Reasons. In the first place, the Countrey is now well inhabited by the Christians, who have great Stocks of all sorts of Cattle, that encrease extraordinarily, and upon that account they are oblig'd to go farther up into the Countrey, because there is the chiefest and best place for their Stocks, and for them that go back into the Countrey, they get the richest Land, for the best lies thereabouts.

Secondly, Farther into the Countrey is the Principal Place to Trade with the Indians for all sorts of Pelt, as Skins and Furs, and also Fat Venison, of whom People may Purchase cheaper by three Parts in four than they can at the City of Philadelphia.

Thirdly, Backwards in the Countrey lies the Mines where is Copper and Iron, besides other Metals, and Minerals, of which there is some Improvement made already in order to bring them, to greater Perfection; and that will be a means to erect more Inland Market-Towns, which exceedingly promote Traffick.

Fourthly, and lastly, Because the Countrey at the first laying out, was void of Inhabitants (except the Heathens, or very few Christians not worth naming) and not many People caring to abandon a quiet and easie (at least tolerable) Life in their Native Countrey (usually the most agreeable to all Mankind) to seek out a new hazardous, and careful one in a Foreign Wilderness or Desart Countrey, wholly destitute of Christian Inhabitants, and even to arrive at which, they must pass over a vast Ocean, expos'd to some Dangers, and not a few Inconveniencies: But now all those Cares, Fears and Hazards are vanished, for the Countrey is pretty well Peopled, and very much Improv'd, and will be more every Day, now the Dove is return'd with the Olive-branch of Peace in her Mouth.

I must needs say, even the present Encouragements are very great and inviting, for Poor People (both Men and Women) of all kinds, can here get three times the Wages for their Labour they can in England or Wales.

I shall instance in a few, which may serve; nay, and will hold in all the rest. The first was a Black-Smith (my next Neighbour), who himself and one Negro Man he had, got Fifty Shillings in one Day, by working up a Hundred Pound Weight of Iron, which at Six Pence per Pound (and that is the common Price in that Countrey) amounts to that Summ.

And for Carpenters, both House and Ship, Brick-layers, Masons, either of these Trades-Men, will get between Five and Six Shillings every Day constantly. As to Journey-Men Shooe-Makers, they have Two Shillings per Pair both for Men and Womens Shooes: And Journey-Men Taylors have Twelve Shillings per Week and their Diet. Sawyers get between Six and Seven Shillings the Hundred for Cutting of Pine-Boards. And for Weavers, they have Ten or Twelve Pence the Yard for Weaving of that which is little more than half a Yard in breadth. Wooll-Combers, have for combing Twelve Pence per Pound. Potters have Sixteen Pence for an Earthen Pot which may be bought in England for Four Pence. Tanners may buy their Hides green for Three Half Pence per Pound, and sell their Leather for Twelve Pence per Pound. And Curriers have Three Shillings and Four Pence per Hide for Dressing it; they buy their Oyl at Twenty Pence per Gallon. Brick-Makers have Twenty Shillings per Thousand for their Bricks at the Kiln. Felt-Makers will have for their Hats Seven Shillings a piece, such as may be bought in England for Two Shillings a piece; yet they buy their Wooll commonly for Twelve or Fifteen Pence per Pound. And as to the Glaziers, they will have Five Pence a Quarry [a square or lozenge-shaped pane] for their Glass. The Rule for the Coopers I have almost forgot; but this I can affirm of some who went from Bristol (as their Neighbours report), that could hardly get their Livelihoods there, are now reckon'd in Pennsilvania, by a modest Computation to be worth some Hundreds (if not Thousands) of Pounds. The Bakers make as White Bread as any in London, and as for their Rule, it is the same in all Parts of the World that I have been in. The Butchers for killing a Beast, have Five Shillings and their Diet; and they may buy a good fat large Cow for Three Pounds, or thereabouts. The Brewers sell such Beer as is equal in Strength to that in London, half Ale and half Stout for Fifteen Shillings per Barrel; and their Beer hath a better Name, that is, is in more esteem than English Beer in Barbadoes, and is sold for a higher Price there. And for Silver-Smiths, they have between Half a Crown and Three Shillings an Ounce for working their Silver, and for Gold equivalent. Plasterers have commonly Eighteen Pence per Yard for Plastering. Last-Makers have Sixteen Shillings per dozen for their Lasts. And Heel-Makers have Two Shillings a dozen for their Heels. Wheel and Mill-Wrights, Joyners, Brasiers, Pewterers, Dyers, Fullers, Comb-Makers, Wyer-Drawers, Cage-Makers, Card-Makers, Painters, Cutlers, Rope-Makers, Carvers, Block-Makers, Turners, Button-Makers, Hair and Wood Sieve-Makers, Bodies-Makers, Gun-Smiths, Lock-Smiths, Nailers, File-Cuters, Skinners, Furriers, Glovers, Patten-Makers, Watch-Makers, Clock-Makers, Sadlers, Coller-Makers, Barbers, Printers, Book-Binders, and all other Trades-Men, their Gains and Wages are about the same proportion as the forementioned Trades in their Advancements, as to what they have in England.

Of Lawyers and Physicians I shall say nothing, because this Countrey is very Peaceable and Healt[h]y; long may it so continue and never have occasion for the Tongue of the one, nor the Pen of the other, both equally destructive to Mens Estates and Lives; besides forsooth, they, Hang-Man like, have a License to Murder and make Mischief. Labouring-Men have commonly here, between 14 and 15 Pounds a Year, and their Meat, Drink, Washing and Lodging; and by the Day their Wages is generally between Eighteen Pence and Half a Crown, and Diet also; But in Harvest they have usually between Three and Four Shillings each Day, and Diet. The Maid Servants Wages is commonly betwixt Six and Ten Pounds per Annum, with very good Accommodation. And for the Women who get their Livelihood by their own Industry, their Labour is very dear, for I can buy in London a Cheese-Cake for Two Pence, bigger than theirs at that price when at the same time their Milk is as cheap as we can buy it in London, and their Flour cheaper by one half.

Corn and Flesh, and what else serves Man for Drink, Food and Rayment, is much cheaper here than in England, or elsewhere; but the chief reason why Wages of Servants of all sorts is much higher here than there, arises from the great Fertility and Produce of the Place; besides, if these large Stipends were refused them, they would quickly set up for themselves, for they can have Provision very cheap, and Land for a very small matter, or next to nothing in comparison of the Purchace of Lands in England; and the Farmers there, can better afford to give that great Wages than the Farmers in England can, for several Reasons very obvious.

As First, their Land costs them (as I said but just now) little or nothing in comparison, of which the Farmers commonly will get twice the encrease of Corn for every Bushel they sow, that the Farmers in England can from the richest Land they have.

In the Second place, they have constantly good price for their Corn, by reason of the great and quick vent [sale] into Barbadoes and other Islands; through which means Silver is become more plentiful than here in England, considering the Number of People, and that causes a quick Trade for both Corn and Cattle; and that is the reason that Corn differs now from the Price formerly, else it would be at half the Price it was at then; for a Brother of mine (to my own particular knowledge) sold within the compass of one Week, about One Hundred and Twenty fat Beasts, most of them good handsom large Oxen.

Thirdly, They pay no Tithes, and their Taxes are inconsiderable; the Place is free for all Persuasions, in a Sober and Civil way; for the Church of England and the Quakers bear equal Share in the Government. They live Friendly and Well together; there is no Persecution for Religion, nor ever like to be; 'tis this that knocks all Commerce on the Head, together with high Imposts, strict Laws, and cramping Orders. Before I end this Paragraph, I shall add another Reason why Womens Wages are so exorbitant; they are not yet very numerous, which makes them stand upon high Terms for their several Services, in Sempstering, Washing, Spinning, Knitting, Sewing, and in all the other parts of their Imployments; for they have for Spinning either Worsted or Linen, Two Shillings a Pound, and commonly for Knitting a very Course pair of Yarn Stockings, they have half a Crown a pair; moreover they are usually Marry'd before they are Twenty Years of Age, and when once in that Noose, are for the most part a little uneasie, and make their Husbands so too, till they procure them a Maid Servant to bear the burden of the Work, as also in some measure to wait on them too.

It is now time to return to the City of Brotherly-Love (for so much the Greek Word or Name Philadelphia imports) which though at present so obscure, that neither the Map-Makers, nor Geographers have taken the least notice of her, tho she far exceeds her Namesake of Lydia [Asia Minor], (having above Two Thousand Noble Houses for her Five Hundred Ordinary) . . . yet in a very short space of time she will, in all probability, make a fine Figure in the World, and be a most Celebrated Emporeum. Here is lately built a Noble Town-House or Guild-Hall, also a Handsom Market-House, and a convenient Prison. The Number of Christians both Old and Young Inhabiting in that Countrey, are by a Modest Computation, adjudged to amount to above Twenty Thousand.

The Laws of this Countrey, are the same with those in England; our Constitution being on the same Foot: Many Disputes and Differences are determined and composed by Arbitration; and all Causes are decided with great Care and Expedition, being concluded (generally) at furthest at the Second Court, unless they happen to be very Nice and Difficult Cases; under Forty Shillings any one Justice of the Peace has Power to Try the Cause. Thieves of all sorts, are oblig'd to restore four fold after they have been Whipt and Imprison'd, according to the Nature of their Crime; and if they be not of Ability to restore four fold, they must be in Servitude till 'tis satisfied. They have Curious Wharfs as also several large and fine Timber-Yards, both at Philadelphia, and New-Castle, especially at the Metropolis, before Robert Turner's Great and Famous House, where are built Ships of considerable Burthen; they Cart their Goods from that Wharf into the City of Philadelphia, under an Arch, over which part of the Street is built, which is called Chesnut-Street-Wharf, besides other Wharfs, as High-Street Wharf, Mulberry Street Wharf, and Vine-Sreet Wharf, and all those are Common Wharfs; and likewise there are very pleasant Stairs, as Trus and Carpenter-Stairs, besides several others. There are above Thirty Carts belonging to that City, Four or Five Horses to each. There is likewise a very convenient Wharf called Carpenter's Wharf, which hath a fine necessary Crain belonging to it, with suitable

Granaries, and Store-Houses. A Ship of Two Hundred Tun may load and unload by the side of it, and there are other Wharfs (with Magazines and Ware-Houses) which front the City all along the River, as also a Curious and Commodious Dock with a Draw-Bridge to it, for the convenient Reception of Vessels; where have been built some Ships of Two or Three Hundred Tuns each: They have very Stately Oaks to build Ships with, some of which are between Fifty and Sixty Foot long, and clear from Knots, being very straight and well Grain'd. In this famous City of Philadelphia there are several Rope-Makers, who have large and curious Rope-Walks especially one Joseph Wilcox. Also Three or Four Spacious Malt-Houses, as many large Brew-Houses, and many handsom Bake-Houses for Publick Use.

In the said City are several good Schools of Learning for Youth, in order to the Attainment of Arts and Sciences, as also Reading, Writing, etc. Here is to be had on any Day in the Week, Tarts, Pies, Cakes, etc. We have also several Cooks-Shops, both Roasting and Boyling, as in the City of London; Bread, Beer, Beef, and Pork, are sold at any time much cheaper than in England (which arises from their Plenty) our Wheat is very white and clear from Tares, making as good and white Bread as any in Europe. Happy Blessings, for which we owe the highest Gratitude to our Plentiful Provider, the great Creator of Heaven and Earth. The Water-Mills far exceed those in England, both for quickness and grinding good Meal, their being great choice of good Timber, and earlier Corn than in the aforesaid Place, they are made by one Peter Deal [Daile], a Famous and Ingenious Workman, especially for inventing such like Machines.

All sorts of very good Paper are made in the German-Town; as also very fine German Linen, such as no Person of Quality need be asham'd to wear; and in several places they make very good Druggets, Crapes, Camblets, and Serges, besides other Woollen Cloathes, the Manufacture of all which daily improves: And in most parts of the Countrey there are many Curious and Spacious Buildings, which several of the Gentry have erected for their Country-Houses. As for the Fruit-Trees they Plant, they arrive at such Perfection, that they bear in a little more than half the time that they commonly do in England.

The Christian Children born here are generally well-favoured, and Beautiful to behold; I never knew any come into the World with the least blemish on any part of its Body, being in the general, observ'd to be better Natur'd, Milder, and more tender Hearted than those born in England.

There are very fine and delightful Gardens and Orchards, in most parts of this Countrey; but Edward Shippey [Shippen] (who lives near the Capital City) has an Orchard and Gardens adjoyning to his Great House that equalizes (if not exceeds) any I have ever seen, having a very famous and pleasant Summer-House erected in the middle of his extraordinary fine and large Garden abounding with Tulips, Pinks, Carnations, Roses, (of several sorts) Lilies, not to mention those that grow wild in the Fields.

Reader, what I have here written, is not a Fiction, Flam, Whim, or any sinister Design, either to impose upon the Ignorant, or Credulous, or to curry Favour with the Rich and Mighty, but in meer Pity and pure Compassion to the Numbers of Poor Labouring Men, Women, and Children in England, half starv'd, visible in their meagre looks, that are continually wandering up and down looking for Employment without finding any, who here need not lie idle a moment, nor want due Encouragement or Reward for their Work, much less Vagabond or Drone it about. Here are no Beggars to be seen (it is a Shame and Disgrace to the State that there are so many in England) nor indeed have any here the least Occasion or Temptation to take up that Scandalous Lazy Life.

Jealousie among Men is here very rare, and Barrenness among Women hardly to be heard of, nor are old Maids to be met with; for all commonly Marry before they are Twenty Years of Age, and seldom any young Married Woman but hath a Child in her Belly, or one upon her Lap.

What I have deliver'd concerning this Province, is indisputably true, I was an Eye-Witness to it all, for I went in the first Ship that was bound from England for that Countrey, since it received the Name of Pensilvania, which was in the Year 1681. The Ship's Name was the *John and Sarah* of London, Henry Smith Commander. I have declin'd giving any Account of several things which I have only heard others speak of, because I did not see them my self, for I never held that way infallible, to make Reports from Hear-say. I saw the first Cellar when it was digging for the use of our Governour Will. Penn.

VI. THE SOUTHERN COLONIES

In the 17th century the colonies that were destined to become the most distinctive region of the United States were sparsely populated, richly endowed, and perhaps too well known for the wrong reasons. What criticisms were made in the 17th century of the southern colonies? What truth was there in these criticisms? Were these criticisms equally true of all the colonies all through the century? How did the colonies overcome these criticisms? Why would an English farmer benefit from moving to a southern colony? Why would an English minister? An indentured servant? a trader? Why were Virginians healthier than Englishmen? Why were English visitors concerned about the medicinal qualities of Carolina plants? How did the settlers learn about New World medicine? What kind of life did Negro slaves have in the 17th century? How effective were southern agricultural practices? What was the moral and religious character of the southern colonies? Is the stereotypical "southern character" visible in the 17th century? Do any of the 17th-century southern characteristics not fit the later stereotype?

By 1656 Virginia had had a long and not altogether happy history, and her reputation in England had seen better days. To set the record straight, John Hammond, an English farmer who had first come to America in 1635 and remained for 21 years, wrote Leah and Rachel, or, the Two Fruitfull Sisters Virginia, and Mary-land: Their Present Condition, Impartially stated and related *(London, 1656). Hammond's simple but direct views are taken from the reprint of the first edition in Peter Force's* Tracts and Other Papers, Relating Principally to the Origin, Settlement, and Progress of the Colonies in North America *(Washington, 1844), vol. 3, pp. 6-20.*

It is the glory of every Nation to enlarge themselves, to encourage their own forraign attempts, and to be able to have of their own, within their own territories, as many several commodities as they can attain to, that so others may rather be beholding to them, then they to others; and to this purpose have Encouragements, Priviledges and Emunities been given to any Discoveries or Adventurers into remote Colonies, by all politique Common Wealths in the world.

But alas, we Englishmen (in all things else famous, and to other Countries terrible) do not onely faile in this, but vilifie, scandalize and cry down such parts of the unknown world, as have been found out, setled and made flourishing, by the charge, hazzard and diligence of their own brethren, as if because removed from us, we either account them people of another world or enemies.

This is too truly made good in the odiums and cruell slanders cast on those two famous Countries of *Virginia* and *Mary-land*, whereby those Countries, not onely are many times at a stand, but are in danger to moulder away, and come in time to nothing; nor is there any thing but the fertility and natural gratefulnesse of them, left a remedy to prevent it.

To let our own Nation (whose common good I covet, and whose Common-wealths servant I am, as born to no other use) be made sensible of these injuries: I have undertaken in this Book to give the true state of those places, according to the condition they are now in; and to declare either to distressed or discontented, that they need not doubt because of any rumour detracting from their goodnesses, to remove and cast themselves and Fortunes upon those Countries, in which if I should deviate from the truth; I have at this present carping enemies in *London* enough, to contradict and cry down me and this, for Impostours. It is not long since I came from thence (God knows sore against my will) having lived there upward of one and twenty years; nor do I intend (by Gods assistance) to be long out of it again: and therefore can by experience, not hear-say (as *Bullock* and other lying Writters have done, who at randome or for their own private lucre have rendred their Books rediculous and themselves infamous lyars, nor will I like them, over extoll the places, as if they were rather Paradices than earthly habitations; but truly let ye know, what they are, and how the people there live.) Which when impartially viewed, will undoubtedly clear up those Foggy Mists, that hath to their own ruine blinded and kept off many from going thither, whose miseries and misfortunes by staying in *England* are much to be lamented, and much to be pittied.

In respect these two Sister Countries (though distinct Governments) are much of one nature, both for produce and manner of living; I shall only at present, Treat of the elder Sister *Virginia*, and in speaking of that include both: And ere I leave off, shall in particular rehearse the unnaturall usage *Mary-land* the younger Sister, hath had, not by *Virginia*; but by those Vipers she hath received and harboured with much kindnesse and hospitalitie.

The Country is reported to be an unhealthy place, a nest of Rogues, whores, desolute and rooking persons; a place of intolerable labour, bad usage and hard Diet, &c.

To Answer these several calumnies, I shall first shew what it was? next, what it is?

At the first settling and many years after, it deserved most of those aspersions (nor were they then aspersions but truths) it was not settled at the publique charge; but when found out, challenged, and maintained by Adventurers, whose avarice and inhumanity, brought in these inconveniences, which to this day brands *Virginia*.

Then were Jayls emptied, youth seduced, infamous women drilled in, the provisions all brought out of *England*, and that embezzelled by the Trustees (for they durst neither hunt fowl, nor Fish, for fear of the *Indian*, which they stood in aw of, their labour was almost perpetuall, their allowance of victual small, few or no cattle, no use of horses nor oxen to draw or carry, (which labours men supplyed themselves) all which caused a mortality; no civil courts of justice but under a Marshall [martial] law, no redresse of grievances, complaints were repaied with stripes, moneys with scoffes, tortures made delights, and in a word all and the worst that tyrany could inflict or act, which when complained of in *England*: (but so were they kept under that it was long ere they would suffer complaints to come home) the bondage was taken of, the people set free, and had lands a signed to each of them to live of themselves, and enjoy the benefit of their own industry; men then began to call what they laboured for their own, they fell to making themselves convenient housing to dwell in, to plant corne for their food, to range the wood for flesh, the rivers for fowle and fish, to finde out somwhat staple for supplie of cloathing, to continue a commerce, to purchase and breed cattle, &c. but the bud of this growing happinesse was again nipt by a cruell Massacre committed by the Natives [in 1622], which again pull'd them back and kept them under, enforcing them to get into Forts (such as the infancy of those times afforded: they were taken off from planting; their provisions destroyed, their Cattle, Hogs, Horses, &c. kill'd up, and brought to such want and penury, that diseases grew rife, mortality exceeded; but receiving a supply of men, amunition and victuals out of *England*, they again gathered heart, pursued their enemies, and so often worsted them, that the *Indians* were glad to sue for peace, and they desirous of a cessation) consented to it.

They again began to bud forth, to spread further, to gather wealth, which they rather profusely spent (as gotten with ease then providently husbanded, or aimed at any publique good; or to make a Country for posterity; but from hand to mouth, and for a present being; neglecting discoveries, planting of Orchards, providing for the Winter preservation of their stocks, or thinking of any thing staple or firm; and whilest Tobacco, the onely Commodity they had to subsist on bore a price, they wholy and eagerly followed that, neglecting their very planting of Corn, and much relyed on *England* for the chiefest part of their provisions; so that being not alwayes amply supplied, they were often in such want, that their case and condition being related in *England*, it hindred and kept off many from going thither, who rather cast their eyes on the Barren and freezing soyle of *New-England*, than to joyn with such an indigent and sottish people, as were reported to be in *Virginia*.

Yet was not *Virginia* all this while without divers honest and vertuous inhabitants, who observing the general neglect and licensiousnesses there, caused Assemblies to be call'd and Laws to be made tending to the glory of God, the severe suppression of vices, and the compelling them not to neglect (upon strickt punishments) planting and tending such quantities of Corn, as would not onely serve themselves, their Cattle and Hogs plentifully, but to be enabled to supply *New-England* (then in want) with such proportions, as were extream reliefs, to them in their necessities.

From this industry of theirs and great plenty of Corn, (the main staffe of life) proceeded that great plenty of Cattel and Hogs, (now innumerable) and out of which not only *New-England* hath been stocked and relieved, but all other parts of the *Indies* inhabited by Englishmen.

The inhabitants now finding the benefit of their industries, began to look with delight on their increasing stocks: (as nothing more pleasurable then profit) to take pride in their plentifully furnished Tables, to grow not onely civil, but great observers of the Sabbath, to stand upon their reputations, and to be ashamed of that notorious manner of life they had formerly lived and wallowed in.

They then began to provide and send home for Gospel Ministers, and largely contributed for their maintenance; But *Virginia* savouring not handsomely in *England*, very few of good conversation would adventure thither, (as thinking it a place wherein surely the fear of God was not) yet many came, such as wore Black Coats, and could babble in a Pulpet, roare in a Tavern, exact from their Parishoners, and rather by their dissolutenesse destroy than feed their Flocks.

Loath was the Country to be wholy without Teachers, and therefore rather retain these then to be destitute; yet still endeavours for better in their places, which were obtained, and these Wolves in sheeps cloathing, by their Assemblies questioned, silenced, and some forced to depart the Country.

Then began the Gospel to flourish, civil, honourable, and men of great estates flocked in: famous buildings went forward, Orchards innumerable were planted and preserved; Tradesmen set on work and encouraged, staple Commodities, as Silk, Flax, Pot-ashes, &c. of which I shall speak further hereafter, attempted on, and with good successe brought to perfection; so that this Country which had a mean beginning, many back friends, two ruinous and bloody Massacres [in 1622 and 1644], hath by Gods grace out-grown all, and is become a place of pleasure and plenty.

And having briefly laid down the former state of *Virginia*, in its Infancy, and filth, and the occasion of its scandalous aspersions: I come to my main subject, its present Condition and Hapinesse (if any thing can be justly called happy in this transatory life (otherwise then as blessings which in the well using whereof, a future happinesse may be expected.)

I affirme the Country to be wholesome, healthy and fruitfull; and a modell on which industry may as much improve it self in, as in any habitable part of the World; yet not such a Lubberland as the Fiction of the land of Ease, is reported to be, nor such a *Utopian* as Sr. *Thomas Moore* [More] hath related to be found out.

In the Countries minority, and before they had well cleared the ground to let in ayre (which now is otherwise) many imputed the stifling of the wood to be the cause of such sicknesse; but I rather think the contrary; for divers new Rivers lately settled, where at their first comming upon them as woody as *James* Rivers, the first place they setled in, and yet those Rivers are as healthy as any former setled place in *Virginia* or *England* it self: I believe (and that not without reason) it was only want of such diet as best agreed with our English natures, good drinks and wholesome lodgings were the cause of so much sicknesses, as were formerly frequent, which we have now amended; and therefore enjoy better healths; to which I add, and that by experience since my comming into *England*, and many (if not all *Virginians* can do the like,) that change of ayre does much alter the state of our bodies: by which many travellers thither may expect some sickness, yet little danger of mortality.

A Geographicall description of the Country I shall not attempt (as having little skill in the Mathematicks) enough of that hath been formerly Written; nor is it a place now to learn to discover. I shall abhor to spirit over any; but go along with such as are voluntarily desirous to go thither, and lead them with my blunt relation (for truth knows little of eloquence) aboard the Ships thither bound, and carrying you into the Country, shew you the courtesie of the place, the disposition of the Inhabitants, the commodities, and give all sorts of people advice how and where to set down for their present benefit and future accommodation.

If any are minded to repair thither, if they are not in a capacity to defray their own charges (if they are I wish they might and so be at their own disposing) let them not be seduced by those mercinary spirits that know little of the place, nor aime at any good of theirs, but onely by foysting and flattering them to gain a reward of those they procure them for; beware them, for it is not only hab nab whether ye go to a good service or a bad, but scandalous to your selves to be so seduced, and it were good and very just that such vagabond people were severely punished, as great betrayers of their own Nation, for ye cannot imagine but their are as well bad services as good; but I shall shew ye if any happen into the hands of such crooked dispensitions, how to order them and ease your selves, when I come to treat of the justice of the Country, which many being ignorant of suffer inconveniences, which by this they may prevent.

Let such as are so minded not rashly throw themselves upon the voyage, but observe the nature, and enquire the qualities of the persons with whom they ingage to transport themselves, or if (as not acquainted with such as inhabit there, but go with Merchants and Mariners, who transport them to others,) let their covenant be such, that after their arrival they have a fortnights time assigned them to enquire of their Master, and make choyce of such as they intend to expire their time with, nor let that brand of selling of servants, be any discouragement to deter any from going, for if a time must be served, it is all one with whom it be served, provided they be people of honest repute, with which the Country is well replenished.

And be sure to have your contract in writing and under hand and seal, for if ye go over upon promise made to do this or that, or to be free or your own men, it signifies nothing, for by a law of the Country (waving all promises) any one coming in, and not paying their own passages, must serve if men or women four years, if younger according to their years, but where an Indenture is, that is binding and observing.

The usual allowance for servants is (besides their charge of passage defrayed) at their expiration, a years provision of corne, dubble apparrel [two suits of clothes], tooles necessary, and land according to the custome of the Country, which is an old delusion, for there is no land accustomary due to the servant, but to the Master, and therefore that servant is unwise that will not dash out that custom in his covenant, and make that due of land absolutely his own, which although at the present, not of so great consequence; yet in few years will be of much worth, as I shall hereafter make manifest.

When ye go aboard, expect the Ship somewhat troubled and in a hurliburly, untill ye cleer the lands end; and that the Ship is rummaged, and things put to rights, which many times discourages the Passengers, and makes them wish the Voyage unattempted: but this is but for a short season, and washes off when at Sea, where the time is pleasantly passed away, though not with such choise plenty as the shore affords.

But when ye arrive and are settled, ye will find a strange alteration, an abused Country giving the lye in your own approbations to those that have calumniated it, and these infalable arguments may convince all incredible and obstinate opinions, concerning the goodnesse and delightfulnesse of the Country, that never any servants of late times have gone thither; but in their Letters to their Friends commend and approve of the place, and rather invite than disswade their acquaintance from comming thither. An other is this, that seldom (if ever) any that hath continued in *Virginia* any time, will or do desire to live in *England*, but post back with what expedition they can; although many are landed men in *England*, and have good Estates here, and divers wayes of preferments propounded to them, to entice and perswade their continuance.

The Country is as I said of a temperate nature, the dayes, in summer not so long as in *England*, in winter longer; it is somewhat hotter in *June*, *July* and *August* then here, but that heat sweetly allayed by a continual breaze of winde, which never failes to cool and refresh the labourer and traveller; the cold seldom approaches sencibly untill about *Christmas*, (although the last winter was hard and the worst I or any living there knew) and when winter comes, (which is such and no worse then is in *England*,) it continues two monthes seldom longer, often not so long and in that time although here seldom hardweather keep men from labour, yet there no work is done all winter except dressing their own victuals and making of fires.

The labour servants are put to, is not so hard nor of such continuance as Husbandmen, nor Handecraftmen are kept at in *England*, I said little or nothing is done in winter time, none ever work before sun rising nor after sun set, in the summer they rest, sleep or exercise themselves five houres in the heat of the day, Saturdayes afternoon is alwayes their own, the old Holidayes are observed and the Sabboath spent in good exercises.

The Women are not (as is reported) put into the ground to worke, but occupie such domestique imployments and houswifery as in *England*, that is dressing victuals, righting up the house, milking, imployed about dayries, washing, sowing, &c. and both men and women have times of recreations, as much or more than in any part of the world besides, yet som wenches that are nasty, beastly and not fit to be so imployed are put into the ground, for reason tells us, they must not at charge be transported and then mantained for nothing, but those that prove so aukward are rather burthensome then servants desirable or usefull.

The Country is fruitfull, apt for all and more then *England* can or does produce, the usuall diet is such as in *England*, for the rivers afford innumerable sortes of choyce fish, (if they will take the paines to make wyers or hier the Natives, who for a small matter will undertake it,) winter and summer, and that in many places sufficient to serve the use of man, and to fatten hoggs, water-fowle of all sortes are (with admiration to be spoken of) plentifull and easie to be killed, yet by many degrees more plentifull in some places then in othersome, Deare all over the Country, and in many places so many, that venison is accounted a tiresom meat, wilde Turkeys are frequent, and so large that I have seen some weigh neer threescore pounds; other beasts there are whose flesh is wholsom and savourie, such are unknowne to us; and therefore I will not stuffe my book with superfluous relation of their names; huge Oysters and store in all parts where the salt-water comes.

The Country is exceedingly replenished with Neat cattle, Hoggs, Goats and Tame-fowle, but not many sheep; so that mutton is somwhat scarce, but that defect is supplied with store of Venison, other flesh and fowle; The Country is full of gallant Orchards, and the fruit generally more luscious and delightfull then here, witnesse the Peach and Quince, the latter may be eaten raw savourily, the former differs and as much exceeds ours as the best relished apple we have doth the crabb, and of both most excellent and comfortable drinks are made, Grapes in infinite manners grow wilde, so do Walnuts, Smalnuts, Chesnuts and abundance of excellent fruits, Plums and Berries, not growing or known in *England*; graine we have, both *English* and *Indian* for bread and Bear, and Pease besides *English* of ten several sorts, all exceeding ours in *England*, the gallant root of Potatoes are common, and so are all sorts of rootes, herbes and Garden stuffe.

It must needs follow then that diet cannot be scarce, since both rivers and woods affords it, and that such plenty of Cattle and Hogs are every where, which yeeld beef, veal, milk, butter, cheese and other made dishes, porke, bacon, and pigs, and that as sweet and savoury meat as the world affords, these with the help of Orchards and Gardens, Oysters, Fish, Fowle and Venison, certainly cannot but be sufficient for a good diet and wholsom accommodation, considering how plentifully they are, and how easie with industry to be had.

Beare is indeed in some place constantly drunken, in other some, nothing but Water or Milk, and Water or Beverige; & that is where the goodwives, (if I may so call them) are negligent and idle; for it is not for want of Corn to make Malt with (for the Country affords enough) but because they are sloathfull and carelesse: but I hope this Item will shame them out of those humours, that they will be adjudged by their drink, what kinde of Housewives they are.

Those Servants that will be industrious may in their time of service gain a competent estate before their Freedomes, which is usually done by many, and they gaine esteeme and assistance that appear so industrious: There is no Master almost but will allow his Servant a parcell of clear ground to plant some Tobacco in for himself, which he may husband at those many idle times he hath allowed him and not prejudice, but rejoyce his Master to see it, which in time of Shipping he may lay out for commodities, and in Summer sell them again with advantage, and get a Sow-Pig or two, which any body almost will give him, and his Master suffer him to keep them with his own, which will be no charge to his Master, and with one years increase of them may purchase a Cow Calf or two, and by that time he is for himself; he may have Cattle, Hogs and Tobacco of his own, and come to live gallantly; but this must be gained (as I said) by Industry and affability, not by sloth nor churlish behaviour.

And whereas it is rumoured that Servants have no lodging other then on boards, or by the Fire side, it is contrary to reason to believe it: First, as we are Christians; next as people living under a law, which compels as well the Master as the Servant to perform his duty; nor can true labour be either expected or exacted without sufficient cloathing, diet, and lodging; all which both their Indentures (which must inviolably be observed) and the Justice of the Country requires.

But if any go thither, not in a condition of a Servant, but pay his or her passage, which is some six pounds: Let them not doubt but it is money well layd out (yet however let them not fail) although they carry little else to take a Bed along with them, and then few Houses but will give them entertainment, either out of curtesie, or on reasonable tearms; and I think it better for any that goes over free, and but in a mean condition, to hire himself for reasonable wages of Tobacco and Provision, the first year, provided he happen in an honest house, and where the Mistresse is noted for a good Housewife, of which there are very many (notwithstanding the cry to the contrary) for by that means he will live free of disbursment, have something to help him the next year, and be carefully looked to in his sicknesse (if he chance to fall sick) and let him so covenant that exceptions may be made, that he work not much in the hot weather, a course we alwayes take with our new hands (as they call them) the first year they come in.

If they are women that go after this manner, that is paying their own passages; I advise them to sojourn in a house of honest repute, for by their good carriage, they may advance themselves in marriage, by their ill, overthow their fortunes; and although loose persons sel-dome live long unmarried if free; yet they match with as desolute as themselves, and never live handsomly or are ever respected.

For any that come over free, and are minded to dyet and quarter in another mans house, it matters not whether they know on what term or conditions they are there; for by an excellent Decree, made by Sir *William Berkly*, when Governour; (as indeed he was the Author of many good Laws:) It was ordered, that if any inhabitant received any stranger Merchant, or border into their houses, and did not condi-tion in Writing with him or them so entertained on what tearms he received them, it should be supposed an invitation, an no satisfaction should be allowed or recovered in any Court of Justice; thereby giving notice that no stranger coming into the Country should be drilled in, or made a purchase of under colour of friendship: but that the Inhabi-tants at first coming shall let them know how they mean to deal with them, that if they like not the terms they may remove themselves at pleasure; a Law so good and commendable, that it is never like to be revoked or altered.

Now for those that carry over Families and estates with a determina-tion to inhabit, my advice is that they neither sojourn for that will be chargeable; nor on the sudden purchase, for that may prove unfor-tunate; but that they for the first year hire a house (for seats are alwayes to be hired) and by that means, they will not onely finde content and live at a cheap rate, but be acquainted in the Country and learn the worth and goodnesse of the Plantation they mean to purchase; and so not rashly intangle themselves in an ill bargain, or finde where a convenient parcell of Land is for their turns to be taken up.

Yet are the Inhabitants generally affable, courteous and very assistant to strangers (for what but plenty makes hospitality and good neighbourhood) and no sooner are they settled, but they will be visiting, presenting and advicing the stranger how to improve what they have, how to better their way of livelihood.

Justice is there duly and daily administred; hardly can any travaile two miles together, but they will finde a Justice, which hath power of himself to hear and determine mean differences, to secure and bind over notorious offenders, of which very few are in the Country.

In every County are Courts kept, every two moneths, and oftener if occasion require, in which Courts all things are determined without exceptions; and if any dislike the proceedings of those Courts, they have liberty to appeal to the Quarter Court, which is four times a year; and from thence to the Assembly, which is once or oftner every year: So that I am confident, more speedy Justice and with smaler charge is not in any place to be found.

Theft is seldome punished (as being seldome or never committed; for as the Proverb is, where there are no receivers, there are no thieves; and although Doores are nightly left open (especially in the Summer time) Hedges hanging full of Cloathes; [silver or pewter] Plate frequently used amongst all comers and goers (and there is good store of Plate in many houses) yet I never heard of any losse ever received either in Plate, Linnen, or any thing else out of their Houses all the time I inhabited there.

Indeed I have known some suffer for stealing of Hogs, (but not since they have been plentifull) and whereas Hogstealing was once punished with death, it is now made penal, and restitution given very amply to the owner thereof.

Cases of Murther are punished as in *England*, and Juries allowed, as well in Criminal causes, as in all other differences between party and party, if they desire it.

Servants complaints are freely harkened to, and (if not causlesly made) there Masters are compelled either speedily to amend, or they are removed upon second complaint to another service; and often times not onely set free, (if the abuse merit it) but ordered to give reparation and damage to their servant.

The Country is very full of sober, modest persons, both men and women, and many that truly fear God and follow that perfect rule of our blessed Saviour, to do as they would be done by; and of such a happy inclination is the Country, that many who in *England* have been lewd and idle, there in emulation or imitation (for example moves more then percept) of the industry of those they finde there, not onely grow ashamed of their former courses, but abhor to hear of them, and in small time wipe off those stains they have formerly been tainted with; yet I cannot but confesse, there are people wicked enough (as what Country is free) for we know some natures will never be reformed, but these must follow the Fryers rule, *Si non caste, tamen cante*; for if any be known, either to prophane the Lords day or his Name, be found drunk, commit whoredome, scandalize or disturb his neighbour, or give offence to the world by living suspiciously in any bad courses; there are for each of these, severe and wholsome laws and remedies made, provided and duly put in execution. I can confidently affirm, that since my being in *England*, which is not yet four moneths, I have been an eye and ear witnesse of more deceits and villanies (and such as modesty forbids me to utter) then I either ever saw or heard mention made of in *Virginia*, in my one and twenty years aboad in those parts.

And therefore those that shall blemish *Virginia* any more, do but like the Dog bark against the Moon, untill they be blind and weary; and *Virginia* is now in that secure growing condition, that like the Moon so barked at, she will passe on her course, maugre all detractors, and a few years will bring it to that glorious happinesse, that many of her calumniators, will intercede to procure admittance thither, when it will be hard to be attained to; for in smal time, little land will be to be taken up; and after a while none at all; and as the Mulberry Trees grows up, which are by every one planted, Tobacco will be laid by, and we shall wholy fall to making of Silk (a Sample of 400l. hath already been sent for *England*, and approved of) which will require little labour; and therefore shall have little use of Servants; besides, Children increase and thrive so well there, that they themselves will sufficiently supply the defect of Servants: And in small time become a Nation of themselves sufficient to people the Country: And this good policy is there used; As the Children there born grow to maturity, and capable (as they are generally very capable and apt) they are still preferred and put into authority, and carry themselves therein civilly and discretly; and few there are but are able to give some Portions with their daughters, more or lesse, according to their abilities; so that many comming out of *England* have raised themselves good fortunes there meerly by matching with Maidens born in the Country.

And therefore I cannot but admire, and indeed much pitty the dull stupidity of people necessitated in *England*, who rather then they will remove themselves, live here a base, slavish, penurious life; as if there were a necessity to live and to live so, choosing rather then they will forsake *England* to stuff *New-Gate*, *Bridewell*, and other Jayles with their carkessies, nay cleave to tyburne [Tyburn, the public hanging place] it selfe; and so bring confusion to their souls horror and infamine to their kindred or posteritie, others itch out their wearisom lives in reliance of other mens charities, an uncertaine and unmanly expectation; some more abhorring such courses betake themselve to almost perpetuall and restlesse toyle and druggeries out of which (whilst their strength lasteth) they (observing hard diets, earlie and late houres) make hard shift to subsist from hand to mouth, untill age or sicknesse takes them off from labour and directs them the way to beggerie, and such indeed are to be pittied, relieved and provided for.

I have seriously considered when I have (passing the streets) heard the several Cryes, and noting the commodities, and the worth of them they have carried and cryed up and down; how possibly a livelihood could be exacted out of them, as to cry Matches, Smal-coal, Blacking, Pen and Ink, Thred-laces, and a hundred more such kinde of trifling merchandizes; then looking on the nastinesse of their linnen habits and bodies: I conclude if gain sufficient could be raised out of them for subsistance; yet their manner of living was degenerate and base; and their condition to be far below the meanest servant in *Virginia*.

The other day, I saw a man heavily loaden with a burden of Faggots on his back, crying, Dry Faggots, Dry Faggots; he travailed much ground, bawled frequently, and sweat with his burthen: but I saw none buy any, neer three houres I followed him, in which time he rested, I entered into discourse with him, offered him drink, which he thankfully accepted of (as desirous to learn the mistery of his trade) I enquired what he got by each burden when sold? he answered me three pence: I further asked him what he usually got a day? he replyed, some dayes nothing some dayes six pence; some time more, but seldome; me thought it was a pittifull life, and I admired how he could live on it; And yet it were dangerous to advise these wretches to better their conditions by travaile, for fear of the cry of, a spirit, a spirit.

The Country is not only plentifull but pleasant and profitable, pleasant in regard of the brightnesse of the weather, the many delightfull

rivers, on which the inhabitants are settled (every man almost living
in sight of a lovely river) the abundance of game, the extraordinary
good neighbour-hood and loving conversation they have one with the
other.

Pleasant in their building, which although for most part they are
but one story besides the loft, and built of wood, yet contrived so
delightfull, that your ordinary houses in England are not so handsome,
for usually the rooms are large, daubed and whitelimed, glazed and
flowered, and if not glazed windows, shutters which are made very
pritty and convenient.

Pleasant in observing their stocks and flockes of Cattle, Hoggs, and
Poultry, grazing, whisking and skipping in their sights, pleasant in
having all things of their own, growing or breeding without drawing
the peny to send for this and that, without which, in England they
cannot be supplyed.

The manner of living and trading there is thus, each man almost
lives a free-holder, nothing but the value of 12. d. a year to be paid
as rent, for every 50. Acrees of land; firing cost nothing every man
plants his own corne and neede take no care for bread: if any thing
be bought, it is for comodity, exchanged presently, or for a day, payment is usuall made but once a year, and for that Bill taken (for
accounts are not pleadable.)

In summer when fresh meat will not keep (seeing every man kils
of his own, and quantities are inconvenient, they lend from one to
another, such portions of flesh as they can spare, which is repaied
again when the borrowers kils his.

If any fall sick, and cannot compasse to follow his crope which
if not followed, will soon be lost, the adjoyning neighbour, will either
voluntarily or upon a request joyn together, and work in it by spels,
untill the honour recovers, and that gratis, so that no man by sicknesse
loose any part of his years worke.

Let any travell, it is without charge, and at every house is entertainment as in a hostery, and with it hearty welcome are stranger entertained.

In a word, *Virginia* wants not good victual, wants not good disposi-
tions, and as God hath freely bestowed it, they as freely impart with
it, yet are there aswel bad natures as good.

The profit of the country is either by their labour, their stockes,
or their trades.

By their labours is produced corne and Tobacco, and all other growing provisions, and this Tobacco however now low-rated, yet a good maintenance may be had out of it, (for they have nothing of necessity but cloathing to purchasse) or can this mean price of Tobacco long hold, for these reasons, First that in England it is prohibited, next that they have attained of late those sorts equall with the best Spanish, Thirdly that the sicknesse in Holland is decreasing, which hath been a great obstruction to the sail of Tobacco.

And lastly, that as the mulbery tree grows up, tobacco will be neglected and silke, flax, two staple commodities generally fallen upon.

Of the increase of cattle and hoggs, much advantage is made, by selling biefe, porke, and bacon, and butter &c. either to shipping, or to send to the Barbadoes, and other Islands, and he is a very poor man that hath not sometimes provision to put off.

By trading with Indians for Skine, Beaver, Furres and other commodities oftentimes good profits are raised; The Indians are in absolute subjection to the English, so that they both pay tribute to them and receive all their severall king[s] from them, and as one dies they repaire to the English for a successor, so that none neede doubt it a place of securitie.

Several ways of advancement there are and imployments both for the learned and laborer, recreation for the gentry, traffique for the adventurer, congregations for the ministrie (and oh that God would stir, up the hearts of more to go over, such as would teach good doctrine, and not paddle in faction, or state matters; they could not want maintenance, they would find an assisting, an imbracing, a conforming people.)

It is knowne (such preferment hath this Country rewarded the industrious with) that some from being wool-hoppers and of as mean and meaner imployment in England have there grown great merchants, and attained to the most eminent advancements the Country afforded. If men cannot gaine (by diligence) [e]states in those parts, (I speake not only mine owne opinion, but divers others, and something by experience) it will hardly be done (unlesse by meere lucke as gamsters thrive, and other accidentals in any other part whatsoever).

Now having briefly set down the present state of *Virginia* not in fiction, but in realitie, I wish the juditious reader to consider what dislike can be had of the Country, or upon what grounds it is so infamously injured, I only therein covet to stop those blackmouthed babblers, that not only have and do abuse so noble a plantation, but abuse Gods great blessing in adding to England so flourishing a branch, in perswading many souls, rather to follow desparate and miserable courses in England, then to ingage in so honourable an undertaking as to travile and inhabite there; but to those I shall (if admonition will not worke on their recreant spirits) only say. Let him that *is filthie be filthie still*.

Jaspar Dankers and Peter Sluyter also looked at the southern colonies of Maryland and Virginia as candidates for their religious community. Their description of Maryland in 1680 is taken from the Memoirs of the Long Island Historical Society, *vol. 1 (1867), pp. 214-221.*

[15 Dec. 1679]: It was flood tide early this morning, and our servant slept a little too long, for it was not far from high water when he appeared. We hurried, however, into the boat and pushed on as hard as we could, but the flood stopped running, when we were about half way. We continued on rowing, and as the day advanced we caught a favorable wind from the west and spread the sail. The wind gradually increasing brought us to Newcastle about eight o'clock among our kind friends again, where we were welcome anew. We were hardly ashore before the wind, changing from the west to the northwest, brought with it such a storm and rain that, if we had still been on the water, we would have been in great peril, and if we had been at Casparus's we would not have been able to proceed in such weather. We here again, so clearly perceived the providence of the Lord over us, that our hearts were constrained to ascend to him, and praise him for what he is and does, especially towards his children. As we have confined ourselves quite strictly to the account of our journey, we deem it serviceable to make some observations upon some general matters concerning Maryland, in addition to what we have before remarked.

As regards its first discoverer and possessor, that was one Lord Baltimore, an English nobleman, in the time of Queen Maria. Having come from Newfoundland along the coast of North America, he arrived in the great bay of Virginia, up which he sailed to its upper-most parts, and found this fine country which he named Maryland after his queen. Returning to England he obtained a charter of the northerly parts of America, *inexclusively*, although the Hollanders had discovered and began to settle New Netherland. With this he came back to America and took possession of his Maryland, where at present his son, as governor, resides.

Since the time of Queen Elizabeth, settlers have preferred the lowest parts of the great bay and the large rivers which empty into it, either on account of proximity to the sea, and the convenience of the streams, or because the uppermost country smacked somewhat of the one from whom it derived its name and of its government. They have named this lower country Virginia, out of regard to Queen Elizabeth. It is the most populous, but not the best land, and has a government distinct from that of Maryland. A governor [Lord Culpepper] arrived while we were there, to fill the place made vacant by the death of his predecessor [Sir William Berkeley].

As to the present government of Maryland, it remains firm upon the old footing, and is confined within the limits before mentioned. All of Maryland that we have seen, is high land, with few or no meadows, but possessing such a rich and fertile soil, as persons living there assured me, that they had raised tobacco off the same piece of land for thirty consecutive years. The inhabitants who are generally English, are mostly engaged in this production. It is their chief staple, and the means with which they must purchase every thing they require, which is brought to them from other English possessions in Europe, Africa and America. There is, nevertheless, sometimes a great want of these necessaries, owing to the tobacco market being low, or the shipments being prevented by some change of affairs in some quarter, particularly in Europe, or to both causes, as was the case at this time, when a great scarcity of such articles existed there, as we saw. So large a quantity of tobacco is raised in Maryland and Virginia, that it is one of the greatest sources of revenue to the crown by reason of the taxes which it yields. Servants and negroes are employed in the culture of tobacco, who are brought from other places to be sold to the highest bidders, the servants for a term of years only, but the negroes forever, and may be sold by their masters to other planters as many times as their masters choose, that is, the ser-vants until their term is fulfilled, and the negroes for life. These men, one with another, each make, when they are able to work, from 2,500 pounds to 3,000 pounds, and even 3,500 pounds of tobacco a year, and some of the masters and their wives who pass their lives here in wretchedness, do the same. The servants and negroes after they have worn themselves down the whole day, and gone home to rest, have yet to grind and pound the grain, which is generally maize, for their masters and all their families as well as themselves, and all the negroes, to eat. Tobacco is the only production in which the planters employ themselves, as if there were nothing else in the world to plant but that, and while the land is capable of yielding all the productions that can be raised anywhere, so far as the climate of the place allows. As to articles of food, the only bread they have is that made of Turkish wheat or maize, and that is miserable. They plant this grain for that purpose everywhere. It yields well, not a hundred, but five or six hundred for one; but it takes up much space, as it is planted far apart like vines in France. The corn, when it is to be used for men, has to be first soaked, before it is ground or pounded, because the grains being large and very hard, cannot be broken under the small stones of their light hand-mills; and then it is left so coarse it must be sifted. They take the finest for bread, and the other for different kinds of groats, which, when it is cooked, is called *sapaen* or *homma*. The meal intended for bread is kneaded moist without leaven or yeast, salt or grease, and generally comes out of the oven so that it will hardly hold together, and so blue and moist that it is as heavy as dough; yet the best of it when cut and roasted, tastes almost like warm white bread, at least it seemed to us so. This corn is also the only provender for their horses, oxen, cows, hogs and fowls, which generally run in the woods to get their food, but are fed a little of this morning and evening during the winter when there is little to be had in the woods; though they are not fed too much, for the wretchedness, if not *cruelty*, of such living, affects both man and beast. This is said not without reason, for a master having a sick servant, and there are many so, and observing from his declining condition, he would finally die, and that there was no probability of his enjoying any more service from him, made him, sick and languishing as he was, dig his own grave, in which he was laid a few days afterwards, the others being too busy to dig it, having their hands full in attending to the tobacco.

A few vegetables are planted, but they are of the coarsest kinds and are cultivated in the coarsest manner, without knowledge or care, and they are, therefore, not properly raised, and do not amount to much as regards the production, and still less as to their use. Some have begun to plant orchards, which all bear very well, but are not properly cultivated. The fruit is for the greater part pressed, and makes good cider, of which the largest portion becomes soured and spoiled through their ignorance or negligence, either from not putting it into good casks, or from not taking proper care of the liquor afterwards. Sheep they have none, although they have what is requisite for them if they chose. It is matter of conjecture whether you will find any milk or butter even in summer; we have not found any there at this season of the year. They bestow all their time and care in producing tobacco; each cask or hogshead, as they call it, of which pays two English shillings on exportation, and on its arrival in England, two pence a pound, besides the fees for weighing and other expenses here, and freight and other charges beyond sea. When, therefore, tobacco only brings four or five pence, there is little or nothing left for the owner.

The lives of the planters in Maryland and Virginia are very godless and profane. They listen neither to God nor his commandments, and have neither church nor cloister. Sometimes there is some one who is called a minister, who does not as elsewhere, serve in one place, for in all Virginia and Maryland there is not a city or a village—but travels for profit, and for that purpose visits the plantations through the country, and there addresses the people; but I know of no public assemblages being held in these places; you hear often that these ministers are worse than anybody else, yea, are an abomination.

When the ships arrive with goods, and especially with liquors, such as wine and brandy, they attract everybody, that is, masters, to them, who then indulge so abominably together, that they keep nothing for the rest of the year, yea, do not go away as long as there is any left, or bring any thing home with them which might be useful to them in their subsequent necessities. It must, therefore, go hard with the household, and it is a wonder if there be a single drop left for the future. They squander so much in this way, that they keep no tobacco to buy a shoe or a stocking for their children which sometimes causes great misery. While they take so little care for provisions, and are otherwise so reckless, the Lord sometimes punishes them with insects, flies and worms, or with intemperate seasons, causing great famine, as happened a few years ago in the time of the last Dutch war with the English, when the Lord sent so many weevils (*eenkor-entjes*) that all their grain was eaten up as well as most all the other productions of the field, by reason of which such a great famine was caused that many persons died of starvation, and a mother killed her own child and eat it, and then went to her neighbors, calling upon them to come and see what she had done, and showing them the remains of her child, whereupon she was arrested and condemned to be hung. When she sat or stood on the scaffold, she cried out to the people, in the presence of the governor, that she was now going to God, where she would render an account, and would declare before him that what she had done she did in the mere delirium of hunger, for which the governor alone should bear the guilt; inasmuch as this famine was caused by the *eenkorens*, a visitation from God, because he, the governor, undertook in the preceding summer, an expedition against the Dutch, residing on the South [Delaware] river, who maintained themselves in such a good posture of defense, that he could accomplish but little; when he went to the *Hoere-kill* [Whore-creek] on the west side of that river, not far from the sea, where also he was not able to do much; but as the people subsisted there only by cultivating wheat, and had at this time a fine and abundant harvest in the fields—and from such harvests the people of Maryland generally and under such circumstances as these particularly, were fed—he set fire to it, and all their other fruits, whether of the trees or the field; whereby he committed two great sins at the same time, namely, against God and his goodness, and against his neighbors, the Dutch, who lost it, and the English who needed it; and had caused more misery to the English in his own country, than to the Dutch in the enemy's country. This wretched woman protesting these words substantially against the governor, before heaven and in the hearing of every one, was then swung up.

In addition to what the tobacco itself pays on exportation, which produces a very large sum, every hundred acres of land, whether cultivated or not, has to pay one hundred pounds of tobacco a year, and every person between sixteen and sixty years of age must pay three shillings a year. All animals are free of taxation, and so are all productions except tobacco.

It remains to be mentioned that those persons who profess the Roman Catholic religion, have great, indeed, all freedom in Maryland, because the governor makes profession of that faith, and consequently

there are priests and other ecclesiastics who travel and disperse themselves everywhere, and neglect nothing which serves for their profit
and purpose. The priests of Canada take care of this region, and hold
correspondence with those here, as is supposed, as well as with those
who reside among the Indians. It is said there is not an Indian fort
between Canada and Maryland, where there is not a Jesuit who teaches
and advises the Indians, who begin to listen to them too much; so
much so, that some people in Virginia and Maryland as well as in
New Netherland, have been apprehensive lest there might be an out-
break, hearing what has happened in Europe, as well as among their
neighbors at Boston; but they hope the result of the troubles there
will determine many things elsewhere. The Lord grant a happy issue
there and here, as well as in other parts of the world, for the help
of his own elect, and the glory of his name.

In 1680 King Charles II sent his ship Richmond *to deliver 45
French Huguenots to Carolina in hopes of settling them there to cultivate silk. The officers of the ship were given "particular Instructions
to enquire into the State of that Country" while on duty in those
waters. When the* Richmond *returned to London two years later,
Thomas Ashe, a young gentleman and "Clerk on Board his Majesties
Ship," published* Carolina; or a Description of the Present State of
that Country, and the Natural Excellencies thereof, *one of several such
tracts designed to advertise the Lord Proprietors' real estate. Ashe's
complete description is given below from the first edition.*

Reader,
  You may please to understand, that the first Discovery of this Country was at the Charge of King Henry the Seventh, as you will find
in this Book; and that as it hath pleased God to add such a Jewel
to the Crown of England, so I doubt not but in a few years it will
prove the most Beneficial to the Kingdom in General of any Colony
yet Planted by the English, which is the more probable from the great
Concourse that daily arrives there, From the other Plantations, as well
as from England, Ireland, etc., being drawn and invited thither by
the Healthfulness of Air, Delicacy of Fruits, the likelyhood of Wines,

Oyls and Silks, and the great Variety of other Natural Commodities within specified, which well considered, will sufficiently evidence the Truth of what I Assert; that I may contribute what lies in my Power for a further Satisfaction to those Gentlemen that are curious concerning the Country of Carolina, they may find a small Description thereof, with a Map of the first Draught, Published by Mr. Richard Blome, and Printed for Dorman Newman, in the Year 1678 in Octavo, and one larger in Mr. Ogleby's *America*; since the publishing of these, there is by Order of the Lords Proprietors newly published in one large Sheet of Paper, a very spacious Map of Carolina, with its Rivers, Harbors, Plantations, and other Accommodations, from the latest Survey, and best Informations, with a large and particular Description of the Entrances into Ashly and Cooper Rivers; this Map to be sold for 1 *s.* by Joel Gascoyne, near Wapping Old Stairs, and Robert Green in Budge Row, London, 1682.

A Compleat Discovery of the State of Carolina, in the Year 1682.

THE Discourses of many Ingenious Travellers (who have lately seen this part of the West Indies) have for Salubrity of Air, Fertility of Soyl, for the Luxuriant and Indulgent Blessings of Nature, justly rendered Carolina Famous. That since my Arrival at London, I have observed many with pleasing Ideas, and Contemplations, as if ravisht with Admiration, discourse of its Pleasures: Whilst others more actively prest and stimulated, have with vehement and ardent Desires willingly resolved to hazard their Lives, Families, and Fortunes to the Mercy of the Wind, Seas and Storms, to enjoy the Sweets of so desirable a Being.

Having spent near three Years Abroad, in which time I had a fair Opportunity of a Survey of great part of our English America. You my Worthy Friend, knowing in what Character I went abroad, and understanding of my being at Carolina, did obligingly request (that at Leisure) I would collect such Notices of my own whilst there, with those Remarques and Observations which I had learnt from the most Able and Ingenious Planters, who have had their Residence on the place from its first being Coloniz'd: You desiring to be assured whether the true State of the Country did answer the Reports of Common Fame. Which in Compliance with, and in Obedience to your Commands, I have undertaken.

Carolina derives her name either from our present Illustrious Monarch, under whose glorious Auspices it was first establisht an English Colony, in the Year One Thousand Six Hundred and Seventy, and under whose benign and happy Influence it now prospers and flourishes. Or from Charles the Ninth of that Name King of France, in whose Reign a Colony of French Protestants were transported thither, at the encouragement of Gasper Coligni, Admiral of that Kingdom; the place of their first Settlement named in Honour of their Prince Arx Carolina, but not long after, that Colony, with Monsieur Ribault their Leader, were by the Spaniard at once cut off and destroy'd. Since which, nor French, nor Spaniard have made any Attempt for its Re-Settlement. Carolina is the Northermost part of the spacious and pleasant Province of Florida; it lies in the Northern temperate Zone, between the Latitude of Twenty Nine, and Thirty Six Degrees, and Thirty Minutes: It's bounded on the East, with the Atlantick or Northern, on the West, with the Pacifick or Southern Ocean, on the North, with Virginia, on the South, with the remaining part of Florida. The Air of so serene and excellent a temper, that the Indian Natives prolong their days to the Extremity of Old Age. And where the English hitherto have found no Distempers either Epidemical or Mortal, but what have had their Rise from Excess or Origine from Intemperance. In July and August they have sometimes Touches of Agues and Fevers, but not violent, of short continuance, and never Fatal. English Children there born, are commonly strong and lusty, of sound Constitutions, and fresh ruddy Complexions. The Seasons are regularly disposed according to Natures Laws; the Summer not so torrid, hot and burning as that of their Southern, nor the Winter so rigorously sharp and cold, as that of their Northern Neighbours. In the Evenings and Mornings of December and January, thin congealed Ice, with hoary Frosts sometimes appear; but as soon as the Sun elevates her self, above the Horizon, as soon they disappear and vanish; Snow having been seen but twice in ten Years, or from its first being settled by the English.

The Soil near the Sea, of a Mould Sandy, farther distant, more clayey, or Sand and Clay mixt; the Land lies upon a Level in fifty or sixty Miles round, having scarce the least Hill or Eminency. It's cloathed with odoriferous and fragrant Woods, flourishing in perpetual and constant Verdures, viz. the lofty Pine, the sweet smelling Cedar and Cyprus Trees, of both which are composed goodly Boxes, Chests,

Tables, Scrittores, and Cabinets. The Dust and Shavings of Cedar, laid amongst Linnen or Woollen, destroys the Moth and all Verminous Insects: It never rots, breeding no Worm, by which many other Woods are consumed and destroyed. Of Cedar there are many sorts; this in Carolina is esteemed of equal Goodness for Grain, Smell and Colour with the Bermudian Cedar, which of all the West Indian is esteemed the most excellent; that in the Caribbe Islands and Jamaica being of a courser kind, Oyl and the Spirit of Wine penetrating it; but with this they make Heading for their Cask, which the sharpest and most searching Liquors does not pierce. With the Berry of the Tree at Bermudaz, by Decoction, they make a very wholesome and sovereign Drink. This Tree in the Sacred Writ is famous, especially those of Lebanon, for their Stately Stature; but those in the West Indies I observed to be of a low and humble height. The Sassafrass is a Medicinal Tree, whose Bark and Leaves yield a pleasing Smell: It profits in all Diseases of the Blood, and Liver, particularly in all Venereal and Scorbutick Distempers. There are many other Fragrant smelling trees, the Myrtle, Bay and Lawrel, several Others to us wholly unknown. Fruit Trees there are in abundance of various and excellent kinds, the Orange, Lemon, Pomegranate, Fig and Almond. Of English Fruits, the Apple, Pear, Plumb, Cherry, Quince, Peach, a sort of Medlar, and Chesnut. Wallnut Trees there are of two or three sorts; but the Black Wallnut for its Grain, is most esteem'd: the Wild Wallnut or Hiquery-Tree, gives the Indians, by boyling its Kernel, a wholesome Oyl, from whom the English frequently supply themselves for their Kitchen uses: It's commended for a good Remedy in Dolors, and Gripes of the Belly; whilst new it has a pleasant Taste; but after six Moneths, it decays and grows acid; I believe it might make a good Oyl, and of as general an use as that of the Olive, if it were better purified and rectified. The Chincopin Tree bears a Nut not unlike the Hazle, the Shell is softer: Of the Kernel is made Chocolate, not much inferiour to that made of the Cacoa.

The Peach Tree in incredible Numbers grows Wild: Of the Fruit express'd, the Planters compose a pleasant refreshing Liquor; the Remainder of the Fruit serves the Hogg and Cattle for Provision. The Mulberry Tree every-where amidst the Woods grows wild: The Planters, near their Plantations, in Rows and Walks, plant them for Use, Ornament and Pleasure: What I observed of this Fruit was admirable; the Fruit there, was full and ripe in the latter end of April and beginning of May, whereas in England and Europe, they are not ripe before the latter end of August. A Manufactory of Silk well encouraged might soon be accomplisht, considering the numerousness of the Leaf for Provision, the clemency and moderateness of the Climate to indulge and nourish the Silkworm: To make tryal of its Success, was the Intention of those French Protestant Passengers transported thither in His Majesties Frigat the *Richmond* being Forty Five, the half of a greater Number design'd for that place; but their Design was too early anticipated: the Eggs which they brought with them being hatch'd at Sea, before we could reach the Land, the Worms for want of Provision were untimely lost and destroyed. The Olive Tree thrives there very well. Mr. James Colleton, Brother to Sir Peter, one of the Honourable Proprietors, brought an Olive Stick from Fyall, (one of the Western Islands) cut off at both Ends to Carolina, which put into the Ground, grew and prospered exceedingly; which gave so great an Encouragement, that since I left the place, I hear that several more were brought there, there being great Hopes, that if the Olive be well improved, there may be expected from thence perhaps as good Oyl as any the World yields.

Vines of divers sorts, bearing both Black and Gray Grapes, grow, climbing their highest Trees, running and over-spreading their lower Bushes: Five Kinds they have already distinguish'd, three of which by Replantation, and if well cultivated, they own, will make very good Wine; some of which has been transported for England, which by the best Pallates was well approved of, and more is daily expected, 't is not doubted, if the Planters as industriously prosecute the Propagation of Vineyards as they have begun; but Carolina will in a little time prove a Magazine and Staple for Wines to the whole West Indies; and to enrich their Variety, some of the Proprietors and Planters have sent them the Noblest and Excellentest Vines of Europe, viz. the Rhenish, Clarret, the Muscadel and Canary, etc. His Majesty, to improve so hopeful a Design, gave those French we carried over their Passage free for themselves, Wives, Children Goods. and Servants, they being most of them well experienced in the Nature of the Vine, from whose Directions doubtless the English have received and made considerable Advantages in their Improvements.

Trees for the Service of building Houses and Shipping, besides those and many more which we have not nam'd; they have all such as we in England esteem Good, Lasting, and Serviceable, as the Oak of three sorts, the White, Black and Live Oak, which for Toughness, and the Goodness of its Grain is much esteemed: Elm, Ash, Beech, and Poplar, etc. Into the Nature, Qualities, and Vertues of their Herbs, Roots and Flowers, we had little time to make any curious Enquiry: This we were assured by many of the knowing Planters, that they had Variety of such whose Medicinal Vertues were rare and admirable. The China grows plentifully there, whose Root infus'd, yields us that pleasant Drink, which we know by the Name of China Ale in England: in Medicinal Uses it's far more excellent. Monsieur Tavernier, in his late Voyages to Persia, observes that Nation, by the frequent use of Water in which this Root is boyl'd, are never troubled with the Stone or Gout: It mundifies [clears] and sweetens the Blood: It's good in Fevers, Scurvy, Gonorrhoea, and the Lues Venerea. They have three sorts of the Rattle-Snake Root which I have seen; the Comous, or Hairy, the Smooth, the Nodous, or Knotted Root: All which are lactiferous, or yielding a Milkie Juice; and if I do not very much in my Observations err, the Leaves of all these Roots of a Heart had the exact Resemblance: They are all Sovereign against the Mortal Bites of that Snake, too frequent in the West Indies: In all Pestilential Distempers, as Plague, Small Pox, and Malignant Fevers, it's a Noble Specifick; when stung, they eat the Root, applying it to the Venemous Wound; or they boyl the Roots in Water; which drunk, fortifies and corroborates the Heart, exciteing strong and generous Sweats: by which endangered Nature is relieved, and the Poyson carried off, and expelled.

Gardens as yet they have not much improved or minded, their Designs having otherwise more profitably engaged them in settling and cultivating their Plantations with good Provisions and numerous Stocks of Cattle; which two things by Planters are esteemed the Basis and Props of all New Plantations and Settlements; before which be well accomplished and performed, nothing to any purpose can be effected; and upon which all Intentions, Manufactories, etc., have their necessary Dependance. But now their Gardens begin to be supplied with such European Plants and Herbs as are necessary for the Kitchen, viz. Potatoes, Lettice, Coleworts, Parsnip, Turnip, Carrot and Reddish: Their Gardens also begin to be beautified and adorned with such Herbs and Flowers which to the Smell or Eye are pleasing and agreable, viz. The Rose, Tulip, Carnation and Lilly, etc. Their Provision which grows in the Field is chiefly Indian Corn, which produces a vast Increase, yearly, yielding Two plentiful Harvests, of which they make wholesome Bread, and good Bisket, which gives a strong, sound, and nourishing Diet; with Milk I have eaten it dress'd various ways: Of the Juice of the Corn, when green, the Spaniards with Chocolet, aromatiz'd with Spices, make a rare Drink of an excellent Delicacy. I have seen the English amongst the Caribbes roast the green Ear on the Coals, and eat it with a great deal of Pleasure. The Indians in Carolina parch the ripe Corn, then pound it to a Powder, putting it in a Leathern Bag: When they use it, they take a little quantity of the Powder in the Palms of their Hands, mixing it with Water, and sup it off: with this they will travel several days. In short, it's a Grain of General Use to Man and Beast, many thousands of both kinds in the West Indies having from it the greater part of their Subsistence. The American Physicians observe that it breeds good Blood, removes and opens Oppellations [constipation] and Obstructions. At Carolina they have lately invented a way of makeing with it good sound Beer; but it's strong and heady: By Maceration, when duly fermented, a strong Spirit like Brandy may be drawn off from it, by the help of an Alembick.

Pulse they have of great Variety, not only of what Europe yield, viz. Beans, Pease, Callavance, Figolaes, and Bonavist, etc., but many other kinds proper to the place, and to us unknown: Green Pease at the latter end of April, at my being there, I eat as good as ever I did [in] England. Strawberries, Rasberries, Billberries, and Blackberries grow frequently up and down the Woods. Hemp and Flax thrives exceeding well; there grows a sort of wild Silk Pods, call'd Silk-Grass, of which they may make fine and durable Linnen.

What Wheat they have planted has been rather for Experiment and Observation, whether it would be agreeable to the Soil and Climate, than for any Substance for themselves, or for Transportation abroad; what they have sown, the Planters assured us grew exceeding well; as also Barly, Mr. [Jonah] Linch an ingenious Planter, having whilst we were there very good growing in his Plantation, of which he intended to make Malt for brewing of English Beer and Ale, having all Utensils and Conveniences for it. Tobacco grows very well; and they have of an excellent sort, mistaken by some of our English Smoakers for Spanish Tobacco, and valued from 5 to 8s. the Pound; but finding a great deal of trouble in the Planting and Cure of it, and the great Quantities which Virginia, and other of His Majesties

Plantations make, rendring it a Drug over all Europe; they do not much regard or encourage its Planting, having already before them better and more profitable Designs in Action. Tarr made of the resinous Juice of the Pine (which boyl'd to a thicker Consistence is Pitch) they make great quantities yearly, transporting several Tuns to Barbadoes, Jamaica, and the Caribbe Islands. Indigo they have made, and that good: The reason why they have desisted I cannot learn. To conclude, there grows in Carolina the famous Cassiny, whose admirable and incomparable Vertues are highly applauded and extolled by French and Spanish Writers: It is the Leaves of a certain Tree, which boyl'd in Water (as we do Thea) wonderfully enliven and envigorate the Heart, with genuine easie Sweats and Transpirations, preserving the Mind free and serene, keeping the Body brisk, active, and lively, not for an hour, or two but for as many days, as those Authors report, without any other Nourishment or Subsistance, which, if true, is really admirable; they also add, that none amongst the Indians, but their great Men and Captains, who have been famous for their great Exploits of War and Noble Actions, are admitted to the use of this noble Bevaridge. At my being there I made Enquiry after it; but the Ignorance of the Planter did not inform me. Sponges growing on the Sandy Shoars, I have gathered good and large; for which Samos in times past was famous, supposed by the Ancients to be the only place in the World where they grew: a courser sort I have seen pull'd up by Fishers, fishing among the Rocks of the Island of Barbadoes. Ambergrise is often thrown on their Shoars; a pretious Commodity to him who finds it, if Native and pure, in Worth and Value It surpasses Gold; being estimated at 5 and 6 Pound the Ounce, if not adulterated. What it is I shall not decide, leaving it to the Judgment of the more Learned, whether it be the Excrement of the Whale, because sometimes in dissecting and opening their Bodies it's there discovered. I think as well it may be argued the Excrements of other Creatures, Birds and some Beasts greedily desireing and affecting it, especially the Fox, who eating it, by Digestion it passes through his Body; after some Alteration it's again recover'd, and is that which we call Fox Ambergrise. Others, that it is a bitumious Substance, ebullating or boiling up from the Bottom of the Sea, and floating on the Surface of the Waters, is condensed by the circumambient Air: of which Opinion is the Learned Sennertus [a famous German physician]. Some that it is a Plant of a viscous oleaginous Body, really growing at the bottom

of the Sea, the swift and violent Motion of the Waters in Storms causing an Eradication or Evulsion of the Plant, forcing it to the adjacent
Shoars; that its most plentifully found after Storms is certain: if true,
as an intelligent man informed me, who lived many years at the Bermudaz, and among the Behama Islands, who saw at the Behama a
piece of Ambergrise weighing thirty pound (for its bigness famous
in those Parts) having perfect and apparent Roots, equal to the Body
in worth and goodness. Others, that it's the liquid resinous Tears of
some odoriferous Tree, hanging over Seas or Rivers, coagulated in
that Form which we find it. Dr. Trapham, an ingenious Physician
in Jamaica, differs little from this last opinion, thinking it the Gum-
mous Juice of some Fragrant Plant which grows on Rocks near the
Sea, whose Trunks broken by the rude and boysterous Waves, emit
that precious Liquor. In Medicinal and Physical uses it has a high
esteem, being prescribed in the richest Cordials, admirable in the lan-
guishes of the Spirit Faintings, and Deliquium of the Heart; given
as the last remedy to agonizing Persons. In Perfumes of Linnen, Wol-
len, Gloves, etc., there is none esteemed more costly or precious.
It's of different Colors, Black, Red, the Nutmeg, and Gray Color are
held the best.

The great encrease of their Cattel is rather to be admired than
believed: not more than six or seven years past the Country was almost
destitute of Cows, Hogs and Sheep, now they have many thousand
Head. The Planter in Winter takes no care for their Provision, which
is a great Advantage; the Northern Plantations obliging the Planters
to spend great part of their Summer to provide Fodder and Provision
for their Cattle, to preserve them from starving in the Winter. The
Cows the Year round brouzing on the sweet Leaves growing on the
Trees and Bushes, or on the wholesome Herbage growing underneath:
They usually call them home in the Evening for their Milk, and to
keep them from running wild. Hogs find more than enough of Fruits
in the Summer, and Roots and Nuts in the Winter; from the abundance
of their Feeding, great numbers forsake their own Plantations, running
wild in the Woods, the Tyger, Wolf, and wild Cat, by devouring
them, oftentimes goes Share with the Planter; but when the Stock
encreases and grows strong, the older surround the younger, and bodly
oppose, and oftentimes attack their Invaders. Their Sheep bears good
Wooll; the Ewes at a time often have 2 or 3 Lambs; they thrive very
well, the Country being so friendly to their Natures, that it's observed,

they are neither liable or incident to any known Disease or Distemper. Of Beasts bearing Furrs, they have great store of Variety, whose Skins serve the Indians for Cloathing and Bedding, and the English for many uses, besides the great Advantage made of them, by their being sent for England. Deer, of which there is such infinite Herds, that the whole Country seems but one continued Park, insomuch, that I have often heard Captain Matthews, an ingenious Gentleman, and Agent to Sir Peter Colleton for his Affairs in Carolina, that one hunting Indian has yearly kill'd and brought to his Plantation more than an 100, sometimes 200 head of Deer. Bears there are in great numbers, of whose Fat they make an Oyl which is of great Vertue and Efficacy in causing the Hair to grow, which I observed the Indians daily used, by which means they not only keep their Hair clear and preserved from Vermine, but by the nourishing faculty of the Oyl, it usually extended in length to their middles. There are Bevors, Otters, Foxes, Racoons, Possums, Musquasses, Hares and Coneys, Squirrels of five kinds, the flying Squirrel, whose delicate Skin is commended for comforting, if applied to a cold Stomack, the Red, the Grey, the Fox and Black Squirrels. Leather for Shoes they have good and well tann'd: The Indians have also a way of dressing their Skins rather softer, though not so durable as ours in England.

Birds the Country yields of differing kinds and Colours: For Prey, the Pelican, Hawk, and Eagle, etc. For Pleasure, the red, copped and blew Bird, which wantonly imitates the various Notes and Sounds of such Birds and Beasts which it hears, wherefore, by way of Allusion, it's call'd the mocking Bird; for which pleasing Property it's there esteem'd a Rarity. Birds for Food, and pleasure of Game, are the Swan, Goose, Duck, Mallard, Wigeon, Teal, Curlew, Plover, Partridge, the Flesh of which is equally as good, tho' smaller than ours in England. Pigeons and Parakeittoes. In Winter huge Flights of wild Turkies, oftentimes weighing from twenty, thirty, to forty pound. There are also great Stocks of tame Fowl, viz. Geese, Ducks, Cocks, Hens, Pigeons and Turkies. They have a Bird I believe the least in the whole Creation, named the Humming Bird; in bigness the Wren being much superiour, in magnitude not exceeding the Humble Bee, whose Body in flying much resembles it, did not their long Bills, between two and three Inches, and no bigger than Needles, make the difference. They are of a deep Green, shadow'd with a Murry, not much unlike the color of some Doves Necks; they take their Food humming or flying, feeding on the exuberant Moistures of sweet odoriferous Leaves and Flowers. I have frequently seen them in many parts of the West Indies, but never observed them to have any Musical Air, but a loud Note to Admiration, crying *Chur, Chur, Chur*, etc., which at the distance of half a mile is plainly heard: their Eggs, of which they produce three or four young at a time, not unlike small white Pease: they continue between the Tropiques the whole year round, as I have observed at Berbadoes and Jamaica; but I am informed, that in the more Northern parts of America they sleep the whole Winter; at Berbadoes the Jews curiously skin these little Birds, filling them with fine Sand, and perfuming their Feathers, they are sent into Europe as pretty Delicacies for Ladies, who hang them at their Breasts and Girdles.

There are in Carolina great numbers of Fire Flies, who carry their Lanthorns in their Tails in dark Nights, flying through the Air, shining like Sparks of Fire, enlightning it with their Golden Spangles. I have seen a larger sort at Jamaica, which Dr. Heylin in his Cosmography, enumerates amongst the Rarities and Wonders of Hispaniola, an Island under the King of Spain, distant between 20 and 30 Leagues from Jamaica: These have two Lights above their Eyes, and a third in their Tails; in dark nights they shine like Candles for which I have often at a distance mistaken them, supposeing them to have been the Lights of some adjacent Plantation; and in this I have not been the first that has been so deceived. Amongst large Orange Trees in the Night, I have seen many of those Flies, whose Lights have appeared like hanging Candles, or pendant Flambeaus, which amidst the Leaves and ripe Fruit yielded a Light truly glorious to behold: with 3 of these included in a Glass Bottle, in a very dark Night I have read very small Characters: When they are kill'd, their Igneous or Luminous Matter does not immediately, (till half an hour, or an hour after their Deaths) extinguish.

As the Earth, the Air, etc., are enrich'd and replenished with the Blessings of the most High, the Seas and Rivers of the same bounty equally participate in the Variety of excellent and wholesome Fish which it produces, *viz.* Sturgeon, of whose Sounds Iceing-glass, of whose Roes Caviare are made: Mullet, a delicious sweet Fish, of whose Roes or Spawn Botargo is made: Whale, Salmon, Trouts, Bass, Drum, Cat-fish, whose Head and glaring Eyes resemble a Cat; it's esteem'd a very good Fish; it hath a sharp thorny Bone on its Back, which strikes at such as endeavour to take it: which by Seamen is held venemous: yet I saw one of our Seamen, the back of whose Hand was pierced with it, yet no poysonous Symptoms of Inflammation or Rancor appear'd on the Wound, which quickly heal'd, that I concluded it was either false, or that of this Fish there were more kinds than one: Plaice, Eels, Crabs, Prawns twice as large as ours in England: Oysters of an Oblong or Oval Form; their number inexhaustible; a man may easily gather more in a day than he can well eat in a year; some of which are margiritiferous, yielding bright round Oriental Pearl.

The Tortoise, more commonly call'd by our West Indians the Turtle, are of three sorts, the Hawks-Bill, whose Shell is that which we call the Turtle or Tortoise Shell; the Green Turtle, whose shell being thin is little regarded; but its Flesh is more esteemed than the Hawksbill Tortoise: The Loggerhead Turtle, or Tortoise has neither good shell or Flesh, so is little minded or regarded. They are a sort of creatures which live both on Land and Water. In the day usually keeping the Sea, swimming on the surface of the Water, in fair Weather delighting to expose themselves to the Sun, oftentimes falling asleep, lying, as I have seen several times, without any Motion on the waters, till disturbed by the approach of some Ship or Boat, being quick of hearing, they dive away. In the Night they often come ashore to feed and lay their Eggs in the Sand, which once covered, they leave to the Influence of the Sun, which in due time produces her young ones, which dig their Passage out of the sand immediately making their way towards the Water. At this Season, when they most usually come ashore, which is in April, May and June, the Seamen or Turtlers, at some convenient distance watch their opportunity, getting between them and the Sea, turn them on their Backs, from whence they are unable ever to rise, by which means the Seamen or Turtlers turn 40 or 50 in a night, some of 2, 3, 400 weight: If they are far distant from the Harbor or Market to which they design to bring them, they kill, cutting them to pieces, which Salted they Barrel: This is the way of killing at the Caymana's, an Island lying to the Leeward of Jamaica. Turtle, Barrel'd and Salted if well conditioned, is worth from 18 to 25 shillings the Barrel. If near their Market or Harbor they bring them in Sloops alive, and afterwards keep them in Crauls, which is a particular place of Salt Water of Depth and Room for them to swim in, pallisado'd or staked, in round above the Waters Surface, where,

upon occasion they take them out, and kill them, and cutting them
to pieces, sell their Flesh for two pence or three pence the pound:
the Belly, which they call the Callope of the Turtle, pepper'd and
salted, or roasted and baked, is an excellent Dish, much esteemed
by our Nation in the West Indies: the rest of the Flesh boil'd, makes
as good and nourishing Broath, as the best Capon in England, especially if some of the Eggs are mixt with it; they are some white,
and others of a yellow or golden Colour, in largeness not exceeding
a Walnut, wrapt in a thin Skin or Membrane, sweet in Taste, nourishing and wholesome: and of this property, that they never grow hard
by boiling: the Liver is black: it freely opens and purges the Body:
if little of it be eaten, it dies the Excrements of a deep black Colour:
The Fat in Color inclines to a Sea Green; in Taste it's sweet and
luscious, equalling, if not surpassing the best Marrow, if freely eaten
it deeply stains the Urine of its Color: It's of a very penetrating piercing quality, highly comended in Strains and Aches: Of it the Turtlers
oftentimes make an Oyl, which in Lamps burns much brighter and
sweeter than common Lamp or Train Oyl. In general, the Flesh is
commended for a good Anticorbutique and an Antivenereal Diet;
many in the former, and some that have been far gone in Consump-
tions, with the constant use alone of this Diet, have been thoroughly
recovered and cured in 3 or 4 months. It hath 3 Hearts, by thin Pel-
licules only separated, which has caused some to Philosophize on its
Amphibious Nature, alluding to those participating and assimulating
Qualities which it has to the rest of the Universe, it swiming like
a Fish, laying Eggs like a Fowl, and feeding on Grass like an Ox.
This I am assured of, that after it's cut to pieces, it retains a Sensation
of Life three times longer than any known Creature in the Creation:
Before they kill them they are laid on their Backs, where hopeless
of Relief as if sensible of their future Condition, for some hours they
mourn out their Funerals, the Tears plentifully flowing from their
Eyes, accompanied with passionate Sobs and Sighs, in my Judgment
nothing more like than such who are surrounded and overwhelmed
with Troubles, Cares and Griefs, which raises in Strangers both Pity
and Compassion. Compleatly six hours after the Butcher has cut them
up and into pieces, mangled their Bodies, I have seen the Callope
when going to be seasoned, with pieces of their Flesh ready to cut
into Stakes, vehemently contract with great Reluctancy rise against
the Knife, and sometimes the whole Mass of Flesh in a visible Tremu-

lation and Concussion, to him who first sees it seems strange and admirable. There is farther to the Southward of Carolina, especially about the Shoars and Rivers of His[pa]niola and Cuba a Fish in Nature something like the former, call'd the Manaty or Sea-Cow, of an extraordinary Bigness, sometimes of 1000 pound weight: It feeds on the Banks and Shoar sides on the Grassy Hertage like a Tortoise; but that which is more wonderful of this Creature is, that she gives her young Ones Suck from her Duggs [teats]; she is headed like a Cow, of a green Colour, her Flesh by some esteemed the most delicate in the World, sweeter than the tenderest Veal, sold at Jamaica, where it's sometimes brought for 6*d*. the pound: It hath a stone in the Head which is a gallant Remedy against the Pains and Dolors of the Stone; so are the Bones of its Body to provoke Urine, when pulveriz'd and exhibited in convenient Liquors. Its Skin makes excellent Whips for Horses, if prudently us'd, which are very serviceable and lasting; with one of these Manaty Strapps, I have seen a Bar of Iron cut and dented: It cuts so severe and deep, that by the Public Authority at Jamaica, Masters are forbidden and prohibited with it to strike their White Servants.

There is in the mouth of their Rivers, or in Lakes near the Sea, a Creature well known in the West Indies, call'd the Alligator or Crocodile, whose Scaly Back is impenitrible, refusing a Musquet Bullet to pierce it, but under the Belly, that or an Arrow finds an easie Passage to destroy it; it lives both on Land and Water, being a voracious greedy Creature, devouring whatever it seizes on, Man only excepted, which on the Land it has not the courage to attacque, except when asleep or by surprize: In the Water it's more dangerous; it sometimes grows to a great length, from 16 to 20 foot, having a long Mouth, beset with sharp keen Teeth; the Body when full grown as large as a Horse, declining towards the Tail; it's slow in motion, and having no Joynt in the Vertebraes or Back Bone, but with its whole length is unable to turn, which renders it the less mischievous; yet Nature by Instinct has given most Creatures timely Caution to avoid them by their strong musky Smell, which at a considerable distance is perceiveable, which the poor Cattle for their own Preservation make good use of: their Flesh cuts very white; the young ones are eatable; the Flesh of the older smells so strong of Musk, that it nauseates; their Stones at least so called, are commended for a rich, lasting perfume.

Mettals or Minerals I know not of any, yet it's supposed and generally believed, that the Apalatean Mountains which lie far up within the Land, yields Ore both of Gold and Silver, that the Spaniards in their running Searches of this Country saw it, but had not time to open them, or at least, for the present were unwilling to make any farther Discovery till their Mines of Peru and Mexico were exhausted, or as others, that they were politically fearful that if the Riches of the Country should be exposed, it would be an Allure to encourage a Foreign Invader, Poverty preserving, Riches oftentimes the cause that Property is lost, usurped and invaded; but whether it be this or that reason time will discover.

The Natives of the Country are from time immemorial, ab Origine Indians, of a deep Chesnut Colour, their Hair black and streight, tied various ways, sometimes oyl'd and painted, stuck through with Feathers for Ornament or Gallantry; their Eyes black and sparkling, little or no Hair on their Chins, well limb'd and featured, painting their Faces with different Figures of a red or sanguine Colour, whether for Beauty or to render themselves formidable to their Enemies I could not learn. They are excellent Hunters; their Weapons the Bow and Arrow, made of a Read, pointed with sharp Stones, or Fish Bones; their Cloathing Skins of the Bear or Deer, the Skin drest after their Country Fashion.

Manufactures, or Arts amongst them I have heard of none, only little Baskets made of painted Reeds and Leather drest sometimes with black and red Chequers coloured. In Medicine, or the Nature of Simples, some have an exquisite Knowledge; and in the Cure of Scorbutick, Venereal, and Malignant Distempers are admirable: In all External Diseases they suck the part affected with many Incantations, Philtres and Charms: In Amorous Intrigues they are excellent either to procure Love or Hatred: They are not very forward in Discovery of their Secrets, which by long Experience are religiously transmitted and conveyed in a continued Line from one Generation to another, for which those skill'd in this Faculty are held in great Veneration and Esteem. Their Religion chiefly consists in the Adoration of the Sun and Moon: At the Appearance of the New Moon I have observed them with open extended Arms then folded, with inclined Bodies, to make their Adorations with much Ardency and Passion: They are divided into many Divisions or Nations, Govern'd by Reguli, or Petty Princes, which our English call Cacicoes [Cassiques]. Their Diet is of Fish, Flesh, and Fowl, with Indian Maiz or Corn; their Drink Water, yet Lovers of the Spirits of Wine and Sugar. They have hitherto lived in good Correspondence and Amity with the English, who by their just and equitable Cariage have extreamly winn'd and obliged them; Justice being exactly and impartially administred, prevents Jealousies, and maintains between them a good Understanding, that the Neighbouring Indians are very kind and serviceable, doing our Nation such Civilities and good Turns as lie in their Power.

This Country was first discover'd by Sir Sebastian Cabott, by the order, and at the expence of King Henry VII, from which Discovery our Successive Princes have held their Claim, in pursuance to which in the Seventeenth Year of His Majesties Reign it was granted unto his Grace George Duke of Albemarle, unto the Right Honourable Edward Earl of Clarendon, William Earl of Craven, John Lord Berkley, Anthony Lord Ashley now Earl of Shaftsbury, to the Honourable Sir George Carteret, and Sir John Colleton, Knights and Baronetts, to Sir William Berkeley Knight, with a full and plenipotentiary Power, to Colonize, Enact Laws, Execute Justice, etc. The Regalia's of Premier Sovereignty only reserved. The Principal place where the English are now settled lies scituated on a point of Land about two Leagues from the Sea, between Ashly and Cooper Rivers, so named in Honour to the Right Honourable the Earl of Shaftsbury, a great Patron to the Affairs of Carolina. The place called Charles Town, by an express Order from the Lord Proprietors in the Year One thousand six hundred and eighty, their Ordnance and Ammunition being removed thither from Old Charles Town, which lay about a League higher from Ashly River, both for its Strength and Commerce. It's very commodiously scituated from many other Navigable Rivers that lie near it on which the Planters are seated; by the Advantage of Creeks, which have a Communication from one great River to another, at the Tide or Ebb the Planters may bring their Commodities to the Town as to the Common Market and Magazine both for Trade and Shipping. The Town is regularly laid out into large and capacious Streets, which to Buildings is a great Ornament and Beauty. In it they have reserved convenient places for Building of a Church, Town-House and other Publick Structures, an Artillery Ground for the Exercise of their Militia, and Wharfs for the Convenience of their Trade and Shipping. At our being there was judged in the Country a 1000 or 1200 Souls; but the great Numbers of Families from England, Ireland, Berbadoes, Jamaica, and the Caribees, which daily Transport themselves thither, have more than doubled that Number. The Commodities of the Country as yet proper for England, are Furrs and Cedar: For Berbadoes, Jamaica and the Caribbee Islands, Provisions, Pitch, Tarr and Clapboard, for which they have in Exchange Sugar, Rumm, Melasses and Ginger, etc., such things which are proper and requisite for the Planter to be stored with before he leaves England for his better Settlement there at his Arrival, chiefly Servants: All kind of Iron Work for the clearing of Land, pruning of Vines, for the Kitchen and for Building. Commodities proper for the Merchant to Transport thither for his Advantage, Cloathing of all kinds, both Linnen and Woollen, Hats, Stockins, Shoes; all kind of Ammunition, Guns, Fowling-pieces, Powder, Match, Bullet, Nails, Locks and Knives; all Haberdashers Ware; Cordage, and Sails for Shipping, Spirits and Spices, viz., Cloves, Nitmegs and Cinnamon. Finally, to encourage People to Transport themselves thither, the Lord Proprietors give unto all Masters and Mistresses of Families, to their Children, Men-Servants and Maid-Servants if above sixteen years of Age, fifty to all such under forty Acres of Land to be held for ever, annually paying a Peny an Acre to the Lord Proprietors to commence in 2 Years after it's survey'd.

Sir, Thus in an Abstract I have given you the Draught of this excellent Country, begining with its Name, Scituation, etc., and when first settled, regularly proceeding to the Nature of the Soil, Quality of the Air, the Diseases and Longaevity of its Inhabitants, the Rarity of its produce in Trees, Fruits, Roots and Herbs, Beasts, Fish, Fowl and Insects; the Nature and Disposition of the Indians, the Progress the English have made since their first Settlement, what Commodities they abound with, in what defective; in all which from the Truth I have neither swerved nor varied: Indeed in some other things I might have farther enlarged and expatiated, which I shall refer to a Personal Discourse, when I have the Honour to wait upon you again; in the mean time I am

Your humble Servant

T.A.

EPILOGUE

Until the final defeat of the French in 1760, the English settlements in North America were effectively confined to the Atlantic Coast by the Appalachian Mountains. But from the earliest years of exploration, men had searched for a passage over the mountains to lands whose richness they could only imagine. In 1670 John Lederer, a 26-year-old German scholar and student of medicine, became the first European to explore the Piedmont and the Blue Ridge Mountains of Carolina and Virginia. Sponsored by Governor William Berkeley of Virginia, Lederer made three expeditions in search of an Appalachian gap, all of which drew up short of making the momentous discovery. On the third expedition he took a party toward a passage in the northwest that he had heard about from the Indians called "Zynodoa" (probably "Shenandoah" and the gap at Harper's Ferry). Upon reaching the Blue Ridge and looking over into the Shenandoah Valley, he decided to turn back, daunted by the sight of a great peak in the distance and a poisonous spider-bite. But his explorations opened the Indian trade routes into the Catawba and Cherokee country and, moreover, nourished the hope that some day English settlements would proliferate beyond the great mountains.

The following passages are taken from *The Discoveries of John Lederer*, translated from the Latin by Sir William Talbot, Baronet (London, 1672).

The third and last EXPEDITION,

From the Falls of *Rappahanock*River in *Virginia*, (due West)
to the top of the *Apalatoean* Mountains.

ON THE twentieth of *August* 1670, Col. *Catlet* of *Virginia* and
my self, with nine English Horse [mounted men], and five Indians
on foot, departed from the house of one *Robert Talifer*, and that night
reached the falls of *Rappahanock*-river, in Indian *Mantepeuck*.

The next day we passed it over where it divides into two branches
North and South, keeping the main branch North of us.

The three and twentieth we found it so shallow, that it onely wet
our horses hoofs.

The four and twentieth we travelled thorow the *Savanae* amongst
vast herds of Red and Fallow Deer which stood gazing at us; and
a little after, we came to the Promontories of Spurs of the
Apalataean-mountains.

These *Savanae* are low grounds at the foot of the *Apalataeans*,
which all the Winter, Spring, and part of the Summer, lie under snow
or water, when the snow is dissolved, which falls down from the
Mountains commonly about the beginning of *June*; and then their ver-
dure is wonderful pleasant to the eye, especially of such as having
travelled through the shade of the vast Forest, come out of a
melancholy darkness of a sudden, into a clear and open skie. To
heighten the beauty of these parts, the first Springs of most of those
great Rivers which run into the *Atlantick* Ocean, or *Cheseapeack* Bay,
do here break out, and in various branches interlace the flowry Meads,
whose luxurious herbage invites numerous herds of Red Deer (for their
unusual largeness improperly termed Elks by ignorant people) to feed.
The right Elk, though very common in *New Scotland* [Nova Scotia],
Canada, and those Northern parts, is never seen on this side of the
Continent: for that which the *Virginians* call Elks, does not at all differ
from the Red Deer of *Europe*, but in his dimensions, which are far
greater: but yet the Elk in bigness does as far exceed them: their heads,
or horns, are not very different; but the neck of the Elk is so short,
that it hardly separates the head from the shoulders; which is the
reason that they cannot feed upon level ground but by falling on their
knees, though their heads be a yard-long: therefore they commonly
either brouse upon trees, or standing up to the belly in ponds or rivers

feed upon the banks: their Cingles or tails are hardly three inches long. I have been told by a *New-England*-Gentleman, that the lips and nostrils of this creature is the most delicious meat he ever tasted. As for the Red Deer we here treat of, I cannot difference the taste of their flesh from those in *Europe*.

The six and twentieth of *August* we came to the Mountains, where finding no horse-way up, we alighted, and left our horses with two or three Indians below, whilst we went up afoot. The ascent was so steep, the cold so intense, and we so tired, that having much ado gained the top of one of the highest, we drank the Kings Health in Brandy, gave the Mountain His name, and agreed to return back again, having no encouragement from that prospect to proceed to a further discovery; since from hence we saw another Mountain, bearing North and by West to us, of a prodigious height: for according to an observation of the distance taken by Col. *Catlet*, it could not be less than fifty leagues from the place we stood upon.

Here was I stung in my sleep by a Mountain-spider; and had not an Indian suckt out the poyson, I had died: for receiving the hurt at the tip of one of my fingers, the venome shot up immediately into my shoulder, and so inflamed my side, that it is not possible to express my torment. The means used by my Physician, was first a small dose of Snakeroot-powder, which I took in a little water; and then making a kinde of Plaister of the same, applied it neer to the part affected: when he had done so, he swallowed some by way of Antidote himselfe, and suckt my fingers end so violently, that I felt the venome retire back from my side into my shoulder, and from thence down my arm: having thus sucked half a score time, and spit as often, I was eased of all my pain, and perfectly recovered. I thought I had been bit by a Rattle-snake, for I saw not what hurt me: but the Indian found by the wound, and the effects of it, that it was given by a Spider, one of which he shewed me the next day: it is not unlike our great blue Spider, onely it is somewhat longer. I suppose the nature of his poyson to be much like that of the *Tarantula*.

I being thus beyond my hopes and expectation restored to my self, we unanimously agreed to return back, seeing no possibility of passing through the Mountains: and finding our Indians with our horses in the place where we left them, we rode homewards without making any further Discovery.

CONJECTURES of the Land beyond
the *Apalataean* Mountains.

They are certainly in a great errour, who imagine that the Continent of North-*America* is but eight or ten days journey over from the *Atlantick* to the *Indian* Ocean: which all reasonable men must acknowledge, if they consider that Sir *Francis Drake* kept a West-North-west course from *Cape Mendocino* to *California*. Nevertheless, by what I gathered from the stranger Indians at *Akenatzy* of their Voyage by Sea to the very Mountains from a far distant Northwest Country, I am brought over to their opinion who think that the Indian Ocean does stretch an Arm or Bay from *California* into the Continent as far as the *Apalataean* Mountains, answerable to the Gulfs of *Florida* and *Mexico* on this side. Yet I am far from believing with some, that such great and Navigable Rivers are to be found on the other side [of] the *Apalataeans* falling into the Indian Ocean, as those which run from them to the Eastward. My first reason is derived from the knowledge and experience we already have of South-*America*, whose *Andes* send the greatest Rivers in the world (as the *Amazones* and *Rio de la Plata*, &c.) into the *Atlantick*, but none at all into the *Pacifique* Sea. Another Argument is, that all our Waterfowl which delight in Lakes and Rivers, as Swans, Geese, Ducks, &c. come over the Mountains from the Lake of *Canada*, when it is frozen over every Winter, to our fresh Rivers; which they would never do, could they finde any on the other side of the *Apalataeans*.